The Peruvian Industrial Labor Force

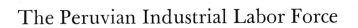

The
Peruvian Industrial
Labor Force

David Chaplin

Princeton, New Jersey
Princeton University Press
1967

Publication of this book has been aided by
the Whitney Darrow Publication Reserve Fund
of Princeton University Press

Printed in the United States of America
by Princeton University Press, Princeton, New Jersey

To my father
Duncan Dunbar Chaplin

Preface

One of the major themes in the literature on the recruitment of an industrial labor force in an underdeveloped "non-Western" area is that it inevitably will be an agonizing process beset by high levels of absenteeism and labor turnover. This may be partly attributed to an anthropological bias in favor of the maintenance, or at least the durability, of traditional culture. It has also been affected by what could be called a managerial bias to the effect that the primary obstacle to the development of manufacturing operations has been intransigence of the workers.

The study will demonstrate that, at least in the case of the Peruvian textile industry, the above perspective is mistaken. This industry has developed in neither the classic Western pattern nor in the fashion described above. Among other generalizations, then, which can be drawn from this evidence is that the process of industrialization, however similar may be its consequences in the long run, can certainly follow a variety of paths.

The major substantive focus will be the Peruvian textile factory labor force and labor market. I am primarily interested in various types of labor mobility, especially that involved in moving from a preindustrial to an industrializing milieu.

The theoretical concern which underlies this study is an interest in middle-level generalizations about social change. The whole field of social change is unquestionably the weakest area of social science theory. My own strategy is to concentrate on the work force as it evolves into an industrial-market-oriented labor force. The central focus is on the dynamics of commercialization. I wish to observe, in the case of Peru, how far the process of commercialization has gone and apparently will go. How many goods and services will enter the market and be evaluated in primarily rational and financial terms? Is the process of rationalization or "disenchantment," as Max Weber[1] put it, bound to continue indefinitely or are there intrinsic "functional" limits required for the continuation of a viable society?[2]

I am also concerned with the dissection of commercialization. Theoretical progress generally moves from unitary global concepts to a more refined analysis of analytical aspects of a phenomenon, if indeed the original concept is still to be viewed as a single entity in any sense. Also, if there are significantly different aspects of commercialization, do all move in the same direction simultaneously or is it possible to have a labor market more commercialized in some respects and less in others?

In order to discuss commercialization, the criterion of rationality must, of course, be specified. The standard used throughout this work will be the desirability, or at least the inevitability, of industrialization. I am not necessarily viewing this process as morally or aesthetically desirable in all respects, worshiping all change as progress, or admiring change for its own sake. Industrialization today has become a necessity in all "developing" countries which have allowed themselves the luxury of a sharp decline in the death rate, to say nothing of their absorption in the goals of economic development by way of the "demonstration effect." Moreover, the increasing mechanization of the primary sector (agriculture and mining), made necessary by the lag in food production and the need for foreign exchange, makes obligatory the opening up of nonagricultural employment opportunities for the

[1] Hans H. Gerth and C. Wright Mills, *From Max Weber: Essays in Sociology* (New York: Oxford University Press, 1946), p. 155. See also Karl Polanyi, "Our Obsolete Market Mentality," *Commentary*, III (February 1947), 109-117.

[2] Max Weber, *The Theory of Social and Economic Organization* (Glencoe, Ill.: The Free Press, 1947), pp. 189, 212.

burgeoning population. Only manufacturing enterprises together with modern services can absorb this surplus labor.

This developmental criterion should not be confused with a United States–oriented managerial bias. The latter perspective could easily lead to a number of serious errors: (1) There is the assumption that free-enterprise, capitalist institutions from the United States (already much modified from their "ideal" nineteenth-century form) must be exported to the currently underdeveloped countries. (2) There is the assumption that managers ought to be given a free hand in structuring the industrial labor force, free of union or governmental interference, and that therefore those currently in these positions should be given more power and authority. There is a question as to the dedication of this group to the ideal norms of an industrial society, since the majority of Peru's textile owners and managers have a very short-sighted mercantile view of their operations. The general emphasis on a disciplined rather than an efficient labor force and a high-mark-up–low-turnover sales policy should disqualify most of Peru's textile manufacturers from playing roles as managerial heroes of industrialization. The pressures toward industrial virtue have come largely from outside and below. (3) A managerial bias can also lead to the assumption that high morale correlates with high productivity and that labor commitment to a concrete manager constitutes commitment to industrial norms. It could be demonstrated in Peru that the degree of worker dissatisfaction with management varies fairly directly with productive efficiency.

Another way of describing the perspective from which this study was undertaken would be to call it an exercise in socio-economics. As a sociologist primarily concerned with the world of work, I am therefore dealing with actions which already have been extensively studied by economists. One of my orientations is to rescue "the social factor" from its role as a residual dumping ground for incomprehensible or economically irrational behavior. Classical economic theory has always been least applicable to the labor market. This limitation becomes all the more evident when Western social scientists study the process of industrialization in "non-Western" areas. In order to comprehend what happens, economists have become either anthropologists or social psychologists, or have retreated to condemnation of such extreme deviations from economic sanity.

It seems to me that the sociologist can contribute to an understanding of the process of industrialization in underdeveloped areas in terms relevant to economic interests. The linking concept is rationalization of which our focal subject of commercialization is a variety. For a sociologist studying partially "economic" phenomena it seems fruitful to study the edges of the labor market—that is, those individuals or places or eras in which the extension of the market is being shifted in or out. Therefore, I am not trying to "do" economics; rather, I am trying to apply the sociological perspective to a substantive problem notably beyond the reach of conventional economic analysis.[3]

There is one respect in which I feel an economic or technological perspective is particularly relevant to a sociological analysis of industrial labor recruitment and commitment. We should have some judgment as to the degree of efficiency of a factory if we are to evaluate workers' adjustment to it as indicating their commitment to industrial norms. In the literature on this subject one rarely finds such a criterion utilized. Instead, an extreme type of technological determinism is in evidence, in which it is assumed that if machines function and some production occurs, everyone working nearby is

[3] In a review of the development of labor market analysis within labor economics, McNulty notes that "an increasing attention by labor economists to labor *market* [his italics] processes and problems . . . represents a narrowing of the labor economists' interests which has been facilitated by the entrance, during the post-war years especially, of the other social sciences into the labor field." Paul James McNulty, "Labor Market Analysis and the Development of Labor Economics," *Industrial and Labor Relations Review*, xix (July 1966), 547.

therefore forced to come to terms with the essence of industrial life. The fact is that many such studies have doubtless dealt with factories with abysmally low levels of efficiency. One can only conclude in such cases that the indigenous culture had won out over what the authors assume to be the inevitable emanation of industrial norms from the machinery itself.

Consequently I have brought in studies of the efficiency of the Peruvian textile industry as a whole and of some of the plants in my sample. Fortunately for my work, a United Nations evaluation of the efficiency of Peruvian textile plants was being carried out during my stay in Peru (1958–1959). Thus, when a plant is referred to as one of the most or least efficient plants in Peru, this is not the impressionistic judgment of an amateur.

The Peruvian textile industry was selected as the subject of my research for a variety of reasons. To begin with, as in most countries, it was the earliest branch of manufacturing to be developed. There is, therefore, a substantial cross-cultural literature on labor recruitment in this industry and for this stage of industrialization. Peru has also been extensively studied by archaeologists and anthropologists, as well as by a series of international and United States technical commissions, but her urban and industrial social problems have, until recently, received little scholarly attention.

Peru is an interesting country for such a study in view of its status as the most promising of the generally "backward" Andean Indian republics in terms of its level of economic development and rate of industrial growth. Unlike Ecuador and Bolivia, it has a wide variety of exports that stabilize the exchange value of its currency as well as provide relatively rich internal sources of potential capital for industrial development. Some of Peru's other relative advantages consist of at least one well-developed seaport, a larger population than Ecuador or Bolivia, and one urban center, Lima–Callao, with sufficient overhead facilities for the extensive development of the secondary manufacturing sector.

Peru is a country generally low on most lists of Latin American countries with respect to economic development. The textile industry, however, is sufficiently developed to permit an examination of the recruitment of industrial labor comparable to the many similar studies already available.

The data on which this study of the recruitment of industrial labor in Peru is based were gathered from 13 of Peru's 40 textile mills between August 1958 and June 1959 with the assistance of a Pan American Union Research Fellowship. Nine of the factories are in Lima, three in Arequipa, and one near Cuzco. The 3,918 worker biographies were obtained from company personnel files, and, wherever possible, directly from personal documents such as birth certificates, previous employer recommendations, school certificates, etc., which are usually placed in the plant office for "safekeeping."

Given the many and time-consuming obstacles to systematic sociological research in Peru I decided to concentrate on a restricted number of fairly "hard" worker characteristics such as age, sex, birthplace, and previous occupation, which I could obtain at first hand rather than, for instance, relying primarily on published data—or a mass survey of the subjective perspectives of Peru's workers. This approach was chosen not from any objection in principle to the alternatives but as one which, given my training and non-team style of operation, seemed a more efficient use of my time. In the concluding chapter free rein will be given to speculative hypotheses which, it is hoped, will inform future investigations in this area.

It is hoped that this study will also contribute toward a yet-to-be written "objective" social history of republican Peru, especially after 1896. Histories in Peru are moving out of the traditional political and military descriptive phase into that of polemic reinterpretations. Social history, in the sense of the record of what the majority at the bottom were actually doing, still tends to be overlooked. In fact, from the sociologist's perspective, much of traditional history is marked by a class bias in favor of the elite. The primary reason for this would appear to be that the ruling elite, or at least some of its servants, usually were the only literate group in the society capable of, and interested in, recording the elite's actions for posterity. For their part, most historians apparently were moved by an overriding concern with the visible centers of power who were, or felt they were, controlling their society's destiny.

Recently some sociologists and sociologically minded historians have begun the study of larger anonymous unheroic masses either from an interest in nonpower phenomena or in terms of a more sophisticated definition of where the center of power really lies.

However, before the type of social history I have in mind can be accomplished, a series of studies such as that of the present effort must be undertaken.

Chapter 1 provides some background material on Peru relevant to the general theme of industrialization. Chapter 2 presents the theoretical model in terms of which the analysis in Chapters 5, 6, and 7 is undertaken. Chapter 3 describes the general history of labor force development in Peru with which the same process in the textile industry will be compared. Chapter 4 deals with the development and current structure of the textile industry. Chapters 5, 6, and 7 analyze published data on the textile labor force and the sample of workers from the 13 plants. Appendix A contains vignettes of each plant and its parent firm as background detail for Chapters 4 through 7. Appendix B goes into a number of methodological problems, some having to do with the available data and some with the construction of indices.

Acknowledgments

My expectations of Latin hospitality were amply fulfilled while I was in Peru. I would, therefore, like to acknowledge the great help of many Peruvians and others, especially the following: Mr. Roger Haour, the United Nations textile productivity specialist, who provided me with an industrial yardstick as well as otherwise virtually unobtainable knowledge about the problems of each firm studied; Sr. Jorge Schofield, then Director of the Textile Research Institute at the National Engineering School, who opened many usually closed doors and gave me in effect a course on production problems in the textile industry; Professor Andrés Ruszkowski, *catedrático* in the Catholic University, who gave me much of my insight into Peru's "social problems"; Sr. Alvaro Llona, one of the first Peruvian lawyers to specialize in labor law, who offered me his invaluable counsel in this highly complex area; and Dr. Antonio Pinilla, former Minister of Labor, then Director of the Instituto de Relaciones Humanas of the University of San Marcos, now Rector of the new Universidad de Lima, who gave me the use of an office and his library, his personal influence, and invaluable advice.

I am also, of course, indebted to various colleagues who have given me the benefit of their suggestions and criticisms, especially Professors Robert Alford, Gabriel Escobar, William Glade, John Korbel, Richard Patch, Frederick Pike, William Sewell, and Richard Tomasson. It goes without saying that they are not responsible for what follows.

Perhaps most to be acknowledged is the open generosity of the owners and managers of the factories I visited. In view of the frankness of our discussions and the confidential nature of the information provided, it seems more appropriate to leave this acknowledgment anonymous.

The assistance of Hugo Vega, Carmen Dandler, and Janice Torney is also much appreciated. My wife's solid Canadian education has also provided me with valuable editorial assistance.

I am also grateful for the financial support afforded by the Pan American Union, the Ford Foundation, and the Wisconsin Alumni Research Foundation for various phases of this work.

DAVID CHAPLIN

Madison, Wisconsin
August 1966

Contents

The Peruvian Industrial Labor Force

CHAPTER 1

Peru

㎧㎧㎧㎧㎧㎧㎧㎧㎧㎧㎧㎧㎧㎧㎧㎧㎧㎧㎧㎧㎧㎧㎧㎧㎧㎧㎧

The Choice of the Country

Peru is an unlikely country for self-generated industrialization. Even by Latin American standards it has only tenuous ties with those aspects of Western civilization on which the Industrial Revolution was based. Yet there is a small and relatively efficient manufacturing industry centered largely in the Lima–Callao area. Within this sector of the economy a few branches are fully developed as far as current local consumer demand is concerned. First among these in size and seniority is the textile industry. Here we find forty mills employing approximately 20,000 of a total of about 160,000 workers in all manufacturing plants in the country. As in so many industrializing countries, textiles have been the leading industry in manufacturing.[1]

Another consideration was the relative wealth of background material on Peru by generations of anthropologists, geographers, and, more recently, economists and international technicians of many specialties. Of particular usefulness were the studies by the Cornell–Vicos group on acculturation in the department of Ancash, the Smithsonian series, and the studies by Dr. Kuczynski-Godard. These publications were very relevant owing to their focus on cultural change, migration, and the effects of industrialization as compared with the more common prewar focus on "unspoiled, real" Indian communities.

[1] The figures given are from *Resultados preliminares del censo de manufactura—primer censo nacional económico, 1963* (Lima: Dirección Nacional de Estadística y Censos, 1965). This enumeration was carried out in 1964 and deals only with firms employing more than five workers.

3

Some Historical Considerations

THE COLONIAL HERITAGE

While Peru was one of the two centers of the Spanish Empire during the colonial era, today it ranks near the bottom among Latin American countries with respect to most indices of industrialization.[2] Peruvian political liberals and Indianists would, of course, assert that the second event followed naturally from the first.

Certainly the colonial era effectively eradicated the Incaic civilization. What is viewed today as Indian in Peru is to a considerable extent medieval Spanish as transmitted by the colonial settlers.[3] The take-over of power was greatly facilitated by a civil war in progress when the Spaniards arrived, while the remaking of Indian society was made easier by the similarity of its political structure to that of Spain, as well as by the variety of acculturation techniques used by the crown and various religious orders.

An effect of colonial policies and actions was the elimination of Indian communities on the coast and the pushing back of the indigenous inhabitants to the higher and more isolated sections of the country.

One of the more successfully implemented of Spain's imperial ambitions in Peru was the suppression of any artisan manufacturing operations which would have competed with plants of the mother country. As will be shown in Chapter 3, it was for this reason that the Peruvian weaving sheds, or *obrajes*, were closed down long before Independence.

POST-INDEPENDENCE

The way in which Independence came to Peru in 1821 re-

[2] United Nations, Department of Economic and Social Affairs, *Analysis and Projections of Economic Development. VI: The Industrial Development of Peru* (E/CN.12/493) (Mexico, December 1959), p. 3.

[3] Richard Patch, "Modern Indians and the Inca Empire," American Universities *Field Staff Newsletter* (October 1958), p. 1.

4

mains one of the many controversial issues of Peruvian history. The record seems fairly clear that Peru was rather forcibly liberated by the revolutionary heroes from Venezuela and Argentina, Bolívar and San Martín. Peru remains one of the Latin American countries with the closest formal ties to Spain, although today only a minority of the old guard elite view these ties sympathetically.

Independence was accompanied by a rash of Anglo-French political reformist decrees designed to separate Church and State, liberate the Indians, free the children of the slaves born after Independence, and develop agriculture, mining, and trade. However, after Bolívar's departure, reaction and chaos followed. The only economic "reform" achieved during the nineteenth century was the opening up of Peru to international trade, which meant English domination. The extreme laissez-faire policies which followed, far from enabling capitalism to play out its "Marxist" progressive role,[4] merely succeeded in removing from the Indians what land the Spaniards had not already taken, thus reinforcing a chaotic feudalism called *gamonalismo* and preventing the development of any native manufacturing.[5] The capitalist "collectivization" of coastal agriculture was not realized until the twentieth century and then largely under foreign auspices. In addition, one of Peru's major historians asserts that the plight of the Indians was even worse after Independence than under Spanish domination.[6] The Crown and several of the religious orders had tried quite sincerely to protect the Indians during the colonial period, whereas after Independence there was no responsible power seriously interested in their situation until perhaps very recently.

[4] José Carlos Mariátegui, *Siete ensayos de interpretación de la realidad peruana* (Lima: Biblioteca Amauta, 1957), p. 92.

[5] Emilio Romero, *El pensamiento económico latino-americano* (Mexico: Fondo de Cultura Económica, 1945), pp. 284-303.

[6] Jorge Basadre, *Meditaciones sobre el destino histórico del Perú* (Lima: Ediciones Huascaran, 1947), p. 115.

The first period of chaotic *caudillismo* (military dictators) ended at mid-century as a guano boom (guano is marine bird manure extremely valuable as a fertilizer) re-established Peruvian contact with Europe and created a period of relative stability with some attempts at social reform. Under President Castilla, Negro slaves were emancipated and special courts, or *fueros,* for the clergy were abolished. He also took the main burden for the support of the Church off the Indians and subsidized the Church directly from government funds which came from the new guano trade. This legal change, however, did not seriously alter the situation of the Indians, since private *patrones* (employers) and the government then inherited these obligations.

The second half of the century saw the development of commercial agriculture along the coast. Cotton plantations arose first, in response to the decline in cotton supplies from the United States during the United States Civil War, followed later by the development of sugar plantations. The irrigation systems required by these plantations exposed the administrative weaknesses of the Peruvian government, in comparison with the efficiency of the Incaic system.[7] The solution developed by the *hacendados* (plantation owners) was the erection of largely independent, self-sufficient "kingdoms" with their own *de facto* laws, courts, and transportation systems connected directly with their private ports and Europe rather than with neighboring towns or Lima.

Sporadic attempts were made to reopen mining operations during the nineteenth century, since most Peruvians still felt that minerals were their only source of real wealth. The major economic debate during the first century after Independence was not over free trade as opposed to the protection of native industry, but as to whether agriculture or mining should be the primary basis of the economy.[8] As it turned out, the ef-

[7] See Karl Witfogel, *Oriental Despotism* (New Haven: Yale University Press, 1957).

[8] Romero, *op.cit.,* p. 274.

fective redevelopment of mining was to await American investments after the turn of the century. From the point of view of the overall development of the Peruvian economy, mining rather than coastal agriculture would perhaps have been the preferable sector, since it would have involved a higher degree of mechanization and more extensive transportation networks deeper into the Indian areas of the country.

The last quarter of the nineteenth century was dominated by what may now be called a salutary disaster. In the 1879 war with Chile, Peru was overwhelmingly defeated, losing her then most valuable mineral deposits, the southern nitrate fields, which had replaced guano as the most easily exploited resource. For the following 15 years the economic and political structure of the country fell back into the chaos of the early years after Independence. Between 1880 and 1890 a political group, differentiated from the military, the Church, and the old landed aristocracy, developed. It could be characterized as representing the urban commercial oligarchy, organized from 1890 to 1920 as the Civilista Party, the first real political party to appear in Peru.

In general, the nineteenth century was an era of isolation from the main currents of Western civilization. Many sections of the country—previously described as active politically, economically, and socially—stagnated. Many mines and isolated haciendas reverted to the hands of the resident Indians when their owners left for the towns. As the government lost effective control over the countryside, highway robberies and bandit gangs were commonplace well into the twentieth century.

Thus, while during the colonial period the popular Spanish expression honoring Peru's wealth was "Vale un Perú" (worth a Peru), during the nineteenth century Raimondi coined the sentence, "El Perú es un mendigo sentado en un banco de oro" (Peru is a beggar seated on a bench of gold).

Ideologically the nineteenth century saw a gradual wean-

7

ing away of Peru's new commercial elite from Spanish to French and finally English influence. French and German interests dominated those public and private schools not run by the Peruvian clergy, while England was overwhelmingly influential in commerce. English domination reached its peak between 1895 and 1930. At the beginning of this period, some London banks bailed the Peruvian government out of its Chilean war debts in return for a long lease on its railroad system, a mortgage on its guano deposits, and control over most of the rest of the government's tax sources, i.e., the private tax-collecting agency, the salt monopoly, and the alcohol tax.

Peruvian writers blame most of Peru's troubles on geography and her Spanish heritage, or, if Hispanophiles, on the Indians. Until 1914, with the opening of the Panama Canal, Peru was indeed off the beaten track of world commerce. There was a very small flow of foreign capital and almost nonexistent immigration of white Europeans. The few who did come, unlike those who came to the United States, were educated and relatively well off and thus entered Peruvian society well above the bottom, exerting, as a consequence, an influence out of proportion to their numbers.

While the Civilista governments did not make any substantial investments in economic or social overhead, they did introduce a number of changes which eventually brought Peru from a chaotic feudal, mercantilist society closer to the nineteenth-century colonial-capitalist economy which she has today. French missions took over the army from 1895 to 1940, while in other areas American advisors were brought in from 1902 on to attempt reform at all levels of public education as well as to build up a navy. American mining investments were encouraged to offset British influence. A brief and calamitous rubber boom occurred near the headwaters of the Amazon, which first raised the as-yet unrealized hopes of Peruvians that their future lay eastward to the jungle (the counterpart of Brazil's current effort to push westward into the same area).

By 1914 a sufficiently large urban, nonagricultural labor force and a close integration with world raw material markets had developed so that the sudden lack of shipping due to the war provided a profound shock to the modern sector of the country. On the one hand, Peru's currency depreciated, and, on the other hand, domestic inflation hit not only imported manufactured goods but many basic food products, since the "excessive" specialization of available coastal land had already made Peru somewhat dependent on imported food. Only the textile mills were benefited by the early war shortages, since most had been operating since 1900 and used mainly native materials for domestic distribution.

The decade from 1920 to 1930 was one of forced-draft development of economic overhead projects, especially highways, port facilities, and public buildings under the dictatorial leadership of President Leguía. His regime was and is reviled by labor and liberal groups, but must, it seems, be accorded a progressive role as far as economic development is concerned.[9] It ended ignominiously in an unprecedented scandal of corruption, and foreign, largely American, intrigue exposed by the Depression. It seems that some United States banks had persuaded the government to undertake an exces-

[9] Although Aprista writers still condemn Leguía as a tyrannous thief because of his persecution of them in the 1920's, some recent reassessments of the *oncenio* (the eleven-year era, 1919–1930) have been kinder to his reputation. See Manuel A. Capuñay, *Leguía* (Lima: 1951); René Hooper López, *Leguía* (Lima: Ediciones Peruanas, 1964). One of the more interesting examples of the early polemical attacks is Abelardo Solís, *Once Años* (Lima: 1934). Apologetic and official party propaganda is well represented by José Reaño García, *Historia del legüiismo—sus hombres y sus obras* (Lima: Ernesto E. Balarezo P., 1928); Partido Democratico Reformista, *Lo que el oncenio hizo por el Perú bajo el mando del Presidente Leguía* (Opúscula No. 2, Lima: Imprenta Gil, n.d., but sometime after 1930); Augusto B. Leguía, *Yo Tirano, Yo Ladrón* (Lima. Editorial "Ahora," S.A., about 1930); Roberto MacLean y Estenós, *Democracia* (Lima: 1926); A. Ulloa Cisneros, *Leguía apuntes de cartera, 1919–1924* (Lima: 1933).

sive number of loans and that more than the usual amount of graft seepage occurred at the end of Leguía's regime.

Peru entered the time of the Depression with a popular military dictator of the nineteenth-century type, Sánchez Cerro, but the army and the commercial oligarchy recovered power shortly thereafter to begin the first serious effort to develop native manufacturing activity as well as embarking on a highway construction program.

The Depression years also saw a brief public emergence of the APRA (Alianza Popular Revolucionaria Americana), an independent, i.e., non-Communist, radical reform party started during the 1920's by Peruvian students and labor leaders.[10] Originally it espoused a strongly socialistic, anti-imperialistic, anticlerical program, but several opportunities to exercise real power, from 1945 to 1948 and from 1956 to 1962 (after long periods of suppression), have caused the Apristas to modify their aims sharply. Both nationalization and anticlericalism have been eliminated in favor of a much modified socialism which consists of copying the most advanced labor and social welfare reforms of Western countries.

The APRA and the Communist Party developed simultaneously and have been played off against each other by strong men in what is by now a classic tactic.[11] The most extreme case of this in Peru was under the dictatorship (relatively mild compared to Batista in Cuba and Pérez Jiménez in Venezuela) of General Odría (1948 to 1956). While officially repressing the Communist Party, as well as the APRA, he actually allowed the Communists to take over or become established in as many labor unions as possible. Between 1956

[10] See Harry Kantor, *The Ideology and Program of the Peruvian Aprista Movement* (Berkeley: University of California Press, 1953).

Alfredo Hernández Urbina, *Los partidos y la crisis del Apra* (Lima: Ediciones Raíz, 1956).

Raúl Haya de la Torre, *Treinta años de Aprismo* (Mexico: Fondo de Cultura Económica, 1956).

[11] See Robert J. Alexander, *Communism in Latin America* (New Brunswick, N.J.: Rutgers University Press, 1957).

and 1962, therefore, a major theme in Peruvian labor affairs was the effort of the Apristas, with some government help, to oust the Communists from the labor movement. The Apristas have been only partially successful and, with the advent of Castroism, have recently lost ground.

World War II was much more profitable for Peru than World War I, even though in both cases war demands raised the potential value of her resources. By 1940 Peru was much better prepared to take advantage of the increased war-created demand for her products. This time the American government was to guarantee purchase of most of her exports as well as subsidize the development of new resources in Peru such as fishing and rubber. So World War II for Peru, as for many other underdeveloped countries, was the period of awakening, if not, in Rostow's terms, of a "take-off."[12] World War II also saw in Peru, as in other Latin American countries, the final replacement of England by the United States as the major investor and foreign cultural influence. With travel to Europe blocked during the war, the post-1940 Peruvian students studying abroad went largely to the United States. A secondary wave, however, went to Argentina, primarily those who lacked the money to go to the United States, or those who could not obtain scholarships. The cost of living is still relatively cheap in Argentina for Peruvians and entrance requirements for foreign students negligible.

The 1945 election in Peru, as in many other Latin American countries, was the most democratic in its history, even though only a minority of the adult males was qualified to vote. (Female suffrage came to Peru in 1955.) The results gave the presidency to a moderate liberal, Bustamante y Rivero, and a majority in the Congress to the APRA. The time proved not ripe for the rash of welfare programs and

[12] See W. W. Rostow, *The Stages of Economic Growth* (New York: Cambridge University Press, 1960).

financial controls instituted by this unstable alliance.[13] The market for Peru's exports fell off at the end of the war while at the same time her pent-up demand for manufactured goods could not be met for several years. The government with its Aprista support proved unable to control the wave of labor unrest which broke out. This was the period in Peru, as all over Latin America, of the Communist Party's greatest pre-Castro-era strength.[14]

In 1948 there was a military coup under General Odría, which restored power not so much to the army as to the commercial "oligarchy." On the advice of Pedro Beltrán, a conservative newspaper editor (*La Prensa*) and confidant of American business interests, an economic advisory mission from the Klein Sax Agency in Washington was called in to recommend (what, as usual in such cases, had already been decided) a program of classic economic reforms, making Peru, in the words of *Fortune* magazine, a "show-case of free enterprise."[15] Exchange controls were dropped, the currency was allowed to depreciate, and the power of labor unions was sharply restricted. However, as in Havana under Batista, the bread-and-butter demands of many urban unionized workers were met during this period, especially just before the peaceful end of this regime (another classic tactic of outgoing *jefes* designed to allow them to leave in a blaze of glory while hamstringing their successors with uneconomic commitments and thus perhaps setting the stage for a popular recall to power).

In 1956 Peru had the unusual experience of seeing a dictator retire voluntarily and allow a free election. Again the Apristas won *de facto* control of the Congress, but this time a compromise was worked out with the commercial "oligarchy"

13 See José Luís Bustamante y Rivero, *Tres años de lucha por la democracia en el Perú* (Buenos Aires: 1949).

14 Alexander, *op.cit.*

15 John Davenport, "Why Peru Pulls Dollars," *Fortune* (November 1956), p. 130.

in which the brother of one of their chief representatives was made President. Labeled *convivencia* (living together), this regime survived and allowed a high degree of personal as well as commercial freedom, but at the expense of popular majority support which the APRA had so long enjoyed. Like the Labor Party in England from 1945 to 1950, the APRA had to condone the suppression of some strikes, and in general support the policies of a president personally detested for different reasons by liberals as well as conservatives. The Apristas' hope was to hold together their support until the 1962 elections—this time to control the government completely. Meanwhile both the Communists and several new liberal parties won over Aprista defectors as well as new voters.

Some Cultural Traits and Institutions

The following summary covers less than half the population—excluding those culturally still Indian and that part of the upper class which is strongly oriented toward one or another foreign culture.

INDIVIDUALISM

Unlike the North American emphasis on egalitarian similarities, Peruvians, as Latins, stress the unique differences—the special spirit or soul of each individual, the dignity of the person. They are highly sensitive and prefer to guard the delicacy of their egos with elaborate social graces which are not merely traditional "survivals." The emphasis on unique personal traits, rather than on objectively measurable status symbols, accompanies an as-yet widespread acceptance of social inequality. The Peruvian's desire is to be treated as a unique human being deserving special consideration rather than "like everyone else."[16] In the United States "an individual despite his personality is deserving of respect because

[16] John Gillin, "Ethos Components in Modern Latin American Culture," *American Anthropologist*, LVII (June 1955), 488.

of his position; there [in Latin America] despite his position he is deserving of respect because of his personality."[17]

CRIOLLISMO

The Peruvian characteristic with perhaps the greatest political and economic significance is called *criollismo*. Most educated Peruvians, at least in writing and in discussions with foreigners, seem ambivalent about this complex of traits. It is apparently a distinctively unique modern Peruvian way of life as opposed to the Spanish, Indian, and foreign traits on which, of course, it was built.

Various writers on the subject are in some agreement as to its current social location and content.[18] It seems that it was derived from nineteenth-century Spanish and French roots and was monopolized by the racially *criollo* (creole) upper class until the twentieth century, when social mobility encouraged lower- and middle-class groups to adopt *criollo* manners. The upper class in turn, invaded as they were by "elite foreigners," split up into groups oriented around one or another Western culture. They have gradually disassociated themselves from one *criollo* trait after another as part of the modern mobile society fashion cycle. The only remaining members of this class to exhibit and indeed set *criollo* standards are rich playboys whose antics establish models for *criollo* emulation. In Lima, therefore, *criollismo* is currently the possession of middle- and lower-class mestizos ("mixtures"—Indian and Spanish) , while in provincial centers, the local elite,

17 Allan R. Holmberg, *Some Fundamental Assumptions of Latin American Culture*, International Management Association Pamphlet (1949), p. 207.

18 See Harry Tschopik, "On the Concept of Creole Culture in Peru," *Transactions of the New York Academy of Sciences*, Ser. ii, No. 10 (1948), 252-261.

José Mejía Baca, *Aspectos criollos* (Lima: 1937).

Ozzie Simmons, "The Criollo Outlook in the Mestizo Culture of Coastal Peru," *American Anthropologist*, lvii (February 1955), 107.

Federico Schwab, "Lo huachafo como fenómeno social," *Peruanidad*, ii (March 1942), 400-402.

naïvely supposing those traits to represent current Limenian high society, are the most *criollo* group.

There is no question, however, that Lima is the center of *la vida criolla*. This way of life includes unique dances, highly seasoned food, and *pisco* (grape brandy) and *chicha* (corn beer). In terms of personal characteristics it involves social poise in all company, verbal suasion, and clever self-aggrandizement, especially if it means getting away with something even at another person's expense. In love affairs *ser un criollo verdadero* (to be real creole) or *muy macho* (very masculine) is to be a Don Juan, in politics it is to be *un comechado* (one who gets ahead with a minimum of effort), in public *un gorrero* (a gate-crasher). These latter traits in part aggravate the general *desconfianza* (lack of public trust) which to North American eyes reaches paranoid proportions in Peru.

There is little security in Peru from the smallest to the most important matters. This situation tends to reinforce kinship and other ascribed personal ties as the only basis for confidence. Therefore, while eventually industrialization may radically reduce the genealogical range and role pervasiveness of kinship, the social disorientation which is a chronic aspect of the transitional stage may postpone the reduction in the importance of this institution. The extension of kinship-style obligations to non-kin would seem to be a part of the same social phenomena, although the selection of *compadres* (see next section) can be objectively "universalistic" in spite of the effusive language of friendship and the traditional roots of this institution.

Criollismo is the antithesis of the Protestant ethic. It is concerned largely with leisure-time activities. In this respect it is a combination of old upper- and lower-class traits. It tolerates work only as an evil necessity and a challenge to one's *ingenio malicioso* (malicious ingenuity).

Needless to say, these characteristics are extremely unsuited to economic development. Some of the conservative older generation as well as younger leftists blame foreigners for the prevalence of graft and extortion in Peru—as well as for most of her other ills. The Leguía era with its scandalous American loans was supposed to have been the origin of this degeneration in public and private morals. "Before that only people of good family with independent means occupied responsible positions and therefore could not be corrupted." This interpretation is surely inaccurate and an example of defensive xenophobia. Even granting this sequence of events, a more likely explanation would be that the universalistic treatment of clients never existed. The earlier corruption consisted of favoritism based on particularistic ties rather than on money. When foreigners presented themselves to the Peruvian government with no one or nothing to recommend them but the color of their money, corruption followed as much by extortion as by bribery. Occasionally one must pay not only for a favorable decision, whether just or not, but also to obtain any action at all, not to mention the necessity to pay officials to avoid being unjustly abused, that is, "protection money."

COMPADRAZGO

Compadrazgo (spiritual kinship) experiences a renewed utility due to *desconfianza*. It involves ceremonialized ties made between adults (*compadres*) with the official goal of obtaining a godparent for a child who then becomes the *ahijado* (godchild) of his *padrino* (godfather).

The most interesting features of this institution are the following: (1) it is flourishing more vigorously in Latin America than in Spain,[19] having been extended far beyond baptism to cover the first nailcutting, first haircut, store openings, and any other "deserving cause"; (2) it flourishes most in transitional areas where it "constitutes one of the most effec-

19 Gillin, *op.cit.*, p. 104.

16

tive mechanisms in the hands of the [socially] ambitious."[20] It could be said that *compadrazgo* is flourishing most intensively just before what will presumably be its demise because of its peculiar usefulness in a socially mobile society with little public justice. Subordinate individuals in all situations feel that talent or their legal rights are no guarantee of justice or success, and that only a powerful patron can provide adequate protection. So one finds factory workers, public and private office employees, domestic servants, etc., trying to establish what today have become rather one-sided relationships in which workers invite a superior to become their *compadre*. For this compliment the *patrón* is expected to provide unlimited assistance and use his political influence to protect and promote the "cause" in question. From the author's point of view, "progressive" factory managers, usually foreign, carefully avoided such "snares." Most Peruvian foremen and managers, however, ask, "But how can you refuse?"

These cultural traits lie at the heart of the question of the purity and extensity of the labor market. They are the basis for the antipathy to some of the means toward the generally desired end of economic development. We shall, therefore, be discussing such limitations on the rationalization of the labor market as paternalism and regional, racial, and sexual preferences affecting recruitment, job placement, and promotion.

Some Relevant Issues and Problems

INDIGENISMO (INDIANISM)

This movement developed largely as a result of the example of the Mexican Revolution and the importation of a version of the "white man's burden," rather than from indigenous roots. The *indigenistas* are a diverse group, however. At one extreme there are sentimental xenophobes who regard the Inca civilization as a lost socialist paradise and propound an

---

[20] François Bourricaud, "Algunas características originales de la cultura mestiza en el Perú contemporáneo," *Revista del Museo Nacional* (Lima, XXIII (1954), 167.

extreme version of the *leyenda negra*—the black legend of Spanish rule. At the other extreme are those who want to help the Indian by getting him to slough off his "Indianness" and join the national culture which they define in European terms. In the middle are a few writers who envision some sort of fusion of cultures, even in the face of the fact that the current Indian culture is only the sad tag end of the Inca civilization, having lost its virtues and preserved in attenuated form its vices. In social structure and costume, in fact, it more clearly resembles medieval Spanish society than the Incaic civilization.[21]

The most striking aspect of the *indigenista* movement is its lack of support from even the more ambitious of the Indians themselves. Bourricaud feels that the primary goal of mestizo support for *indigenismo* was embarrassment of the Aprista–Prado *convivencia* regime and the rural landed aristocracy in general. There seems also to be no conscious resistance on the part of Indians to losing their "Indianness."[22] It would be difficult to be a Rousseauan primitivist in a country in which the bottom half of the population so devalues its own existence. As in other Latin American Indian countries, the peasants are officially honored but personally despised.

The major attempt to do something for the Indians has been the *comunidad indígena* law. It provides for the registration of so-called Indian communities, presumably survivals of the pre-Columbian Ayllu. (These were small communities presumably based in part on kinship ties. Land was owned by the community with plots assigned to families and some fields and pasture land worked in common. The persistence of any traditionally communal ayllus today is a matter of dispute among the experts.) If it had been successful this program could have perpetuated the absence of Indian participation in Peruvian life. In fact, as usual, the results of this "reform" have been quite different. The communities best able to take advantage of the law's privileges have been the settlements that were least Indian. Some of them have been able to re-

---

[21] Patch, *op.cit.*   [22] Bourricaud, *op.cit.*, pp. 169-170.

cover some land from nearby large private landowners. The prevalence of private property norms within these communities, however, has meant that the law has accelerated their involvement with the national economy.

Peru has always been officially a highly centralized country in all respects.[23] However, during much of its first half century of independence, by default as well as in reaction to colonial rule, the provincial centers enjoyed a considerable degree of political autonomy, at the cost of cultural and economic isolation. The country was eventually unified through a French type of centralized political control during the Leguía era (1919–1930). All public officials of any importance, even mayors (until 1963), were appointed from Lima. Most taxes still come from import–export duties collected by the national government and therefore regressively, like a sales tax, fall most heavily on the poor. Peru imports not only luxuries but even some basic foodstuffs, since the efficient sector of Peruvian agriculture is devoted to export crops.

At various times in Peru's history both self-defined liberals and conservatives have been for and against centralization.[24] It seems to have been a matter of whether one's party was in or out of favor in Lima. Since Western-style twentieth-century liberals have been out of favor most of the time, they have usually been against Lima's monopoly of power, which has "parasitically" drained the lifeblood of the country for its own enrichment.[25] Currently, however, since a liberal regime is

[23] Like many other Latin American capitals, Lima (1) is Peru's largest city, (2) is its fastest growing city, (3) contained, in 1940, 40 percent of all population in centers over 2,500, (4) contained a significant percentage of the entire national population (8.6 percent), (5) is ten times the size of the next largest city. Kingsley Davis and Ana Casis, "Urbanization in Latin America," *Milbank Memorial Fund Quarterly*, XXIV (April 1946), 2.

[24] Mariátegui, *op.cit.*, p. 169.

[25] Jorge Basadre, *La multitud, la ciudad, y el campo* (Lima: Editorial Huascaran, 1947), p. 157.

in power, the tables are turned. When asked directly about this issue, most of this writer's governmental acquaintances said in effect, "Yes, it's true Lima is grossly oversized and we should do more for other areas, but not by letting the local *gamonales* (rural plutocrats) and *tinterillos criollos* (shyster lawyers) have anything to say about it. Because Lima has everything, there is no responsible local leadership left."

The stagnation still found in provincial centers is only partly due to the central government's clear preference for channeling most funds to Lima. An equal factor, and in the past a more important one, has been the nature of the islands of economic activity which have existed in rural areas of Peru. Both the commercialized haciendas and the mines, originally out of necessity, have developed as self-sufficient worlds unto themselves. Each would construct a company town complete with all urban facilities including private transportation facilities leading directly to the nearest port— all of this the private property of the *hacendado* or mine owner. This policy was followed not only where no other facilities were available but even near Trujillo, an Aprista center, where there was a sizable town nearby. There were political as well as technological advantages for these firms in remaining as isolated as possible from ordinary Peruvian society. The result was that nearby towns would stagnate since their normal hinterlands would be unavailable as a source of food or labor or as a consumers' market.

Lima, the "primate" city. It is undeniably true that since the start of the colonial empire, Lima has drawn more in taxes and resources from rural and provincial Peru than it has returned. The greater part of the nonagricultural investments which have been made outside Lima have come from foreign sources of capital. In part, for these reasons the social distance between rural and provincial Peru and its capital has increased rapidly since 1900. Also it must be noted that Lima is an island of intense urban concentration in a rural ocean —the symbol of a dual culture. In Lima the immigrant slums ring the outside of the city, instead of swelling out from the central business district as in the United States. These *barriadas clandestinas,* or squatter villages, are at best semiurban phenomena since they usually lack any government-supplied urban utilities or services because of the government's fear of encouraging more migration.

Most of these *barriadas,* which encircle Lima on the north and east, have arisen since 1940, when an earthquake, together with the war-induced increase of migrants, created a desperate housing shortage. The government reacted, not with a housing program but merely with a rent-freeze law in order to give quick, easy protection to tenants. To this day, according to law, no one may be evicted without the government's permission nor rents raised during any tenancy. Rents may be raised between tenants, however; thus the rents on new and transferred dwellings are abnormally high to compensate for the frozen rents on other property.

As a result of the clustering of migrants from the same areas, locality clubs tend to develop in the *barriadas.* The net effect of these clubs is to speed up acculturation to urban life. Nevertheless, locality clubs are somewhat dysfunctional for urban adjustment. They promote marriage ties among people from the same backgrounds and carry over in Lima factions based on provincial feuds. They also carry the small-town lack of privacy into an environment which would otherwise provide an escape from such inhibiting intimacy. However, membership in these clubs is, of course, voluntary. The socially prominent members tend to be rather exploited by the lower-class members as group patrons, but in these cases such individuals are usually compensated by having an assured body of clients or political supporters, which is often their object in joining such clubs.

Therefore, in some respects this state of semiurbanity in the slums both eases and delays acculturation. In other respects, however, it hastens it, since the worst of the slums are generally worse than any rural habitations. Hence, an indeterminate disillusioned percentage return to rural areas while the majority seek to get out of the slums into the heart of the city or to new suburban housing developments. The returning group, however, scarcely leaves behind a dent in the excessive labor supply in Lima.

The apparently universal adjustment to this type of oversupply is a proliferation of traditional service occupations, especially petty retailing and domestic service. The implications of both of these occupations for the process of acculturation to "industrial" mores are problematical. On the one hand, both are traditional in form; on the other hand, the thousands of petty street peddlers are certainly classic commercial entrepreneurs working in a rather pure and elastic market. But their desperation leads inevitably to the intrusion of a traditionalistic particularism, namely, begging, which is the selling of themselves as pitiable rather than their products as valuable. Those few who succeed in this general occupation end up as bourgeois merchants whose habits and philosophy are extremely antithetical to industrialization, as, for example, in the Poujadist movement in France.

Domestic servants, on the other hand, except in the homes of the traditional elite or foreigners from servantless countries, are apt to suffer the most abusive treatment of any laborers in Peru. They are in such oversupply that the poorest white-collar mestizo family can and "must" afford at least one Indian maid. The turnover in this occupation is extremely high, only a small percentage remaining even a year with such employers. This occupation seems to be the most effective "make or break" experience. Domestic servants either return to their provincial homes or leave for factory or construction work.

The central question then is whether this "exploitation" by Lima of rural Peru has been largely a dead-end process. Has the capital exported or funneled to Lima been squandered on expenses, such as real estate speculation, of no long-run use to Lima or Peru as a whole? Or, on balance, has this "exploitation" been a process of creating a metropolitan center with sufficient minimum economies of scale and a cultural climate propitious for industrial development?

It would seem that rapid industrial growth today requires the accumulation of capital at such a rate that not all a developing country's citizens can enjoy, at the same time, a continuous real increase in income until the crucial "take-off" stage has been passed. This statement assumes, of course, that the major resources for such growth are not going to be found in foreign gifts or some new "gold mine." This point of view is not intended to defend the manner in which wealth has been extracted from the lower class and rural inhabitants of Peru. In fact, such exploitation has certainly reached the point of diminishing returns. The government must soon undertake long overdue social overhead investments outside Lima.[26]

But it is still my contention that Lima's size and location have been essential to what industrial development has been achieved. It is impossible, of course, to prove *ex post facto* historical hypotheses, but the minimum population size required to utilize and maintain efficiently various urban facilities has been established, at least for some "Western" countries. Furthermore, since numbers of people as well as median income determine the effective size of a market, a poorer population needs to be more numerous than a wealthier one at the same level of gross demand. I am speaking, of course, of those services not highly tied to class tastes. Lima has relatively efficient public utilities which in some cases were the decisive factor in decisions of industrialists to locate there rather than in provincial towns (aside from the question of nearness to markets), even when the other areas had ostensibly compensatory advantages.

More difficult to demonstrate is the ideological and social climate required for industrialization. Economic changes inspired by other countries have occurred in rural areas as a consequence of the development of commercial haciendas and mines, but until recently such potential centers of new ideas

26 United Nations, *op.cit.,* pp. 43, 152.

have had a minimal external social impact. Profits were sent abroad; communication and transportation facilities often connected these outposts more conveniently with Europe than with nearby towns or Lima. Most of the administrative personnel were foreign, and no planned efforts were made to educate Peruvian employees beyond the narrowest requirements of their jobs. In Lima, on the other hand, adequate and willing clerical employees are available. (The distaste Peruvian white-collar workers have for provincial posts surpasses that of foreign employees. Of course, the foreigners are paid more, but in most cases these bonuses for nonpermanent foreign employees make up for real expenses.)

Lima, by serving as the primary receiving area for internal migration, has been able, locally, to offset the nationally worsening dependency burden inevitable in the early phase of such rapid population growth. Thus, while the average age temporarily declines and the dependency burden of children rises sharply in the country as a whole, by age-selective migration Lima gains a population which at least as far as its age distribution is concerned is much more "efficient." This is especially important because the Andean republics have received so little foreign white immigration and none of it at the blue-collar-worker level.

On these general grounds, then, it is arguable that a high degree of urban concentration is not only common but favorable to industrialization in an underdeveloped country. It is, however, at best only a necessary condition, not a sufficient one.

It would follow, then, that the logical locale for manufacturing ventures would be in the most modern urban complex. I shall, therefore, be comparing the textile factories in Lima with those established in rural areas as illustrative of the advantages of an urban location.

TRANSPORTATION PROBLEMS

Until the 1930's, overland transportation throughout Peru was extremely difficult and slow, hampered by mountainous or jungle terrain, bandits, and tolls for the use of what primitive roads did exist. The exceptions to this situation were, of course, the railroads. The first main line, and still one of the world's most spectacular, is the Central Railroad running from Lima to the central sierra mining areas, and only incidentally to Huancayo and a few other nonmining centers. It was started in 1867 with loans from guano exports and built by a fabulously corrupt and clever American engineer, who used Chinese coolies rather than Peruvian Indians for his labor force.[27] His sudden death, and Peru's defeat in the Chilean war, ended this line at Chilca in 1883 until the British continued it to Huancayo after the great "bailing out" loan of 1895 gave them control over most of Peru's railroad lines for 66 years. The British also carried the Mollendo–Puno line, built in 1876, on to Cuzco in 1908, where the picturesque Santa Ana spur to the jungle and Macchu Pichu was added.

The central line has predictably structured the economic and urban development along its route, but no overall "transportation determinism" is possible since the southern line has only recently begun to drain off the Indians of the southern plateau, through whose heartland it passes. Also, all of Peru's railroads, except part of the southern line, run east and west to the coast, not north and south, which would have been much more effective in unifying the country, as the Pan-American Highway has subsequently demonstrated.[28] In addition, there are five different gauges to complicate any eventual program which might try to integrate the entire system. In fact, no major effort is being made to improve the railroad system. In 1954, there were 3,536 kilometers of public railroads, representing an almost unbroken decline in trackage since the 1929 peak of 4,500 kilometers.[29]

[27] See Watt Stewart, *Henry Meiggs, the Yankee Pizarro* (Durham, N.C.: Duke University Press, 1947).

[28] Federico Basadre, *Comparación entre ferrocarriles y caminos en el Perú* (Lima: Sociedad de Ingenieros, 1927).

[29] Ministerio de Hacienda y Comercio, *Boletín de estadística peruana 1954* (Lima: 1954), p. 198.

Highways, because of their recent construction and the intrinsically more flexible nature of automotive transportation, are currently the socially significant routes. Work on highway construction is often the first paid job of Indians in isolated areas and new roads are used as soon as the locally made wooden bus bodies can be mounted on imported truck chassis. A common "transitional" occupation noted on many personnel cards in the textile sample was *ayudante de camión,* that is, the chore boy who loads the baggage on the roof and picks up and delivers packages en route. Drivers often find they have to recruit a new boy for each trip.

Highway construction outside the city of Lima began during the 1920's under the dictatorship of Leguía through a special law requiring every male over 21 to work on road construction or hire a substitute. The first overdue step was the removal of tolls, followed by the construction of the main north–south coastal route, the Pan-American Highway. More recently, since World War II, east-west feeder roads have been built from the sierra out to the coastal highway. By 1946 there were 2,600 kilometers of paved roads, one of which accomplished the feat of reaching the jungle at Pucallpa, which is on a tributary of the Amazon. The current highway program is at the direct and indirect expense of the railway system, since its lines are paralleled in every case by major highways and its revenues specially taxed for road construction.

Hammel observed that the local effect of paving the roads near Ica, a department just south of Lima, was to channel all traffic to these routes, the overall result being more traffic over fewer roads, which effectively leaves to stagnation villages not in the path of the roads and rejuvenates similar communities through which they happen to pass. Since most travel goes to and from Lima, cross routes fall into disuse. Marriage patterns, if not endogamous, follow suit, shifting from intervillage to rural-urban.[30]

[30] Eugene A. Hammel, *Wealth, Authority and Prestige in the Ica Valley, Peru* (Albuquerque: University of New Mexico Press, 1962).

Therefore, as Cole notes, although one of the primary objectives of road building was to develop isolated, moribund, outlying regions, the result in Peru has been to drain off the labor force from these areas. This is clearly due to the lack of a program of diversified and dispersed industrial development.[31]

PERUANIDAD (PERUVIANISM)—AND THE REVOLUTION?

In concluding this discussion of current Peruvian issues and problems, reference should be made to discussions of the "meaning" and direction of Peruvian history.

Underlying most recent analyses of Peru is the implied question, "When is the revolution going to occur?" Bolivia is currently enduring a prolonged period of unrest, Mexico has had a real social revolution,[32] and Peru, on the basis of many indices, is overdue for such a transformation.[33] While preferring not to discuss the matter, most prudent men of wealth, especially those with land and hence with firsthand experience with occasional Indian violence, are said to have banked funds abroad for a sudden flight. On the other hand, I feel, Carleton Beals' 1934 picture is overdrawn as well as outdated.[34] The Indians of the sierra, miserable and abused though they be, are not a restive "Mongol horde" on the verge of descending to the coastal plains in a bloody effort to eradicate whites and Western civilization. The social lines and ties of importance in Peru are primarily cultural rather than racial. The groups most likely to cause violence are not Indians but *cholos*[35] and mestizos, as recent labor troubles have

[31] J. P. Cole, *Estudio geográfico de la gran Lima* (Lima: Oficina Nacional de Planeamiento y Urbanismo, 1957), Sección 2, p. 11.

[32] George I. Blanksten, "Technical Assistance and the Political Instability of Latin America," *Economic Development and Cultural Change*, II (June 1954), 350.

[33] Jesús Veliz Lizárraga, *El Perú y la cultura occidental* (Lima: Biblioteca de Ensayos Sociológicos, 1957), p. 106.

[34] Carleton Beals, *Fire on the Andes* (New York: Lippincott, 1934), p. 22.

[35] *Cholos* are racially Indian, but acculturating to the dominant Latin culture by wearing shoes, speaking Spanish, and expressing rising ambi-

indicated. Indian violence is typically an unorganized burst of anger in a local setting as in the occasional lynching of a white plantation or mine foreman.

My own view on the likelihood of a violent transformation is that Peru may escape the need to industrialize under a brutally totalitarian government after a radical revolution. The country may be able to continue as at present under an administration of Machiavellian "foxes" gnawing away the power of conservative, anti-industrial groups by indirect means. But the race between economic and demographic growth has yet to be decided.

As for explicit discussions of the meaning of Peru's history, it would seem that the majority of nationally and internationally recognized historians would not quarrel in substance with the following quotation, though perhaps they would take issue with its tone:

> Many Peruvians have pointed out that the history of Republican Peru is anything but "glorious" being largely a sorry chronicle of political opportunism and corruption, economic shortsightedness and backwardness, social disunity, incoherence, cultural nemesis and sterility; her nineteenth century literature "trivial and florid" concerned largely with Lima high life and religion.[36]

In the effort to overcome the sense of cultural inferiority and pessimism which a study of Peru's history can impart, major historians such as Basadre have turned from the liberal

---

tion in all fields. They are a "marginal group in revolt." Mestizos are racially part Indian, part Latin, with a full sense of national membership. See Aníbal Quijano, "La emergencia del grupo 'cholo' y sus consecuencias en la sociedad peruana" in Asociación Colombiana de Sociología, *Sociología y sociedad en latinoamérica* (Bogotá, Colombia: 1965), pp. 403-446; and Gabriel Escobar M., "El mestizaje en la región andina: el caso del Perú" in *Revista de Indias* (Madrid: No. 95-96, January–June, 1964), pp. 197-220.

[36] J. N. Plank, "Peru, A Study in the Problem of Nation Forming" (unpublished Ph.D. dissertation, Department of Political Science, Harvard University, 1958), p. 27.

criticism of their youth to playing the role of responsible propagandist, speaking today hopefully of the at least metaphysical reality of *peruanidad* (Peruvianism).[37] The current younger generation of critical writers, however, is still plagued by painful doubts as to the quality of Peru's membership in Western civilization.

After observing that the process of industrialization has meant the linking of "civilized" with "industrialized," and hence the denigration of the "developing" world as made up of "natives," Veliz Lizárraga goes on to say:

> This type of discrimination . . . influenced Indo-America and especially Peru in the form of a self-devaluation of our people and our cultural values—an attitude which is growing. Since Independence we blame our racial heritage for our political, social, economic, and cultural evils. With this self-denigrating attitude our developing mestizo element is seen as an obstacle which prevents us from progressing and which justifies . . . Western racist theories. From this comes the determination to westernize our habits and customs. The foreignized mentality of our ruling class until now has its explanation in this devaluation and inferiority complex toward the West. For these reasons there has arisen a desire to populate Peru with European immigrants, if possible Saxons, in order to make the country progress and to improve the "race"[38] [translation].

There is no question about the desire of educated Peruvians to be accepted as participants in Western civilization. Until the early 1960's there was not, in Peru, any serious East-West division of orientation as in many Asian and African countries. (The most effective United States propaganda line has been

[37] See Jorge Basadre, *La promesa de la vida peruana* (Lima: Librería Editorial Juan Mejía Baca, 1958).

[38] Veliz Lizárraga, *op.cit.*, p. 68.

See also Luís Alberto Sánchez, *El Perú: retrato de un país adolescente* (Buenos Aires: Ediciones Continente, 1958).

to brand Russia and hence communism as "Eastern" and therefore, by implication, as not part of Western civilization. Russia likewise has had some success in Peru in emphasizing its Western-type cultural achievements. However, there are still no diplomatic relations with the Communist nations.)

The commitment to Western civilization is not, however, to those values and institutions which resulted in the Industrial Revolution. Spain, after all, has only recently entered the twentieth century. In Peru, this commitment is based first of all on a desire to appear "cultivated" and secondly on a fear of being associated with anything Indian.

Current Social and Economic Structure

Peru is the fourth largest country in Latin America, after Brazil, Mexico, and Argentina, with a population of 10,420,357 in 1961. Its coast is a long, narrow strip of the world's driest desert—absolutely barren without irrigation. This peculiar situation arises from the coldness of the Antarctic Humbolt current which provides no moisture for the western slopes of the Andes to condense into rain. There are thus no navigable rivers on the coast, merely a series of short, irregular streams. Most of those which run all year have been stretched out to irrigate the nearby valley and supply a port at the river's mouth.

The sierra or mountainous region (27 percent of Peru in territory and 60 percent in population) runs the length of Peru from north to south, widening out in the south into the *altiplano,* a high plateau from 11,000 to 16,000 feet.

The jungle, *la selva,* is the largest and the least populated area of Peru and is one of the most inaccessible of the world's jungles.

DEMOGRAPHIC CHARACTERISTICS

The 1940 census director, Alberto Arca Parró, and most white Peruvians were pleased to see that at last Peru was only 45 percent Indian by race. However, most authorities insist that Indians by race still constitute well over 50 percent of the population.[39] For most purposes ethnic-behavioral differences are more significant than visible racial characteristics. Peruvians are not segregationists in the South African or North American sense, although shadings of color are often a matter of invidious distinctions.

As for the distribution of population, the coast has been populated primarily by whites and Negroes since before Independence, with the addition of Chinese and Japanese after 1850. The Indian population is concentrated in the sierra, the degree of "Indianness" varying fairly directly with altitude, with the exception of the larger mining towns. There is also a north–south differentiation, with mestizos, in a cultural as well as racial sense, predominating in the north and Indians in the central part and especially in the southern plateau or *altiplano* region.[40]

There is a peculiarly discontinuous vertical distribution of population owing to the barren Pacific slope of the Andes. In 1940, 28 percent lived between sea level and 250 meters, 5.8 percent between 251 and 1,750 meters, and the majority, 63 percent, between 1,751 to 4,500 meters. Life of any kind in western Peru can survive only near the few rivers on the Pacific slope or near the permanent snowline, hence the peculiar absence of population between 250 and 1,750 meters. This gap is significant in limiting migration to long distances because of the lack of "intervening opportunities."

In 1940, 42 percent of the population over 15 years of age was defined as literate.[41] By 1961, the 17+ age group demonstrated a 60 percent literacy figure on the basis of a somewhat different definition. In 1940, 24 percent of the children aged 6 to 14 were not in school on the coast and 71 percent

[39] John Howland Rowe, "The Distribution of Indians and Indian Languages in Peru," *Geographical Review*, XXXVII (April 1947), 202.

[40] International Labor Office, *Indigenous People* (Geneva: 1953), p. 60.

[41] *Censo nacional de población* (Lima: Dirección Nacional de Estadística, 1940), I, 179.

were not being educated in the sierra.[42] Among those over 6
years of age, 61 percent of all males and 39 percent of all
females were literate.[43] The 1961 data, which are neither
defined nor presented in a comparable fashion, reveal that
82 percent of those 17 years or older living in urban areas
were literate, with 39 percent the figure for rural areas.

In 1959 the United Nations Economic Commission for
Latin America estimated Peru's rate of natural increase at a
very high 25 per 1000. However, the 1961 census subsequently
revealed that the actual rate of natural increase was 30 per
1000 arising from a birth rate of 45 per 1000 and a death
rate of 15 per 1000.[44] The apparent stability of the birth rate
together with a decline in death rates is illustrated by the following figures from the United Nations report[45] (crude rates
per 1000).

Period	Birth	Death	Natural increase
1940-45 (U.N. estimate)	43.0	24.5	18.5
1945-50 (U.N. estimate)	43.0	23.3	19.7
1950-55 (U.N. estimate)	43.0	23.0	20.0
1955-60 (U.N. estimate)	43.0	19.0	24.0
1960-65 (U.N. estimate)	43.0	17.4	25.6
1961 (Official census)	45.0	15.0	30.0

With a life expectancy of 40 years and a current rate of
population increase in excess of 3 percent per year, Peru has
clearly lost the ability to decide on any course of action other
than rapid industrialization if a mass welfare goal is assumed.

According to official figures nearly 60 percent of Peru's inhabitants were living in rural areas in 1940 and working in
directly agricultural occupations. However, a careful reading
of the definition of urban places used in the 1940 census indicates that in United States terms the urban percentage is

[42] *Ibid.*, p. 180.   [43] *Ibid.*, p. 264.

[44] *Sexto censo nacional de población* (Lima: Dirección Nacional de
Estadística y Censos, Marzo 1965), Tomo i, p. 10.

[45] United Nations, *op.cit.*, p. 4.

approximately one half of these figures, that is, 18 instead of 36 percent.[46] By 1961, the date of the only enumeration since 1940, the Peruvian census officially lists 47 percent of Peruvians as living in urban areas.[47] Again, however, if more demanding criteria are employed, it turns out that only 32 percent live in "populated centers" over 5,000, or 39 percent in centers over 2,000.[48]

Since 1940, Lima has grown at a rate almost twice as fast as Peru as a whole, from 562,885 to 1,578,729. The primary source of this rapid growth has apparently been migration, although a recent study suggests that the urban rate of natural increase in preindustrial societies may be underestimated.[49] It was 12.8 in Peru in 1940 and 30.3 in 1955.[50] Therefore, it may not be the case in the early stages of rapid urban growth that birth rates in the largest cities are the lowest in the country, nor are the death rates there always as high or higher than in rural areas or small towns.

Throughout Latin America, "a really massive movement of people into cities did not begin until well after 1920."[51] García Frías estimates that in 1939, 41 percent of Limenians were born in other departments compared to 45 percent in 1940, with 147,785 migrants coming to Lima between 1931 and 1941.[52] Cavanaugh estimates that of Lima's growth between 1940 and 1954, 240,000 was due to natural increase and 260,000 to internal migration.[53]

[46] See Appendix B on Methodological Procedure and Problems.

[47] *Sexto censo nacional de población*, p. 34.

[48] *Ibid.*, p. 30.

[49] William Petersen, "The Demographic Transition in the Netherlands," *American Sociological Review* (June 1960), p. 334.

[50] Joseph Cavanaugh, *Socio-demographic Characteristics of Lima, Peru* (Lima: Foreign Operations Administration, 1955), p. 5.

[51] Harley L. Browning, "Present Trends in Latin American Urbanization," *Annals of the American Academy of Political and Social Science*, cccxvi (March 1958), 112.

[52] Roque García Frías, "Crecimiento de la población de Lima, ciudad, capital," *Estadística peruana*, Año i, No. 1 (January 1945), p. 41.

[53] Cavanaugh, *op.cit.*, p. 112.

ECONOMIC STRUCTURE

The stage of industrialization. Since economists have contributed the most powerful concepts to the study of economic development as one type of social change, I shall attempt to place Peru, 1900 to 1960, in these terms.[54] In general, Peru's case again demonstrates the fact that these stage concepts should be viewed as analytical aspects of growth and not physically delimited concrete eras.[55]

It appears that in Peru, as compared to the classic English case, the stages are much closer to each other in time and in some cases superimposed or altered in sequence. Furthermore, there seems to be no universal causal chain of stages. The precondition era has in a sense occurred once and for all for the whole world. Since the stimulus for development in most current cases is largely external, one finds limited sectors of "maturity" and "mass consumption" even before the "take-off" has occurred.[56]

Peru is probably an extreme case of a country which postponed many of the "precondition" steps often deemed necessary. There has yet to be a strongly nationalistic, antilandholder, prodevelopment government with the power to enact an effective program. Industrial development is occurring largely at the instigation of foreigners.

The leading sector might have been railroad construction during the 1870's and early 1900's, but this growth petered out without stimulating the development of much local supporting industry. The major era of textile mill development was from 1896 to 1914, but again, as Rostow observed,

> The development of a cotton textile industry sufficient to meet domestic requirements . . . has not generally imparted a sufficient impulse in itself to launch a self-sustaining

[54] See Rostow, *op.cit.*; Colin Clark, *The Conditions of Economic Progress* (New York: St. Martins, 1957).

[55] Wilbert E. Moore, "A Reconsideration of Theories of Social Change," *American Sociological Review*, xxv (December 1960), 815.

[56] See Rostow, *op.cit.*

growth process. . . . It has marked more typically the pre-take-off period as for example in India, China and Mexico.[57]

In Rostow's terms, Peru is yet to enter the "take-off" era. Only Mexico and Argentina in Latin America have entered it, while Brazil and Venezuela are approaching it. Peru is still absorbed in the "primary growth" sector, exploiting easily processed and accessible raw materials.

Peru, like most of Latin America, has in Kerr's terms the least propitious political climate for rapid economic growth.[58] On the assumption that rapid industrialization can only or can best be achieved through high mass motivation and authoritarian controls, a country should have both an internally powerful centralized government and an external threat to justify extraordinary controls and policies glorifying collective over personal ends. In these terms Japan had both the control and the threat while Spain had controls only and Italy a threat only. Latin America's failure to industrialize during the nineteenth and early twentieth centuries could then be explained by the absence of either external threat or internal control. This interpretation is similar to Rostow's "reactive nationalism" as a prerequisite ideology and historical event allowing for eventual self-generated industrialization.[59]

The Latin love of rhetoric and the world-wide commitment to the materialistic and idealistic implications of economic development make an evaluation of Peru's verbal commitment to industrialization very difficult. The language of radical reform and materialistic progress is exploited indiscriminately by men of many shades of political opinion. Moreover, vague commitment to ends guarantees no unanimity as to means. In Peru one can expose a real lack of agreement even with some of the ends of industrial development on the part of

[57] *Ibid.*, p. 153.

[58] See Clark Kerr, John T. Dunlop, Frederick Harbison, and Charles A. Myers, *Industrialism and Industrial Man* (Cambridge: Harvard University Press, 1960).

[59] Rostow, *op.cit.*, p. 26.

various powerful interest groups. This resistance is partly sentimental, a natural preference of the elite for the good old days of cheap, faithful domestic and public servants, and partly economic, a preference for a "colonial" type of economy in which rural landowners constitute the aristocracy of wealth as well as social position.

In Peru one also finds, in addition to the social and ethnic divisions aggravated by economic change, a clash among the elite groups with respect to differing foreign cultures of orientation and hence different styles of economic development.

Land. Latin America is often characterized as being fortunate in still having enough land for its people, in being under-populated relative to the Orient.[60] Such a judgment assumes much about the social and technological problems in opening up the Amazonian jungle. In Peru's case, it seems that there has been for some years an absolute shortage of usable land.[61] Both the modern commercial plantations and the Indian farmers have reached the economic limits of land utilization. Only "uneconomic" subsidies, a considerable real increase in the cost of food, or perhaps a radical reduction in the cost of desalinating water will make the irrigation of new land commercially profitable.[62]

The amount of land under cultivation has not increased since 1929. In the sierra there is 0.23 of a hectare of cultivatable land per capita, 0.54 on the coast, and 0.08 in the heavily Indian southern department of Cuzco.[63] This situation is due in part to the extremely forbidding nature of Peru's topography and climate.

[60] Luís Alberto Sánchez, "Latin America and the War," *Latin American Viewpoints*, Pamphlet Series II (Philadelphia: American Academy of Political and Social Science, 1942), p. 5.

[61] Thomas R. Ford, *Man and Land in Peru* (Gainesville, Fla.: University of Florida Press, 1955), p. 96.

[62] Klein-Sax Economic Mission to Peru, "A Brief Report of Peruvian Production and Prices," May 29, 1951 (mimeographed).

[63] Francisco Ponce de León, *Bosquejo del problema de la propiedad de la tierra en el Perú* (Lima: 1946), p. 161.

Evidence of Peru's export-cash-crop–dominated agricultural sector is its inability to produce enough of the basic foods for its own people. Wheat, rice, and meat have been imported in increasing quantities since World War I. There exists a law setting aside a certain percentage of all new land opened up by irrigation for food, but, in the face of a currently higher per-acre profit from sugar or cotton, this law is usually circumvented.

The distribution of wealth and income. With a population growth of at least 3 percent a year, it would, of course, be of supreme interest to know if real income were increasing faster than or only as fast as population growth, or possibly lagging behind it. The usual inflationary pressures brought about by the growth of population, the "demonstration effect" of imported consumer goods, the rigidity of supply in general, and the government's deficit financing policy give Peruvians the impression that real average incomes are falling. From the point of view of the strategy of industrialization, such a lag at this stage may not be a fatal sign in itself as long as the labor force in the modern sector of the economy is enjoying an increase in consumption power. However, it is just this group which most feels it is slipping behind. According to a United Nations report,

> The characteristics displayed by the Peruvian economy in 1955 were those typical of an underdeveloped country. So low was the figure for average *per capita* income even in comparison with that registered in most of the other Latin American countries, that it was less than two-thirds of the estimated average for the region as a whole.[64] (Peru $187, Latin America $314, gross per capita product.)

In 1949 the Pan American Union Report calculated the net per capita income at only 682 soles a year. On the basis of an exchange rate of 15 soles to the dollar this would have been equivalent to $45 (which is not comparable to the United

[64] United Nations, *op.cit.*, p. 1.

Nations gross product figure). Complicating the estimation of real income during this period is the movement into the market of new workers formerly not working for money.[65] This could have a depressing effect both on these artificial averages and on the real median level of living.

A study of the distribution of the landholdings of the top 1 percent of Peruvian property owners in 1930 "illustrates the hypothesis" that economic development increases inequality— at least during this period.[66] Unfortunately no comparable data are available for a later period.

It is not being suggested that this apparent trend will continue indefinitely according to the Marxian prediction. It is just that Peru is now at the stage England was passing through when Marx reached his conclusions. He overgeneralized them in terms of historical trends, but probably undergeneralized them by limiting himself to capitalist societies.

However, this general pattern of increasing inequality is also illustrated for a later period by the Central Bank's figures on regional mean per capita income in 1955, 1956, 1959, and 1960.[67] Distribution of mean per capita income by geographic regions:

	1955	1956	1959	1960	1959 population (estimated)
Coast	54.09%	56.16%	57.31%	61.62%	33.37%
Sierra	40.51	38.65	38.18	33.77	53.14
Jungle	5.40	5.19	4.51	4.61	13.49
	100	100	100	100	100

The most populous area, the sierra, fell back relatively.

65 See Wilbert E. Moore, "The Exportability of the 'Labor Force' Concept," *American Sociological Review*, XVIII (February 1953), 68-72.

66 See David Chaplin, "Industrialization and the Distribution of Wealth in Peru." Research Paper #18 (mimeographed), distributed by the Land Tenure Center, University of Wisconsin, August 1966.

67 Banco Central de Reserva del Perú, *Renta nacional del Perú, 1942-1956* (Lima: 1958), p. 67; *Renta nacional del Perú, 1952–1960* (Lima: 1962), p. 35.

The poverty of the sierra is, of course, exaggerated due to the inevitable exclusion from this accounting of goods and services not passing through any commercial market. This deficiency is greater in the poorer and more isolated regions. Estimates of the proportions of Peruvians "outside the national economy" in the 1950's range from one third to one half of the population. This miscalculation of the extent of poverty is presumably bound to decline as commercialization proceeds and as the population in the commercialized areas grows relative to that in the relatively untouched areas because of emigration from the latter as well as the rural areas' slower decline in mortality.

The 1959 United Nations study of Peru's industrial development concluded that, although Peru's consumption outstripped its gross product, a situation made possible by post-1950 inflow of foreign capital and a favorable balance of trade, the added consumption was not enjoyed by the lower classes.[68] In fact, even within the officially registered industries, "where better levels and more stable systems of remuneration are usually to be found, real *per capita* (white-collar) salaries were lower in 1955 than in 1947 in all sectors except trade, the reduction being particularly severe in agricultural activities and manufacturing industry. . . . Consequently, this sector did not even succeed in maintaining its real income at the same level."[69]

This report did note that with respect to (blue-collar) wages, "the situation was apparently much more favorable, since considerable real improvements were registered here."[70] It should be noted that this favored group is limited to unionized workers in the larger factories in the Lima–Callao area who have managed, with the help of a series of supreme decrees raising wages, to more than hold their own.

[68] United Nations, *op.cit.*, p. 11.   [69] *Loc.cit.*   [70] *Ibid.*, p. 43.

CHAPTER 2

A Frame of Reference

General Aspects of Labor Mobility

Before taking up the general history of Peruvian labor market development and the case of the textile industry, a frame of reference should be delineated. Not every one of its elements could be tested with the data at hand. But for the sake of logical coherence, it seems desirable to work out a general framework for the study of labor force development in industrializing societies.

My primary focus is on labor mobility as a crucial aspect of Peru's industrialization. With reference to the following typology of labor mobility I shall focus on the situs, migration, employer, employment, and membership (in the labor force) aspects of social mobility, touching only parenthetically on the question of status mobility owing to the nature of the data at hand.

A TYPOLOGY OF LABOR MOBILITY

1. Situs (milieu) —change of cultures or major economic sector; a radical change of referent groups
2. Migration
3. Employer—change of specific work organization only
4. Status
   a. Stratification aspect—prestige dimension
   b. Employment aspect—whether employed or unemployed (if willing and able to work)
   c. Membership in the labor force—availability for paid "outside" work.

My model will be that of a labor market in its transitional state of development in an industrializing society. All markets for goods, liquid capital, land, or labor in an industrializing economy are by definition becoming commercialized or, in the terms to be used in this study, purified and extensive. This means that all goods and services of economic value are ideally available to anyone (extensity) for the going price through the medium of a contract unfettered by obligations or considerations not directly relevant to the values exchanged (purity).

Applied to labor, these two central concepts can be more fully defined as follows. *Extensity*, the more objectively measurable of the two, has in turn two aspects. (1) The first aspect is that of the number and types of workers who (and which) participate in the commercial paid labor force, as opposed to working on an unpaid basis in the work force. This concept requires the delineation of a list of possibly job-relevant traits such as age, sex, marital status, ability, education, etc. Then the question of the proportion of all of the possible workers with these traits who are in the labor force arises. For instance, usually a high percentage of "normal" adult males in industrial societies engage in paid labor. The question of the limits of the extension of the labor market (the central focus of this study) thus arises more with respect to "marginal minority" groups such as women, racial and ethnic minorities, and people with "work handicaps"—the definition of which is highly influenced by cultural norms even in the case of an obvious physical handicap such as lameness or deafness. This first aspect, then, deals with *how many* and *what types* of potential workers actually participate in the commercial labor market. (2) The second aspect of extensity concerns the number of types of services available. Aside from the above question of the types of *workers* available, there are the questions of what are they willing to do for the right price, and how many people can be persuaded to offer this particular service. More or less than are needed? All that could offer it? An extreme but relevant example in the United States would be prostitution. With the loosening of sex norms and the decline of the double standard the professionals are being driven out by the "amateurs." Sex is thus retreating from commercialization in this sense (its increasing exploitation in advertising is another matter).

Purity also has several aspects. (1) First of all, it refers to the criteria of employment—or degree of universalism in Parsonian terminology. As explicated by Marion Levy, universalism involves selecting members of any group solely on the basis of criteria germane to the manifest functions or conscious purposes of that group. It also includes "no social barring" or a willingness to look anywhere to find qualified members without respect to any irrelevant characteristics. A modified form of universalism tends to be the norm in much United States industrial employment in which considerable categories of otherwise qualified applicants are excluded on the basis of sex, race, religion, etc. However, within the "acceptable" group the best qualified are hired. (2) The second aspect of purity, as used here, refers to the "functional specificity" or contractually limited nature of the employment relationship once it is established. Nepotism and *compadrazgo* constitute two major impurifying factors in Peruvian labor–management relations.

Maximal rationalization, therefore, would mean that every individual would make himself continually available to anyone for any service he was capable of performing, that every object of any value to anyone was always available for any use, and that the exchange itself was completely impersonal and germane solely to the buyer's use and seller's interest in price.

The economic function of a pure and extensive industrial labor market, then, would be continuously to reallocate workers physically and occupationally into the situations where their efforts will be most productive for the economy as a whole and, presumably in a free market of relatively equal parties, be most rewarding for themselves.

Socially, the function of a free and pure labor market would be to permit the socialization and motivation of workers into new roles by means of the self-selection from the old culture of those voluntarily ready to leave, for whatever individual reasons. These mobiles are then, in theory, rewarded for choosing an industrial occupation once the move has been made. Such a model assumes a mobility of labor primarily "pulled" by a perceived advantage rather than merely "pushed" as a lesser of evils by a deteriorating home situation.

In Peru's case I am interested in seeing when and how one sector of the labor market becomes relatively more purified and extended. It could proceed along these lines parallel to comparable changes in the markets for land, goods, and capital, or it could precede or follow them. Within the labor market, purification could again parallel, precede, or follow extension. And lastly, the labor market could develop along these lines evenly throughout the process of industrial development, approaching an ideal type of extreme purity and extensity at industrial "maturity." (Since industrial societies have institutionalized internal sources of change we have no way of knowing if or when such a stage will ever be reached.) However, some other sequence may become apparent.

Purity and extensity, in fact, are often found not to vary together. In underdeveloped countries experiencing a population explosion prior to economic development, the number of types of workers, as well as the absolute number available in the largest urban centers, greatly exceeds demand. At the same time new skill demands arise which exceed the supply of qualified workers. Hence, increasing extensity does not result in a purification of all urban industrial labor but rather accompanies a sharp split along skill and status lines.

It could not be asserted, however, that all the workers fortunate enough to be working on "islands of impurity" are "rationally" protected by possessing an industrially relevant and scarce skill or that all with this skill were on these islands. The categorical and political manner in which whole sectors of industry are protected clearly makes such narrowly tech-

43

nical rationality impossible. In Peru the utility of this protection is best revealed in the occasional management-initiated efforts to change the legal definition of categories of workers from *obreros* (blue-collar workers) to *empleados* (white-collar workers). This redefinition in general favors the workers by upgrading their occupations. However, technically virtuous behavior is not the only rational action feasible. A manufacturer can choose to protect himself from the consequence of an inefficient labor force by resigning from competition in his output markets through the pursuit of protective legislation against imports and restrictive laws or practices against competitive domestic products. This, in fact, is very much the case in the Peruvian textile industry.

A more general reason for an inverse relationship between extensity and purity would be that, as more and more types of goods and services enter the market, a pressure towards impurification would exist due to the greater "distance" of the new entries from traditional productive or commercial activities. Prime cases are the entry of women into previously masculine occupations and the loss, or release, of more familial services to the market, as in day nurseries. One thus finds consumer services purchased with the growing proportion of discretionary income to be especially prey to particularistic pressures.[1]

This study will attempt only to suggest at what stage of industrialization the textile labor market in Peru is apparently at its purest and most extensive and what the sources of the impurities and limitations are. The analysis will be made in terms of the observed characteristics of age, sex, birthplace,

[1] In a society such as the United States under growing pressure to desegregate its commercial establishments there thus exist two increasingly conflicting forces—Negro demand for commercial universalism and increasingly affluent white particularization of "luxury" services—which in turn will eventually be regarded as necessities. Psychiatric and psychoanalytic care would be a case in point. (See August B. Hollingshead and Frederick C. Redlich, *Social Class and Mental Illness* [New York: John Wiley & Sons, 1958].)

previous employment, and factory position in the light of a typing of the firms by their labor policy, location, and history.

As for the effect of changing market conditions, historically it would seem that if a labor sellers' market existed owing to a labor shortage, labor would attempt to purify contractual relations by emphasizing direct financial rewards. Management, on the other hand, faced with a labor shortage or too high a level of turnover, tries to impurify the labor market by pulling workers out of competition through tying them to the organization by means of a variety of indirect monetary and nonmonetary devices.

Faced with a labor surplus, we find labor emphasizing security even at the possible expense of income, while management attempts to purify the contractual relationship by relating itself to workers only by means of a free-market-determined wage with a daily "shape up" and piece-rate wages as the concrete form of this extreme.

Contractual impurity thus varies directly with the leverage that labor, as seller, has in the labor market whether created by scarcity of numbers, by scarcity of skills, or by "political" power from unionization or a "laboristic" government.

Within the firms one would expect to see the strongest pressure for germane traits (to the job at hand) and market-determined wages and working conditions to appear at the middle level of highly skilled foremen, workers, technicians, and plant managers, with the top managerial and low-skilled blue-collar worker levels open to differing types of particularistic impurities such as sex-stereotyping, nepotism, provincial favoritism, and ascribed ownership control,[2] again affecting both their social characteristics and income. In general the problem here can be stated as follows:

1. Few relevant selection criteria are known in Peru for either top management or ordinary workers, and even if

[2] Wilbert E. Moore and Arnold S. Feldman, *Labor Commitment and Social Change in Developing Areas* (New York: Social Science Research Council, 1960), p. 35.

they were known, no organized labor market communications system exists to allow an effective selection from all "available" and qualified recruits.

Top management is open to nonfunctional limitations on access to these positions in that its authority is never purely functional, i.e., solely germane to the technical problems of management in a particular type of industry. One could argue, however, that these ascribed limitations of sex, race, class, etc., are "functional," especially in highly stratified societies, in that they constitute leadership in the eyes of workers as well as customers. This is, in fact, the case with many occupations. The utilization of ascribed traits normally excludes many categories of otherwise possibly qualified applicants even in industrial societies, but among the remaining acceptable candidates the more qualified are usually chosen. This is simply the general limitation on extensity to be found in any culture. The types of people excluded from any one comparable position in different societies would, however, vary, but some categorical exclusion would generally exist—especially in high leadership positions. In Weberian terms, charismatic and traditional elements necessarily are components of the authority of top management even in the most bureaucratized of organizations.[3] Thus, in no general sense would the specific exclusive traits be functional—only so in terms of the culture in question.

2. In underdeveloped non-Communist countries business organizations in urban areas are especially likely to be under heavy pressure from a wide variety of conflicting pressures as the focus of norms relevant to the new and old culture as well as some peculiar to this stage of development. Some examples of these norms are the following: conflicts within the family of the owners based on "personalities," or a preference for profit gained by legal manipulation and political influence as opposed to productivity, wide distribution, and a low

---

[3] Max Weber, *Theory of Social and Economic Organization* (Glencoe, Ill.: The Free Press, 1947), p. 335.

mark-up; conflicts between family obligations and family members representing the above norms; and conflicts among related owners, each owning other enterprises competing or doing business with the firm in question. As Parsons and Smelser "concede to Marxism, . . . in a sense capitalism became the refuge of kinship prerogatives after its [the family's] direct control of the state had weakened."[4] Only the subsequent separation of ownership and control has completed the economic purification of business norms—insofar as businesses can be consistently unifunctional. In a capitalist economy free competition is supposed to eliminate the structural weakness inherent in an owner's treating his firm as his personal property and thus appointing his relatives. However, in Peru there are too many alternative methods of organizational survival besides mere efficiency. Most definitive perhaps is the unwillingness of the government to have a body of unionized workers suddenly unemployed.

This study in part will make use of some of the "pattern variables" as developed by Parsons, e.g., functional specificity-diffuseness, and universalism-particularism.[5] As abstract analytical aspects of social interaction, it is understood that no concrete social relationship can embody these norms. No durable social structure could exist in which all physically capable persons continuously offered any goods or services as demanded for a market price inasmuch as the noneconomic functional requisites of all societies impose limits on the purification and extension of the labor market.[6] In this sense these modifications are also economic. If there is to be any production of consumers' goods, there must be consumers. This could be done by decreasing the working time for all somewhat, or by having specialized "parasitical" consumers,

---

[4] Talcott Parsons and Neil J. Smelser, *Economy and Society* (Glencoe, Ill.: The Free Press, 1956), pp. 286-287.

[5] Talcott Parsons, *The Social System* (Glencoe, Ill.: The Free Press, 1951), p. 136.

[6] *Ibid.*, pp. 26-36, 157-161. Moore and Feldman, *op.cit.*, pp. 7, 43, 56-57.

or, when the productive system becomes highly efficient, both.[7]

Labor Turnover

Another focus of this study of a more practical nature will be that of the level of labor turnover. There is a large body of literature describing the agonizing problem of recruiting and committing labor to industrial employment in under-developed non-Western countries. In general, it is assumed that a period of high labor instability is inevitable owing to the strangeness of industrial work patterns and the fixed level of aspirations which causes such so-called "target" workers to quit once they have earned enough to return to their village and buy a cow or some land, dower a wife, etc.

This focus on labor turnover is a reflection of a central sociological concern with basic group structure. The essential elements of a group are its size, organization, activity, membership criteria, *and* rate of change. Some at least cyclical change in any group is minimally unavoidable due to retire-

---

[7] Slavery offers an interesting example of the limits of extensity as well as a source of impurity. It would be inefficient as a device for reducing labor costs and increasing discipline in industrial work for the following reasons: (1) Economic: The costs of socialization and maintenance of an entire subsociety have to be borne by the employers and not, as in a free market, by the workers themselves, or by the entire society through taxation. The costs of quality inspection and social control would alone be prohibitive given the problem of motivation and the more precise nature of factory work as compared to agriculture, since the inspectors and guards would have to be paid. (2) Normative: The permanent and continuous interaction of the slaves and their employers would intro-duce "affective particularism" or personal biases, whether positive or negative, which would conflict with managerial objectivity. Also, the unlimited control of the owners would doubtless result in the univer-sally noted use of slave women as mistresses as well as the disruption of slave family life, all of which tends to make the slave labor force together with the owners or supervisors analogous to a corporate family. Also, since new recruits would be obtained from the offspring of those already purchased, the likelihood of an age, sex, or skill fitted to special-ized industrial jobs would be low. Of course, the employers could always fall back on the slave market again for a worker with all the desired qualifications, but then the primary economic gain from a slave labor force—its "free" self-reproduction—is lost.

48

ments and replacements. Beyond this rate of turnover some higher level of change seems to be necessary in an industrial organization if an undue amount of deviation from the ideal type norms of industrialism is not to occur.

A formal organization with too little turnover will probably suffer the following consequences:

1. There will be a lack of a wide spread of age groups such that eventually a large proportion will be retiring all at once, thus requiring large-scale replacements from outside at all levels, rather than a phased promotion from within. An alternative would be to have a staggered set of age "cohorts" so that the annual rate of age retirements is held near a biological minimum.

2. The "informal" network of personal friendships, grapevines, secondary goals, and activities will come to take on as much importance as the organizations' official goals and structure. Such tendencies seem to be progressive so that, to survive (if this is deemed desirable), formal organizations require periodic "house cleanings" or even purges in extreme cases to "shape things up" and to get "back on the track." At the other extreme, too high a level of change would lower efficiency, since most members of such an organization would have just arrived or be more concerned about their next job than about their present one.

In view of the available data, the rates of turnover to be discussed in Chapter 6 will refer more to groups of workers and eras of labor recruitment than to firms as such. This is because, on all workers ever employed, data were available for only three plants. In addition, not enough reliable other data were available for these plants to allow correlations of turnover rates with, for instance, business cycles, employee morale, or changes in administrative labor policies usually linked to the level of turnover.

Limitations on Labor Mobility

As for the institutional obstacles to labor mobility of various types, as gleaned from literature on the United States, it seems that most organized groups, by design or accident, are contributing to a decreasing rate of mobility in the American labor force.[8]

The security of both workers as individuals and unions and companies as institutions is acquiring a greater value than short-run efficiency or profit.

We could generalize on the sources of impurities in labor markets as a basis for comparison with Peru as follows: (1) preferences of individual workers; (2) preferences of individual employers; (3) preferences of organized workers; (4) preferences of organized employers; and (5) preferences of other parties—especially the government.[9]

Managerial groups often restrict mobility by "gentlemen's agreements" against pirating and area wage-scale busting, and by personal prejudices against categories of otherwise qualified workers.

The effect of union policies on labor mobility varies with the type of union and types of mobility. Industrial unions in the United States restrict migration, situs, and interfirm mobility in favor of status mobility or seniority. But it is difficult to separate the stabilizing effect of these unions from the generally greater stability which characterizes larger industrial firms. Industrial unions allow the outside labor market to affect the wage structure only at the bottom entry positions.

Craft unions, on the other hand, increase migration and interfirm mobility but decrease situs (in this case, entry into the craft) and status mobility. They do this by purifying their labor market within a closely guarded geographical and

8 Clark Kerr, "The Balkanization of the Labor Market," in E. W. Bakke *et al.*, *Labor Mobility and Economic Opportunity* (New York: The Technology Press of Massachusetts Institute of Technology and John Wiley & Sons, 1954), p. 92.

9 *Ibid.*, p. 96.

craft area. This situation develops most easily where many small employers face one large craft union. Needless to say, industrial unions are more characteristic of an industrial society, although artisan laborers and craft unions are not simply "survivals" of a preindustrial era.

Governments affect labor mobility in the following major respects:

1. Requirements for the funding of all fringe benefits whether provided by the government or by the employer.

2. Policies with respect to making movement easier by improving transportation, reducing its cost, and arranging to relieve the worker of the payment of the entire immediate cost of moving. A higher wage after the move is often assumed to cover this expense, but in realistic terms, blue-collar workers need help before and during a move.

3. Housing policies which prevent whatever increase may be earned from being entirely used up in inadequate, expensive living quarters.

4. Provision of employment service activities to integrate supply with demand.

In the case of Peru, there is a shortage only of skilled labor; and at the blue-collar level the shortage seems to have been overrated. There are official policies with respect to all of the points listed above, some of which should increase labor mobility. However, they generally work in the opposite direction.

From the foregoing it can be suggested that a completely open and pure industrial labor market would be as unlikely as a completely closed one. The normal processes of retirement and entry constitute minimal points of contact between even the most restricted industrial employer and the outside labor market.

It would be theoretically interesting if sociology could establish a "law" of *the* optimal level of turnover, but certainly no single rate could possibly be established for all formal organizations, or even for categories limited by size and function, that would maximize all of the legitimate goals being sought, to say nothing of the methodological problems involved. Kerr[10] and Palmer[11] are in favor of the maximum possible openness in the labor market for the sake of the freedom and welfare of individual workers and the progress of the economy.

I would like to suggest, however, that during the early transitional stage of industrialization in countries like Peru it may be desirable, as well as currently inevitable, that a combination of limitations restrict the wage-depressing effects of a labor surplus. The resulting "bias" generally keeps wages above their "true market" level among urban factory workers, for whom progress is so necessary from an industrialization standpoint, and whose status, compared to traditional preindustrial *or* white-collar occupations, would otherwise be too low. In addition, the full effect of the labor surplus which has become normal in currently underdeveloped countries could, in the absence of market impurities, drive wages below the subsistence level and thus impede economic development.[12]

This position, of course, leaves open the question of what happens to those disemployed by such a system. Stated briefly, it seems to be the case that, no matter what type of political or economic system is involved, the standard of living of the entire population cannot be raised throughout the early stages of industrialization. Some groups, perhaps the majority, will suffer a relative if not an absolute decline in income. This seems more probable today than in the case of Western development, since population growth in currently underdeveloped areas is so high and so far in advance of industrial

[10] *Ibid.*, p. 102.

[11] Gladys Palmer, "Social Values in Labor Mobility," in E. W. Bakke, *op.cit.*, p. 111.

[12] Harvey Leibenstein, "The Theory of Underemployment in Backward Economies," *Journal of Political Economy*, LXV (April 1957), 91.

growth. Those groups or sectors which seem destined to be most "exploited" are lower-class women and virtually all rural inhabitants except for a handful of land- and mine owners and their more skilled employees.

The Question of Status Mobility

As has been stated above, I have not attempted to handle the prestige aspect of social mobility. This limitation is not a challenge to the important place class stratification occupies in sociological research, nor is it due to a feeling that subjective attitudes cannot be measured through their behavioral manifestations. It was felt that with the time and facilities available the substantial fund of information in company personnel files should serve as the primary source of data. A questionnaire was used with considerable success in one factory, but it was designed (1) to be a validity check on the personnel files and (2) to provide more information relevant to the non-prestige aspects of social mobility.

Aside from this problem of the intrinsic limitations imposed by the nature of the data used, there would be other problems involved in studying class mobility in a society such as Peru:

1. For the rural migrants a major change in cultural situs or milieu was involved, thus making highly problematical the question of vertical mobility. Subjectively, there is no general agreement from the view of either the rural or urban culture as to whether an ex-farmer has gone up or down in becoming a factory worker. The work is manual in both cases with the increased money income of the factory worker just compensating in many cases for the loss of status in the preindustrial culture. The determination of the type of mobility that has occurred is a matter of the point at which the migrants considered change their values from those of a preindustrial society to those of an industrial society.

2. Inflation complicates the evaluation of status by de-

creasing the consumption power of all holders of fixed-price assets or earners of fixed incomes, or, in the term used by Thorp and Quandt, "passive income claimants,"[13] making this group as a whole feel as if they were moving downward. To compensate for this, more extra jobs (*cachuelos*) are taken on involving the giving up of leisure for status climbing or merely status maintenance. This creates problems of determining which job is regarded as the primary "status" occupation.

3. Education, very highly regarded for its practical money-earning as well as status-giving aspects, is rapidly losing the latter advantage as it becomes "debased" by mass availability especially at the university level. To be a graduate of the ancient University of San Marcos (founded in 1535), once an honor, is now almost a stigma in upper-class Peruvian circles.

4. Already the skilled factory workers earn more than do the average clerical workers in the same firms, a situation thought to represent an advanced stage of industrial development.

5. In general the evolution of the relationship of occupation to family status, from the preindustrial rural situation, in which family tradition determines occupation, to the industrial situation, in which family status is determined by occupation, leaves occupation as a highly problematic index of general social standing in the transitional stage. On the one hand, occupations at this stage are becoming a separate aspect of the blue-collar worker's life; on the other hand, the income generated by whatever sources of income exist becomes the primary basis for social status. By default, and on a traditional basis, such workers look to their leisure consumption pattern rather than their occupation as their primary basis for social status.

In fact, it would appear that one has in the transitional

[13] Willard L. Thorp and Richard E. Quandt, *The New Inflation* (New York: McGraw-Hill Book Co., 1959), p. 195.

stage an addition to the two subcultures usually considered, the preindustrial and industrial, to make a minimum of three in any otherwise previously unified society. *Indios, cholos-*mestizos (the social category of the textile factory workers), and *criollos* in Peru are at least three distinctive subcultures which complicate the assignment of status traits with a wide predictive value. It is characteristic of transitional men that they are for many purposes subjectively and objectively marginal even if they are in the majority. They are not sure where they stand, nor can observers tell them.

CHAPTER 3

Peruvian Labor History and Structure

𝕽𝕽𝕽𝕽𝕽𝕽𝕽𝕽𝕽𝕽𝕽𝕽𝕽𝕽𝕽𝕽𝕽𝕽𝕽𝕽𝕽𝕽𝕽𝕽𝕽𝕽𝕽𝕽𝕽𝕽

Before going into the structure of the textile industry and the data on workers, it should be of interest to review very briefly the historical and contemporary context of the development of Peru's industrial labor force.

The Colonial Era

Although Incaic social structure is known only by conjecture or through the fragmentary reports of a few Spaniards and literate Indians during its collapse, it seems clear that comparable types of "collectivistic" work obligations existed in both medieval Spain and the Inca empire. All the Indian workers in Peru, by the contemporary labor force definition, owed the central government so many days labor on different types of projects of "state-wide" interest.

Kubler notes: "During the protracted disorders following the conquest, extravagant demands were made upon Indian labor . . . a modification of the pre-conquest *mita* was accordingly introduced as a measure for stabilizing food production, in which only a limited number of Indians was expected to appear for hire at stated intervals."[1] The Incaic *mita* was a system of forced annual labor levies on a per capita and territory basis. (The totalitarian type of political organization which underlay this system in the Inca empire was the major factor in the amazingly easy conquest of millions of Indians by a few hundred Spaniards.)

The *mitayos* were paid partly in cash, which was then used for their tribute. This tribute went to the *encomenderos*, who

[1] George Kubler, "The Quechua in the Colonial World," in Julian Steward (ed.), *Handbook of South American Indians*, Bulletin No. 143. (Washington: Bureau of American Ethnology, 1946), ii, 371.

were newly rich creole aristocrats, but at rates set by the government, and with it came the obligation of "instructing the Indians in the Christian religion and incorporating them in Western civilization."[2] Free service was thus supposed to have been suppressed. Actually this burden was merely added to their traditional obligations. As Kubler observed, "The colonial perception of tribute pertained only to Indians. As tribute the levy was juridically regarded as a 'just token of the vassalage owed by natives to the Sovereign,' against which the Crown was empowered to charge ecclesiastical, administrative and educational salaries and expenses for the benefit of the Indians."[3] In this respect the Spaniards found a much more amenable type of "Indian" than the English encountered in North America.

An important difference between the Incaic and Peruvian colonial labor organization was that the former was apparently much more efficient. "Hydraulic" agriculture in Witfogel's view seems to impose a widespread need for an effective centrally organized political system.[4] The Spanish, however, were not interested in supporting a nation of 8 to 20 million Indians with extensive internal trade by means of an agricultural surplus. Their concern was largely in extracting as much wealth from the mines as possible. Thus the whole structure of the Inca government, especially that relating to irrigation and labor organization, was allowed to decay or was directly attacked once it had served to facilitate the Spanish conquest of the Inca empire. This policy, along with disease and warfare, apparently reduced the Indian population to an estimated 5 to 10 percent of its former size

[2] General Felipe de la Barra, *La abolición del tributo por Castilla y su repercusión en el problema del indio peruano* (Lima: Ministerio de Guerra, 1956), p. 5.

[3] George Kubler, *The Indian Caste of Peru 1795–1940* (Washington: Smithsonian Institution, Institute of Social Anthropology, 1952), No. 14, p. 3.

[4] See Karl Witfogel, *Oriental Despotism* (New Haven: Yale University Press, 1957).

within 50 to 100 years. Thus the Spanish colonial system stands condemned in the *leyenda negra* (black legend) by humanistic as well as materialistic criteria because it supported so much smaller a population at apparently a lower level of existence.

The conquistadors, however, were not allowed to restructure the Indian labor force by themselves. Had they been left free to do so, they would probably have further decimated those Indians they controlled while leaving in safe isolation those beyond their reach. The Church, together with the Spanish monarchy, had somewhat different objectives.[5] After the virtual eradication of the Caribbean aborigines by the earliest Spanish New World arrivals, the monarchy and Church made a sustained but never really successful effort to protect the continental Indians from the *criollos*, i.e., American-born whites, as well as to convert them. Their objective was also to limit the power of this new landed aristocracy by controlling their real source of power and wealth, their laborers.[6] Therefore, the Crown stepped in as labor contractor and utilized precolonial work obligations by gathering Indians into government-controlled *reducciones* (settlements) by 1614, or by controlling them indirectly in *encomiendas* (estates) similar to the later British indirect-rule policy in Africa.

The *encomienda* system was a "classic" labor recruiting device in its use of the head tax. The tribute required of all adult males could be paid either in kind or in money, by working for a *patrón*, religious, royal, or private.

Gradually these *encomiendas*, originally intended as commissions to convert Indians, evolved into hereditary private estates as the Crown met the need to reward its soldiers of fortune. After Independence, these landowners acquired *de*

[5] Elman R. Service, "Indian-European Relations in Colonial Latin America," *American Anthropologist*, LVII (June 1955), 413.

[6] Eric R. Wolf, "Types of Latin American Peasantry," *American Anthropologist*, LVII (June 1955), 456.

facto ownership rights over their resident Indians, who could then even be rented out to others for the benefit of their *patrón.*

These policies applied primarily in the sierra, since most of the Indians originally on the coast had been killed off or had intermarried, producing the mestizo class of urban artisans. For the coastal haciendas of the colonial and early republican eras, Negroes were preferred. It was felt they were more appropriate in view of the climate, and since they were far from their native land, they were easier to control. Like Negro slaves in the United States, Negroes in Peru were readily acculturated into creole society.[7]

The Huancavelica mercury mine offers a good example of the results of the various pressures at work during the colonial era in the utilization of Indian labor.[8] It was originally supported equally by the creoles and Madrid because mercury was essential in the process then used to work raw ore down to pure silver. At its peak it had 3,823 Indian *mitayos,* 560 white overseers, and 713 mestizo foremen, middlemen, etc. In all there were 30 creole guilds controlling different aspects of the grossly inefficient and scandalously cruel (even by contemporary standards) mining operation. The Crown tried to reform this extreme support for the *leyenda negra* repeatedly but succeeded only shortly before the end of Spanish rule in 1795. Its "reform" placed recruitment and management in the hands of native *caciques,* or bosses, in an attempt to end the abuses of the creole-run *mitas.* With Independence the marketing organization tying the production of mercury to that of silver mining broke down. Thus most of Peru's mines stagnated during the nineteenth century, being worked only by thousands of individual placer miners—Indians and mestizos using the most primitive techniques.

In addition to the agricultural and mining use of Indian

[7] Service, *op.cit.,* p. 415.

[8] See Arthur Preston Whitaker, *The Huancavelica Mercury Mine* (Cambridge, Mass.: Harvard University Press, 1941).

labor, there were also *obrajes*, or work houses, where Indians behind in their tribute payments were locked up in sheds filled with hand looms to work off their "indebtedness."[9]

Even under this system these textile sheds were so productive that Spain in the late eighteenth century forced them to close in order to give Spanish factories control of the Peruvian market. Thus the urban mestizo artisan weaver began to disappear even before Independence. In England, on the other hand, the status and prosperity of artisan handweavers was never higher than during the earlier stages of the development of the textile industry.[10] In Peru there were no artisan guilds to attack the early factories, and thus no machine breakings or riots against industry per se. The only vocal enemies of the early mills were importers of foreign textiles, but eventually this group became a source of entrepreneurs in textile manufacturing.

The Republican Era

During the republican nineteenth century in Peru, the Indians were even more abused once the interceding hand of the Crown was gone, and with it all Loyalist clergy. In the colonial era the most humane and efficient use of labor had been on the Jesuit-run haciendas,[11] which were expropriated in 1767 when the Jesuits were expelled from Spanish America. The Indians on the very extensive Church properties during the republican era enjoyed no such protected status.[12] Their tribute in fact continued to be the Church's primary source of income.

The system of colonial tribute had been replaced by the *contribución de indigenas*, or caste tax, which was officially

[9] Alejandro Garland, *Reseña industrial del Perú* (Lima: 1905), p. 113.

[10] Neil J. Smelser, *Social Change in the Industrial Revolution* (Chicago: University of Chicago Press, 1959), pp. 136-137.

[11] K. V. Fox, "Pedro Muñiz, Dean of Lima, and the Indian Labor Question," *Hispanic American Historical Review*, XLII (February 1962), 70.

[12] Service, *op.cit.*, p. 416.

abolished in 1854 but actually continued to operate long after.[13] The burden of this taxation persuaded many Indians to become free mestizo artisans. This social transformation, in addition to the exodus of the *criollo* elite already mentioned, altered the reported "racial" status of Peru's nineteenth-century population according to the two censuses taken during that century.[14] Many rural areas became more Indian while other previously Indian areas appeared to have become more mestizo.

During his brief regime in Peru, Bolívar, as one of his many imposed liberal reforms, proclaimed the freedom of the sons of all slaves and abolished Indian tribute and free services. But by 1835 the slave trade had been re-established, while the emancipation of the Indians had never taken effect. However, by 1849 the British managed to cut off Peru's supply of Negroes, thus forcing her to look to other races in other parts of the world.

During the following 25 years, about 100,000 Chinese males were imported to satisfy Peru's agricultural and railroad construction needs.[15] This trade started in 1849 when two *criollo* merchants obtained a government monopoly for the importation of coolies on the basis of eight-year contracts. The demand for coastal plantation labor had risen sharply in the 1860's due to the United States Civil War–induced demand for Peruvian cotton, and to the quite effective emancipation of Negro slaves in Peru in 1854.

Most of the coolies were prisoners taken in clan feuds who had been sold to Chinese merchants in Macao, already held by the Portuguese. Others were debtors escaping creditors or were simply "shanghaied." Again the British stepped in and closed this supply of labor in 1874, partly because of the loss

13 Kubler, *The Indian Caste of Peru, 1795–1940*, pp. 5-6. See also de la Barra, *op.cit.*

14 Kubler, *The Indian Caste of Peru, 1795–1940*, p. 36.

15 Watt Stewart, *Chinese Bondage in Peru* (Durham, N.C.: Duke University Press, 1951), p. 75.

of about 10 percent of each shipload, and partly because of the abusive working conditions within Peru. Most of the haciendas where the Chinese worked were beyond the reach of groups in Lima that wished to protect the Chinese and save Peru's international reputation. Pass systems were general, with all workers being locked up each night under the "divide and conquer" surveillance of Negro foremen.[16] It seems that Oriental workers brought out the worst in Peruvians, since they were denied even the meager protection of the old paternalistic *patrón-peón* relationship. This extreme impersonality was possible because in most cases both the managers, usually Europeans, and the workers were foreigners to each other as well as to Peruvians. The managers received mandates from Peruvian owners which the latter did not care to have to carry out themselves. "Many managers were foreigners by birth, as Europeans were thought best adapted to the work. . . . They were more able to exact obedience and industry from the workers and were more fertile in resources than their own easy going countrymen. . . . They were often promised a share in the profits of the plantation."[17] After the British embargo, the Grace Company tried to re-export coolies left over from United States railroad gangs, but the Chilean War sabotaged this plan. Thereafter a few free Chinese immigrated until all Oriental immigration was cut off after World War I.

At the present time, however, one finds virtually no Orientals as plantation peons. Most Chinese are petty merchants. This is partly because all Chinese immigration was cut off in 1922. Perhaps a more important factor was that since no Chinese females were imported, a pressure toward acculturation occurred through miscegenation. Once local ties were established, most fled to the cities. Even today there is a difference between the integration of the Chinese communities and those of the Japanese in Peruvian society. The Japanese

16 *Ibid.,* p. 100.
17 *Loc.cit.*

came over as free immigrants with families, and enough money and education to enter Peruvian society above the manual level. Before the Japanese were expropriated during World War II, they owned a number of large cotton plantations in the north of Peru.[18]

With the closing of the coolie trade in 1874, and the development of sugar and cotton plantations, the chronic shortage of rural coastal labor reappeared, to be aggravated after the turn of the century by the reopening of the mines in the mountains, which absorbed the normal supply of Indian *enganchados* (literally "hooked ones," that is, workers recruited through devious or coercive techniques).[19] It was not until the late thirties that mechanization and increased migration turned a chronic shortage into a politically revolutionary labor surplus in the coastal haciendas.

By 1910 an abortive rubber boom had depopulated, for purposes of labor recruitment, most of the jungle areas in the headwaters of the Amazon, even up into the Urubamba valley. The sierra Indians lived in special terror of the rubber recruiters because of jungle diseases and dangers. By 1912, however, the easier extraction and exportation of Malayan rubber ended the Peruvian rubber boom.

As in the case of Peru's previous attempts at recruiting nonwhite labor, this effort became an international scandal, resulting in several investigations by American and international commissions. Unfortunately, as the United States Congressional Committee Report noted.

> . . . those in control of the Putumayo concession are among the wealthiest and most influential men in this part of Peru and in fact of the whole country. . . . This universal system of peonage, an old institution, well-established, recognized by law, . . . has come to be the basis on which the rubber business almost entirely rests. The system of advancing

[18] See Mischa Titiev, "The Japanese Colony in Peru," *The Far Eastern Quarterly*, x, No. 3 (1951), 227-247.
[19] Garland, *op.cit.*, p. 42.

supplies, necessities and luxuries to the peons and rubber gatherers is universal. . . . It is to the patron's interest to get those working for him hopelessly into his debt . . . [since] the Indians very honorably respect . . . their personal debts.[20]

However, they also observed that: "Some instances are known where the labor of so-called cannibal tribes has been successfully secured by decent treatment at what are stated to be reasonable rates of compensation."[21] In this part of Peru the courts allowed employers to erase debts by acquiring the services of the debtors' children as wards.

During the period from 1905 to 1915, Indians living around Cuzco and Sicuani in Puno had yet another source of harassment. Lacking the brigades of coolies used to build the Central Railroad 50 years before, the government, on behalf of the British Railroad Company, was obliged to impress enough workers to complete the railroad from Mollendo to Cuzco. The most difficult stretch from the point of view of the sierra Indians was the extension from Cuzco to Santa Ana since it involved descending into the "eyebrow of the jungle."

As for independent nonagricultural artisans, until recently, migratory rug weavers, like the mattress-makers, traveled to the homes of the upper class and wove on the spot to fit the customer's particular specifications.[22]

As was noted above, the urban mestizo weavers were eliminated long before the first textile mills were established. In Indian areas much clothing is still homemade, but here weaving is rapidly declining from a full-time male occupation to a part-time female chore.

---

[20] H.R. Doc. 1366, "The Putumayo Affair—Slavery in Peru," 62nd Congress, 3rd session (1913), p. 14. (See also P. Alberto Gridilla, *Un año en el Putumayo* [Lima: 1953]; Carlos Rey de Castro, *Los pobladores del Putumayo* [Barcelona: 1914]; Carlos Rey de Castro, *Los escándalos del Putumayo* [Barcelona: 1913].)

[21] H.R. Doc. 1366, "The Putumayo Affair—Slavery in Peru," p. 15.

[22] Isaiah Bowman, *The Andes of Southern Peru* (New York: Henry Holt, 1916), p. 70.

Most industries except for textiles suffered during World War I. The inflation which accompanied the end of the war hurt all workers; as Rowe observed, "even the highly paid dock workers who were out of work preferred to sit on the docks rather than take mine or hacienda work."[23]

Mine laborers were still largely *enganchados* with maximum wages fixed by a gentleman's agreement among the mine owners. Competition did exist, however, in fringe benefits and living conditions. Haciendas also relied on *enganchados* but paid by the day.

Although Leguía (1919–1930) inaugurated the registration of Indian communities, his need for labor for his ambitious public works projects caused him to issue a decree in 1920 calling for the conscription of able-bodied Indians between 18 and 60 for road work. One could escape this obligation by paying a small fine or hiring a substitute. Just such governmental conscription was officially prohibited in 1930.

Stein noted in 1952, however, that this system of *corvée* labor was still an important factor in the lives of the Indians in the Callejón de Huaylas in the Andean north central department of Ancash. "*La República* labor tribute is imposed from the outside and is thus not a spontaneous labor organization. *Hualcainos* who can afford the expense often prefer to pay the fine when there is pressing household work to be done. Some, of course, are habitually attracted to . . . [this] labor force because of the accumulated fine money and its promise of a drunken party after the work is done."[24] *La República* is used for "public projects such as roads, bridges and irrigation." The few independent peasants "feel that they are compelled to carry the burden of this labor; *patrones* try to free their peons from this work so that they will be free

[23] See L. S. Rowe, *Early Effects of the War upon the Finance, Commerce and Industry of Peru* (New York: Carnegie Endowment for International Peace, Oxford University Press, 1920), p. 38.

[24] William W. Stein, *Hualcan: Life in the Highlands of Peru* (Ithaca, N.Y.: Cornell University Press, 1961), p. 111.

to labor on the haciendas."[25] Worse still is the feeling on the part of the Indians that all this work "benefits the mestizo directly since it is always done in mestizo areas."[26]

As shall be explained more fully, Peruvian textile mills, in general, did not have to utilize these coercive tactics to obtain and hold a labor force. Their urban location, slow growth, and relatively high wages enabled them to recruit enough workers easily even before migration from rural areas, or the "revolution of rising expectations," was a feature of Peruvian life.

The only one of these "classic" techniques put to consistent use by an industrial textile mill was a modified version of the *encomienda* system. In effect this gave landholders virtually complete use of the services of the resident Indians. The earliest textile mill in continuous operation, Oropesa, took advantage of these traditional work obligations by purchasing a hacienda from the Beneficencia Pública[27] in order to inherit a *faena* (work gang) of workers for the factory along with the usual free household services of their wives and children (*pongaje*).

Current Rural Labor Structure

The substantial number of ethnographic studies carried out since 1944 in Peru, first by the Smithsonian Institution and Maxime Kuczynski-Godard and later by Peruvian anthropologists, provide us with an extensive description of current rural labor practices.[28] Recently several preliminary efforts

[25] *Ibid.*, p. 45.

[26] Mario C. Vázquez, "A Study of Technological Change in Vicos, Peru: Cornell-Peru Project" (Unpublished Master's thesis, Department of Anthropology, Cornell University, 1955), p. 51.

[27] The Beneficencia Pública is a semipublic charitable society established in Peru in the 1820's as, among other things, an alternative to the Church as a recipient of inheritances and manager of charity and social service.

[28] "Socio-Economic Development of Andean Communities," Reports 1-7, Cornell-Peru Project, Department of Anthropology, Cornell Univer-

have been made to pull together the terminology used[29] and to systematize the scattered reports. This literature could be summarized as follows: *Indigenistas* and "cooperative" enthusiasts notwithstanding, cooperative unpaid communal labor for the common good in the tradition of the Incaic *ayllu* seems to have virtually died out. The major factors accounting for the deep penetration of commercialized labor are that, except for the jungle tribes (with whom this study is not concerned), Peru's Indians are not part of a primitive folk society, but the survivors of a great agrarian civilization profoundly transformed by 400 years of Hispanic and then "Western" influence. The most significant changes of the past 100 years have been the privatization of landholding, elimination of entail, equal division of inheritances among all children, and population growth with its resulting diminution of average holdings.[30] This decrease in the property of the average landholder is not inconsistent with an increase in the inequality of land distribution. A great many more people own less on the average, while a very small number own relatively more. These factors, in the context of the long-standing, if shallow, participation in a commercial market for goods, make the commercialization of labor inevitable. More specifically, the increasing inequality in the distribution of land makes unnecessary the exchange of neighborly peer services. As Martínez notes, not only communal labor but even individual reciprocity (*ayne*) has declined, since "with an average extension of one half a hectare per family, the great majority of indigenous *Taraqueños* have no need of utilizing the *ayne* except on rare occasions." Those who have appreciable

---

sity (1963–1965). (Also see the bibliography for all references by Kuczynski-Godard, Gillin, Castro Pozo, Kubler, Tschopik.)

[29] Richard J. de Luca, "Glossary of Terms Used in Land Tenure and Related Labor Situations in Peru," Land Tenure Center, University of Wisconsin (mimeographed).

[30] Thomas R. Ford, *Man and Land in Peru* (Gainesville: University of Florida Press), pp. 41, 46, 66.

amounts of land prefer to hire the land-poor as day laborers, paying them in kind or in very low wages.[31]

The next step away from the *ayne* is called the *minca* in which those better off discharge whatever exchange labor obligation they may have by hiring a replacement. Martínez also noted the transformation of *compadrazgo* in this area in the Indians' preference not to hire out to their mestizo *compadres* or *padrinos* since in this case they would have to work for even less than the prevailing low wage.[32]

Typical of the agricultural labor pattern of the coastal truck gardens is the situation observed by Vásquez in the valley of Viru in the Department of La Libertad.[33] Here 3.4 percent of the landowners (nine individuals or firms) owned 78 percent of the irrigated land. However, 68 percent of this land was exploited indirectly through a number of share-cropping arrangements. Of this absentee property, 93 percent belong to the top nine landowners and was worked as follows: tenants, 32.61 percent; *colonos*, 64 percent; *aparceros*, 3.23 percent; undetermined, 0.16 percent.

Coloniaje (or *Yanaconaje*) is the oldest and most extensive system in current use. Under it the owner advances land and water rights for a fixed or indefinite period in exchange for a fourth or a fifth of the gross production. Most of the *colonos* already have some land of their own. They are a lower middle class of peasants far below the owners of the large estates but much nearer the tenants. They in turn employ *aparceros* and landless peons. They function as foremen between the owner or the tenant's plantation manager and the actual field hands.

Aparceros are the actual laborers hired by owners, tenants, or *colonos*. In the case where *colonos* make the arrangements no salary is paid but a further division of the harvest is made

[31] Hector Martínez, "El indígena y el mestizo de Taraco," *Revista del Museo Nacional* (Lima), XXXI (1962), 185.

[32] *Loc.cit.*

[33] Mario C. Vázquez, "Campesinos Andinos en un Valle Costeño del Perú," *Extensión en las Américas*, IX, Nos. 1 and 2 (1964), 13.

after the owner takes his share. In all cases the *aparceros* are "grub staked" to room and board, which is then deducted from their share at the moment of the division of the harvest.

In those plantations run directly by their owners, three types of wage labor are employed: (1) full-time attached workers who receive housing and food and, presumably, all the national welfare fringe benefits; (2) seasonal migrant labor paid a higher cash wage with no other benefits; (3) daily "shape-up" type peons who pick up odd jobs in the medium- and small-owner or *colono*-managed farms. They are the lowest paid and most recently arrived from the sierra. This section of the coast has seen a 20 percent increase in its rural population in the past 20 years, unlike the country as a whole, which experienced an 11 percent reduction in rural population during the same period. This is a consequence of the predominantly truck gardening function of this area. In other coastal valleys devoted largely to sugar cane, the process of mechanization has foreclosed future employment opportunities. In the latter case the only employment is paid labor. In Viru, on the other hand, absentee ownership, mixed vegetable crops, and a surplus of labor have perpetuated the sierra pattern of sharecropping instead of permitting the development of a purely cash-based labor system. However, the close connection between this truck-garden area and the urban markets of Trujillo, Chimbote, and Lima involves all of the workers in a commercial goods market. Moreover, if medium-scale peasant capitalists are a desirable source of economic development, this valley is more promising than the sugar cane areas, where there are only a few owners and a mass of rural proletarians as permanent field hands.

One feature of Peru's sugar plantations which differs from those in Cuba is that they operate throughout the year owing to their dependence on irrigation. They can thus employ a full-time corps of resident workers in contrast to the average four-month seasonal work year of the Cuban *guajiro* (cane cutter). This is one of the reasons why Castroite labor organizers were not successful in breaking the APRA's hold over these elite rural proletarians.

Erasmus, in an essay which attempts a synthesis of rural labor organization in Latin America, divides uncommercialized labor into two types—festive and exchange. Festive labor tends to occur on holidays, between different social levels, utilizing large numbers of workers, in which a strong element of prestige display is involved on the part of the host; Exchange labor tends to involve less than ten men, who are peers concerned with fairly predictable planting and harvesting chores.[34]

Festive labor tends to die out first, as Erasmus sees it, not only because machine technology makes labor-intensive systems unnecessary but also because the host–guest boss–worker role conflict inevitably results in low-quality, high-cost work. Exchange labor he found more persistent among poor peers especially for unpredictable emergencies.

An alternative explanation can be offered for the undoubted decline of festive labor parties. In the first place, the government has been increasingly pre-empting this "right" for highway construction and similar projects. Prestige-seeking local elites have not, however, been left without an opportunity to impress their inferiors. Most anthropologists pay considerable attention to the persistent phenomena of *cofradías, mayordomías* and other festive occasions in which men of some wealth can allow others to consume conspicuously. In fact, the pressure on such people to redistribute their wealth in this fashion is so great that the "stingy" ones who refuse must constantly moan about being on the verge of bankruptcy.[35] Festive displays have thus been "purified," or decommercialized of any economically productive element, leaving labor to

[34] Charles J. Erasmus, "The Occurrence and Disappearance of Reciprocal Farm Labor in Latin America," in Dwight B. Heath and Richard N. Adams (eds.), *Contemporary Cultures and Societies of Latin America* (New York: Random House, 1965), p. 174.

[35] François Bourricaud, "Castas y clases en Puno," *Revista del Museo Nacional* (Lima), XXXII (1963), 315.

be employed primarily on a paid contractual basis. As will be noted later, the process of commercialization is not a simple unilineal "all-corrupting" growth. The family, for instance, ceases to be a unit of production once the subsistence farm and domestic putting-out stage of industry is passed and thus in this respect moves out of the commercial market. *Compadrazgo,* on the other hand, seems to suffer a high degree of "abuse" during the early stages of industrialization as each side of this transitionally cross-class tie tries to take advantage of it. Ultimately, as the present author observed in a study of this institution in Lima in 1965, this once "spiritual" institution returns to its traditional function within the developing urban middle class—namely searching for a godfather of high character for one's child, rather than using children as an excuse to seek a wealthy protector for oneself or, on the other side, obtaining cheap and loyal domestic servants or workers.

Exchange labor ("free" reciprocity among equals) has the advantage of being cheap, or at least apparently so where people do not think in terms of the alternative value of their own time and the virtue of high-quality work, since (1) one works beside his helpers on his own project and (2) the helpers perform well in order to receive equal treatment. This form of labor, however, suffers several fatal defects: (1) it is highly inconvenient in terms of time scheduling; (2) it works only among men in the same type of low-skilled job; (3) it generates no cash income per se, thus leaving participants at a disadvantage in the face of desirable consumer goods which must be bought.

Commercialized farm labor then begins, as one party to a once-free reciprocal labor exchange prefers to specialize in management and thus discharge his obligation in cash instead of return labor. Then, as his labor needs exceed the availability of poorer neighbors, he must attract migrants whom he could not conveniently compensate in a nonmonetary fashion.

Richard N. Adams offers a more analytical typology of rural labor organizations also relevant to my perspective.[36] Labor relationships may be personalistic, based on *mutual privileges*. Exchange labor, in Erasmus' terms, is the prime case of this type, in which two peasants choose to help each other on a voluntary reciprocal basis. Such expectations can exist between smaller plantation owners and poorer peasant neighbors. In such cases the worker feels he is doing his "employer" a favor. The more common rural type, however, would be the paternalistic type in which the employer exercises *rights* by virtue of tradition and his greater power, while the worker enjoys only what *privileges* the employer may care to grant him. In the fully "industrial" type of labor–management relationship, very rare in rural areas, both sides exercise only contractual rights enforced by a third party.

The paternalistic relationship is the source of the major type of "exploitation" by management. But the "abuse" of labor should in turn be subdivided into emancipated worker orientation, in which the one-sided definition of the terms of work are resisted, and traditional worker orientation, in which a modernized management, which refuses to meet traditional diffuse privilege expectations, is resented for its "inhumanity." (The most common version of this type consists of management's expecting traditional "paternalistic-servile" behavior from workers but being unwilling to reciprocate in like fashion.) This worker resentment is very common in Peru and is comparable to the first stage of industrial protest in England.[37] There early unrest consisted of worker resentment at not being taken care of by factory employers, as landed aristocrats were supposed to have watched after their serfs or tenant farmers.

It is doubtful if labor protest in Peru will ever achieve the

[36] Richard N. Adams, "Rural Labor," in J. J. Johnson (ed.), *Continuity and Change in Latin America* (Stanford, Calif.: Stanford University Press, 1964), pp. 47-78.

[37] Reinhard Bendix, *Work and Authority in Industry* (New York: John Wiley & Sons, 1956), pp. 46, 51, 60.

same degree of "rugged individualism" and independence from paternalism that was prevalent in England in the nineteenth century. Moreover, many employers are not attempting to structure the industrial labor force in this direction.

Adams also observes that throughout Latin America, there are few workers left who have never worked for wages.[38] The already highly mobile rural labor force with its wide variety of sources of income, no one of which is adequate, could well be called a semiproletariat.

With respect to the textile factory workers to be studied, these references to current rural labor practices in Peru indicate that no factory workers are moving from the Stone Age to the twentieth century in the sense that they must learn not only how to operate machines but even the meaning of money and labor contracts. The major factor retarding the full commercialization of labor in the highlands (it has been contractual on the coast for over 50 years) has been the failure of most of these plantations to commercialize their agricultural operation. The highland *hacendado* has generally preferred not to work his land for a cash crop but to lease it out under a wide variety of sharecropping devices which will ensure him some money income but, more important, guarantee him control over a large number of people whose services he can use as domestics, as artisans, or as labor to rent to other plantation owners. The shortage of land, while forcing some to migrate to cities, has the more immediate effect of holding rural workers in these nonwage labor systems as the only alternative. Moreover, those who leave for the cities are generally not the most wretched of the landless peasantry but rather those with above average education and outside wage labor experience.

Labor Protest and Organization

As was mentioned above, Spain's preferential treatment of its own artisans and merchants discouraged the development

[38] Adams, *op.cit.*, p. 61.

of such groups in Peru except in noncompetitive groups such as bakers and musicians, i.e., perishable or nontransportable goods and services. After Independence the growth of Peruvian manufacturing was equally discouraged by the complete lack of protective legislation as well as the upper-class preference for imported goods.[39] Six factories were opened during the first guano boom (1845-1850), time and transportation cost at least being in their favor. One was a cotton textile mill in the town house of the famous mistress of a colonial viceroy. But all these efforts failed within five years.

The first recorded strikes, over wages, were in 1872 by the workers recruited to tear down Lima's medieval city walls to make way for a Parisian type of urban renewal—à la Hausman minus the apartment buildings.[40] There were also a few riots in Callao by the carpenters' guilds against imported furniture during the last quarter of the nineteenth century.

Throughout the nineteenth century, there were also numerous "Indian uprisings" in rural areas. These were, however, uncoordinated, purely spontaneous local affairs, and so served only to accelerate the flight of the gentry to the cities—primarily Lima.

The first "general" strike in Peru occurred in Lima in 1912, but the first wave of successful unionization occurred during and shortly after World War I. Among the first to be organized (and still the strongest and best paid unionists) were the longshoremen, followed by the railroad workers and the textile factory workers.

A clear view of this stage of labor organization in Peru is still difficult to obtain since, as in most countries, labor history escapes the notice of standard histories and thus is recorded primarily in partisan tracts. Conditions in Peru at this time (1917-1920), or more precisely in Lima, were certainly conducive to labor unrest, with war inflation followed by a sharp

[39] Jorge Basadre, *La multitud, la ciudad, y el campo* (Lima: Editorial Huascaran, 1947), p. 180.
[40] *Ibid.*, p. 183.

postwar drop in wages. Foreign influence was important though difficult to pin down. The Mexican and Russian revolutions and the students' reform movements throughout Latin America created intellectual leadership for the labor movement for the first time.

During the 1920's, however, the government was the primary structuring agent. The postwar labor protests against the cost of living and for the eight-hour day built up to a climax during the 1919 election. Leguía, in a bid for wider support (after his installation by means of the usual military *golpe* or coup) in 1920 freed the jailed labor leaders, mostly from the textile workers' union, and proclaimed the eight-hour day, at least in the infant, foreign-owned Lima manufacturing plants. By this time a Labor Bureau had been established with the power to set wages, freeze hours, and forbid layoffs and firings, the classic governmental techniques for buying off labor protest at the expense of a group, the early factory owners, who were not yet part of the Peruvian political elite.

The first Worker Congress in 1921 exposed the anarchistic political leanings of the majority of union leaders, most of whom belonged to "craft" unions. (The small size and the organization of the textile factories placed the machine tenders in a craft-like situation in United States terms.) During the twenties, the Communists and the APRA battled for control of the whole movement, with the APRA gaining an undisputed victory. A one-time Marxist, Ricardo Martínez de la Torre (no admitted relation to Haya de la Torre) analyzed the situation in the following characteristic terms:

> . . . those false writers, mental masturbators, who adulate the ignorance of the *mestizo serrano*, [who are] envious, owing to their impotent indolence, of any culture or ennobling discipline, [those who] foment the vain cretinism of the enslaved feudal latifundist sierra, . . . [demonstrate] a false suicidal provincialism which is afraid of its own shadow. . . . This tactic of dissipating in the provinces the

75

exemplary effort demonstrated by the proletariat of the Capital . . . is one of the many means by which the spiteful opportunism of the petty bourgeoisie, incubated in our conservative universities, reveals itself. [It is] dyed with the false reformist and treacherous uneasiness of recently arrived twisted nationalist demagogues, who preach in falsetto and claim to be discoverers of a surprising American "reality" which only exists in their disoriented revolutionary bohemia.[41]

This colorful analysis, nevertheless, correctly reflects the social origin of the APRA and its pragmatically successful tactics. The APRA had a program which captured the imagination of both the workers and the intellectuals and thus has inoculated Peru until recently against the appeal of a party-line Communist party. As Martínez de la Torre sees it, Latin elites characteristically react to worker unrest not by direct opposition but by fostering fascistic groups, who, using Marxist jargon, can soak up resentments without changing the society.

An interesting managerial experiment during the twenties was a movement led by Ricardo Tizón y Bueno. In an attempt to offset union influence he established *sociedades mutualistas*, company unions and sports clubs. Tizón y Bueno was Peru's first management representative to the International Labor Office and had previously been one of the few *criollo* managers of Peru's largest textile factory. Even this attempt was too progressive for Leguía, who in his antilabor era had Tizón y Bueno deported.

When the Depression and Peru's crippling foreign debt displaced Leguía, the APRA had the support of most organized

[41] Ricardo Martínez de la Torre, *Apuntes para una interpretación marxista de historia social del Perú* (Lima: Empresa Editorial Peruana S.A., 1947), I, 35.

See also Frederick B. Pike, "The Old and the New APRA in Peru: Myth and Reality," *Interamerican Economic Affairs*, XVIII, No. 2 (Autumn 1964), 3-45.

workers and thus might have obtained an electoral majority. They were predictably defrauded of victory on several occasions, but during the thirties the process of unionization spread rapidly to the mines and a few haciendas.

During the latter half of the thirties, under the administration of General Benavides, fear of the APRA led the conservative elite to employ, for the first time, the tactic of deliberately fostering Communists in order to split the labor movement.[42] During the Second World War, prosperity mitigated the government's efforts to repress the APRA as local factory owners connived with their workers to raise actual take-home pay above the frozen wage rates in the face of a labor shortage. In spite of their governmental support, the Communists lost control of the combined labor movement during the free election of 1945. After three years of rapid growth, the Apristas, who represented most of organized labor, were again repressed under the Odría regime until 1956, when they finally obtained a government largely dependent on their support. Today the APRA formally dominates the combined labor movement, but has lost effective control over the crucial mining, longshoremen's and bank clerks' unions. In general, the Apristas dominate northern unions, the Communists control southern unions, while in Lima power is split. The stronghold of *Aprismo sindical* remains the Textile Workers' Federation, led by its old guard of mestizo heroes of the twenties and thirties. Its ex-president, Arturo Sabroso, was once Peru's delegate to the International Labor Office—a symbol of APRA's power and relative respectability during the *convivencia* era (1956–1962).

The current Communist strategy in their southern stronghold in Cuzco is collaboration and indoctrination. Thus, local factory owners find them easiest to deal with as union chiefs since they value discipline over bread-and-butter benefits. So the Communist labor leaders trade labor peace for mana-

[42] U.S. International Cooperation Administration, *Summary of the Labor Situation in Peru* (Washington, D.C., October 1958), pp. 8-9.

gerial cooperation in the hiring, firing, and promotion of workers. Thus, the recruitment preference of the Aprista union chiefs is different from that of the Communists. The former seek emancipated urban workers from Lima or the larger mestizo towns—especially if they already belong to the party. The Communists' current emphasis on internal control leads them to prefer the least sophisticated *serranos* as rank-and-file members, which conforms as well to the preference of the majority of managers.

Labor and Social Welfare Legislation

GENERAL POLICY

One of the major differences in the development of the labor force in currently underdeveloped countries, as compared to Western industrialization, is the role "progressive" labor and welfare legislation plays. In general, labor protective laws have preceded rather than followed the formation of an industrial labor force in Peru.[43] Along with aspiring to the latest consumer goods ahead of their economy's ability to produce them, Peruvians desire the latest social welfare and labor legislation.

Most of the laws before 1945 were passed not at the instigation of unions or popular parties, but by governments representing the dominant "commercial oligarchy." Such governments would seem to be examples of shortsighted wily compromisers who for lack of principles open the door to basic changes which seal their own doom. They wished to counter the appeal of radical parties largely at the expense of the owners of manufacturing operations, most of whom are not yet part of "the oligarchy." International and Western managerial representatives to the International Labor Office conventions have their own goals in supporting such recommendations. They wish to equalize labor cost as a factor in international trade and competition.

[43] Wilbert E. Moore, *Industrialization and Labor* (Ithaca, N.Y.: Cornell University Press, 1951), p. 144.

78

A quite different local motivation also plays an important role in the development of Peruvian social and labor legislation. Many idealistic Peruvians, especially those not in positions of managerial responsibility, would like to spare Peruvian workers from all of the exploitation and abuses which accompanied the Industrial Revolution in the West. A purely universalistic contractual relationship in Peru is still viewed by the majority of people as "exploitation," since many of the norms on which it would be based are contrary to the "Peruvian way of life."

In general it seems Peruvians do not accept the market mechanism, the "law of supply and demand," as a valid basis for labor policy. There appear to be two main bases for this attitude. Neither traditional nor modern Catholic social doctrine accepts the market evaluation of labor. The more general orientation is a distaste for objective competition in all spheres of life. This operates as a self-fulfilling prophecy enabling a Peruvian "cynically" to reject this "law" as a fraud. The general, and often correct, assumption is that if prices or wages are unfavorable to you, some person or group of people has deliberately arranged to exploit or cheat you. Marxism thus appeals to a wide spectrum of people who would otherwise have little in common. There is of course little free business competition within Peru except among the marginal petty street merchants. But this orientation has as much a cultural as an experiential basis.

As for the actual form of Peruvian labor law, we must first note the comment that "unlike most Latin American countries, Peru has no general labor code; . . . in many cases decrees are overlapping, contradictory or no longer applicable. . . . Some legislation compares favorably with that of the most economically advanced countries of the world though not necessarily tailored to Peru's stage of development."[44] Such an evaluation, of course, is based on the assumption

[44] U.S. International Cooperation Administration, *op.cit.*, p. 25.

that currently underdeveloped countries (1) should not award benefits they could not afford if completely enforced and (2) should recapitulate the later-stage arrival of such welfare benefits as in the case of Western countries. Aside from the problem that no such course is politically feasible in democratically governed countries, it can be argued that since such "progressive" laws are actually very unevenly enforced, only the workers in the economically progressive sectors of the economy will, in fact, be benefited.

A prominent feature of Peruvian labor law which further complicates labor relations is the lack of a principle of precedence.[45] Each new case is in effect unique; the few lawyers in Peru who specialize in labor law find the study of previous decisions of no help. The outcome of administrative and most judicial decisions is thus completely "political," that is, effective power, not any abstract ideal of justice, prevails. In addition, the enforcement by labor inspectors of protective laws is reputedly very corrupt; inspectors often obtain many times their own salary from bribes and extortion.

UNION–MANAGEMENT RELATIONS

In general, union–management relations in Peru have functioned through governmental intervention rather than through direct local collective bargaining except under the restrictive regime of General Odría, when little could be achieved by overt political pressure on the government. Most unions have had more success by striking and then having the government impose a politically pressured solution by decree on management. An extreme example of this type of decree was the nationwide 10 percent wage hike awarded to all employees in 1957.

Unions, even under a semi-"laboristic" regime, are closely controlled by the government through the secret police (cur-

[45] Moises Poblete Troncoso and Ben A. Burnett, "Latin American Labor Law: A Synthesis," *Interamerican Economic Affairs*, II, No. 2 (Autumn 1958), 3-18.

rently in the background) and the Ministry of Labor and Indian Affairs. All locals must register with the Ministry and organize themselves on the basis of a standard charter, with all books open for continuous inspection. No union leaders may be foreigners, and all leaders and members are in theory investigated by the police. On the other hand, no union official may be fired. Unions can be dissolved by the government for a variety of reasons, and all actions of unions are subject to governmental review.

In line with the absence of communication between unions and management, there are no dues check-off systems or adequate grievance procedures. Conciliation and arbitration are mandatory but are usually by-passed because companies turn down the initially extravagant demands of unions, thus permitting the unions to go on strike.

Under nondictatorial regimes strikes are highly restricted in theory but not in practice. Strike votes must be 75 percent favorable, government-run, and repeated every four days. Since strike funds are usually low, large-scale flash strikes are used to obtain maximum political impact at the least expense to the workers. Pay for the strike period is allowed if the strike is judged legal.[46]

The current form of labor–management conflict in Peru has been described by Payne as "democracy by violence." He contrasts this "political bargaining" system with collective bargaining or protection through legal enactment as the only feasible style of operation for a country like Peru. Moreover, it has proved quite successful for the highly organized industrial workers in the Lima–Callao area.[47] "The unions have a key resource not available to employers: violence. When

[46] Jorge Ramírez Otarola, *Codificación de la legislación de trabajo y de previsión social del Perú* (Lima: 1955), pp. 585-586.

[47] James L. Payne, *Labor and Politics in Peru* (New Haven: Yale University Press, 1965), p. 17.

See also François Bourricaud, "Syndicalisme et politique: le cas peruvien," *Sociologie du travail*, October–December 1961, No. 4, pp. 33-49.

this resource is properly mobilized it tends to outweigh any that employers might bring to bear. Arguments about inflation, invoking friendships (with Ministry of Labor officials), and perhaps even bribes would not prevent a substantial union victory when the executive is threatened by violence."[48]

Payne's field data come from the 1961 *convivencia* era of a relatively peaceful and "laboristic" democracy in which the APRA party exerted as much influence as it had ever had or probably ever will have. He assumes that the executive is terrified of being overthrown by either the left, or more likely the right, if civilian unrest gets out of hand; hence the president forces employers to give in to some union demands.

This explanation does not hold for the Odría military dictatorship period from 1948 to 1956 in which the APRA was sharply repressed, the C.T.P. (Confederación de Trabajadores del Peru) was dissolved, and the Communists helped to infiltrate previously Aprista unions. Nor does it adequately explain labor laws as opposed to the settlement of specific strikes, since much of the labor and welfare legislation, as will be explained below, was enacted by dictators or by presidents not under the immediate pressure of strikes or labor violence.

WAGES AND WORKING CONDITIONS

Wages and working conditions are all, according to the constitution, determined by the government. In practice, however, only politically effective unions have obtained special decrees setting wages and working conditions in their own industry. This is notably the case with the Textile Workers Federation, which has the only escalator clause in Peru.[49] During the *convivencia* era (1956–1962) it was also the most favored union in most other respects, since it has always been the core of the labor support for the APRA. If it were not for the fact that the textile industry is currently "overdevel-

[48] *Ibid.*, p. 276.
[49] Ramírez Otarola, *op.cit.*, p. 426.

oped" and facing a world-wide overproduction crisis, textile workers might be the most highly paid workers in Peru.

In 1948, a profit-sharing plan whereby all companies worth more than 50,000 soles would distribute 30 percent of net annual profits was proposed but set aside during the Odría regime. Under the Prado regime, all firms whose net profit after taxes was 10 percent of their capital paid a bonus based on seniority and status. *Obreros* received a bonus of ten days' pay and *empleados* a month's pay.

As in other Latin American countries, the distinction between manual and nonmanual occupations, already sharp enough due to the two major races and cultures in Peru, is made even more distinct and rigid in all aspects of labor and welfare laws.[50] One of the "functions" of this separation is to weaken the labor movement politically, since *obreros* (blue-collar) and *empleados* (white-collar) at the same plant may not join the same union even if they wish to. In general, the *empleados* are greatly favored. This system is modified, however, by increasing intergenerational mobility across the line through education. Also, the borderline is lowered and confused by the occasionally successful efforts of craft unions to get their *obrero* members' jobs redefined as *empleado* positions. The white-collar sector is the fastest growing sector of the labor market, another of the "premature" features of Peru's economic development.

In addition to the many special decrees fixing wages in particular industries or even firms, the general wage law prohibits any reduction of pay and any deductions as disciplinary measures.

One feature of Peruvian labor costs very lightly touched on and considerably underestimated in an International Labor Office report[51] are the *cargos sociales* or social charges, the fringe benefits awarded all workers by government decree

[50] Raúl R. Ferrero and Carlos Scudellari, *El derecho del trabajo en el Perú* (Lima: Centro de Estudios Económicos y Sociales, 1955), p. 17.

[51] International Labor Office, *Textile Wages* (Geneva: 1952).

rather than through plant- or industry-wide collective bargaining. The reason for this de-emphasis would seem to be that most of these labor and welfare laws are decreed into law directly from the latest and most general of the I.L.O.'s recommendations. These social charges are estimated to amount to a 41.4 percent additional employer expense for *obreros* and 39.7 percent for *empleados*. In Mexico, according to the same study, the average social charges only amount to an additional 20 percent.[52]

To highlight the contrast a few of the more significant benefits are listed below.

LABOR REGULATIONS[53]

(1959)

Obreros	*Empleados*
COMPARABLE	REGULATIONS
Fifteen days of paid vacation annually, which is "obligatory, irrenouncable and noncumulative."	Thirty days of paid vacation, 15 of which may be worked for double pay.
One paid holiday a year.	Twenty paid holidays a year.
Severance pay of seven days for each year of service in firms capitalized at under 500,000 soles, 15 days if over this size, and the right to three months' notice of dismissal.	Severance pay of one month's salary for each year of service, and the right to three months' notice of dismissal.
Pensions from a government controlled fund at age 60 of 60 percent of average wages for previous five years or 40 percent for invalidism.	Pension after 35 years at the best salary at the employer's expense (no adequate funding required).
Year-end bonus of three days to two weeks depending on seniority.	Year-end bonus of from 25 to 100 percent of one month's salary depending on seniority.

[52] Rómulo A. Ferrero and Arthur J. Altmeyer, *Estudio económico de la legislación social peruana y sugerencias para su mejoramiento* (Lima: 1957), p. 118.

[53] See Ramírez Otarola, *loc.cit.*

84

NON-COMPARABLE REGULATIONS

Obreros	*Empleados*
Free schools and lodging if over ten kilometers from a town.	Free life insurance at the employer's expense equal to one-third of four years' salary.
For each six days of consecutive work, a day's wage is added, i.e., the Sunday wage law, or *salario dominical*.	Thirty percent salary increase after 30 years' service.

Government hospitalization exists in physically and socially separated institutions for almost all categories and classes of workers, and is paid from a 3 percent tax on the payrolls of all firms worth over 50,000 soles ($2,000 in 1959).

Obreros	*Empleados*
Obreros receive complete medical, surgical and dental care, cash payments limited to 26 weeks and up to 70 percent of wages. In maternity cases all medical and allied services are provided by the government.	*Empleados* have a comparable but separately financed and administered fund.

An especially interesting source of additional benefits is the concept of *derecho adquirido*. By law, as well as tradition, any bonus or benefit of any kind bestowed more than twice becomes an "acquired right" no longer terminable by management. Needless to say, this tends to discourage the offering of any additional noncontractual inducements.

Another important regulation sharply limits the discharging of workers. Any worker may be freely discharged within his first 90 days, but thereafter only, with the permission of the Ministry of Labor, for stealing, disrespect, more than three days' unexcused absences, chronic drunkenness, or dealing in the employer's business on his own account. In addition he must be given three months' notice or, as usually happens, paid three months' salary in addition to severance pay for seniority or "indemnization," which is discussed below. For many firms this rigidifying factor is a major cause of low labor productivity. For others this limitation is by-passed in a variety of ways. A common way is to keep most workers on an *eventual* or temporary basis, as though they were temporarily hired for construction work.

Obreros let go after 90 days have to be paid 15 days wage per year of work (for firms over 500,000 soles), while *empleados* receive a month's pay for each year of service. This severance pay ("indemnization") is also received at regular retirement, making for a very sizable bonus.

A very effective wage device, used also in Colombia, Mexico, and Venezuela, is the *salario dominical*, or Sunday wage. All workers who put in six consecutive days of work receive an extra day's wage—in effect, for the day off on Sunday. This single device introduced under Odría in 1950 has reduced absenteeism up to 20 percent in many plants, according to factory managers with whom I talked.

Working mothers are entitled to 72 days of maternity leave at 70 percent of full pay, plus one hour per day off thereafter for nursing their children. Also, women must not work over 45 hours a week but must be paid for the usual 48-hour work week. As we shall see, the percentage of women has dropped sharply in the Peruvian textile industry because, overall, female workers are more expensive than male.

An additional regulation of interest is one prohibiting the pirating away of foreign technicians hired directly from abroad. This was a concession to some of the larger foreign-owned firms but is particularly ineffective, and in my view happily so. It is true that some foreign firms lose time and money on foreign employees who default to work for smaller Peruvian employers, but since the latter firms otherwise have no direct access to this international labor market, this practice would seem to be very helpful to the economic development of Peru by lowering barriers to labor mobility.

Although not relevant to our sample, some of the post-1959 changes in Peruvian labor law are of interest in terms of our general discussion. In brief, the sharp distinction, extreme even within Latin America, between *obreros* and *empleados* has been greatly reduced. Medical facilities are still segregated, but vacations, minimum salaries and wages, separation payments, and annual bonuses have been equalized by bringing *obreros* up to the *empleados* level. (See Ley 13683, August 25, 1961, on *obrero* vacations; Decreto Ley 14192, August 21, 1962, on minimum pay scales; and Decreto Supremo, July 25, 1959, Ley 13842, January 12, 1962, on separation "indemnization.") [54] The distinction between these groups continues to be the object of a "game" in which on balance more *obreros* jobs are reclassified as *empleados* than vice versa. The most significant change, both in practice and in terms of our theoretical perspective, has been the opening up of the *empleado* labor market. Previously it was extremely disadvantageous from both his and his employer's point of view, for a clerk or technician or manager to change jobs. With unfunded pension systems, employees lost their credits on changing jobs. Since most employers did not set aside the required reserves for pensions, they preferred to fire employees just short of retirement ages. To counter this, generous indemnization payments were required. Thus both preferred a low rate of turnover.

Today pension rights for employees are properly funded by the government. (See Ley 13724, July 11, 1962, and Ley 14069 on the *Caja de Pensiones del Seguro Social del Empleado.*) (An understandable distrust of such funds still exists ever since the previous exhaustion of *obrero* trust funds by Odría to buy submarines to defend Peru against the Chileans.) Credit toward pensions now accumulates continuously. In addition, there is a ceiling on the maximum size of separation bonuses—thus making it easier to discharge or lay off workers.

[54] Jorge Ramírez Otarola, *Codificación de la legislación del trabajo y de previsión social del Perú* (2nd ed.; Lima: Editorial Antonio Lulli, 1963).

These changes constitute an exceptional development toward labor market extension and purity. One consequence has been the recent establishment of a society of textile engineers, unthinkable only a few years ago when being seen with employees of competing firms was sometimes cause for dismissal. Peruvian plants are still generally not open for public visits. Most owners assume they will lose valuable trade secrets, although one can argue it is their weaknesses which most need to be hidden.

Another area of legislation illustrating the incessant game between the generally paternalistic government and "devious" employers is that of regulations affecting the trial period of employment after which it is legally possible, but can be politically difficult, to fire workers. In 1962, the concept of "indemnization" or a separation bonus was extended even to the trial period (Decreto Ley 14218, October 19, 1962). A most interesting though very dubious clause in this law states, in effect, that any worker gaining appointment through a competitive test shall not have to suffer any trial period. This will presumably have one or both of the following consequences: (1) prevent the use of these tests until just before the trial period is up (if so, the government will doubtless follow past practice and expressly forbid this) ; (2) corrupt the marking or handling of such tests and thus make them prematurely suspect. The government's intention was laudable even if its respect for the scientific status of commercialized psychological testing is excessive.

CHAPTER 4

The Textile Industry

The Choice of Industry

Three factors have led to the choice of the textile industry in Peru as the field of research: its position as a leading sector in the development of manufacturing industry; its current importance; and the availability of data.

LEADING SECTOR

The textile industry was in the "West," and now is in currently underdeveloped countries, a leading sector in the development of manufacturing industry because (1) it exploits a readily available agricultural raw material; (2) it supplies a well-established consumer good; (3) it can effect immediate and radical cost reductions in competition with even the most efficient hand looms run by the most poorly paid weavers. (This does not mean that the textile factories in developing countries, even with ostensibly cheap labor, could compete against imported factory-made cloth without heavy tariff protection or subsidies.) The major difference, of course, is that in England the textile industry was *the* leading industry serving as the primary source for industrialization, whereas in Peru and most underdeveloped countries, mining, railroads, and mechanized agriculture preceded the growth of a textile industry. However, in Peru these earlier industries developed mostly in isolated rural areas and thus did not directly give rise to unions and modern industrial legislation. Thus, the Peruvian textile industry played a role comparable to that of the English textile industry, i.e., it provided the locus and milieu for the recruitment of an urban industrial labor force.

A comparison of the Peruvian case with the English is appropriate not only for the above reasons, but also for the reason that the very machinery, engineers, and foremen in Peru were—and to a large extent still are—English. These expatriates had a type of training consisting largely of practical experience, which tended to make them more stereotyped in their technical as well as labor policy than was and is the case with German or American textile experts, who generally are products of technical schools and universities and thus a bit more flexible.

CURRENT IMPORTANCE

Even after 40 years of growth of other manufacturing operations, the textile industry is still the second largest branch of manufacturing—following that of food processing—employing 15.8 percent of all workers in the so-called manufacturing sector. There are in Peru approximately 21,000 textile factory workers out of 160,000 in all manufacturing establishments.[1] (A more extensive discussion of the structure of textiles in the context of other industries will be found in Chapter 7.)

These figures, while highlighting the importance of the textile industry, also reveal the low level of Peruvian industrial development. A country in which the major branches of manufacturing are made up of small factories processing food and fibers has only begun the process of industrialization so far as the development of manufacturing is concerned. In other respects, Peru is "ahead of itself," i.e., in terms of social legislation and the development of a major city with a substantial middle class.

SOURCE MATERIAL AVAILABLE

As a result of the importance of the textile industry and of the fact that (as in most other countries) it is in serious financial straits, there now exist a large number of reputable and detailed studies on this branch of manufacturing, starting with a United Nations study in 1949,[2] and concluding,

[1] Dirección Nacional de Estadística y Censos, *Resultados preliminares primer censo nacional económico, 1963* (Lima: 1965), Table 1.
[2] See United Nations, Department of Economic and Social Affairs,

as of 1959, with a continuing United Nations study whose purpose was to recommend specific laws and actions for all of Peru's manufacturing activities. Various investigations were in process or had recently been completed prior to my arrival in Peru in 1958, and they provided an excellent fund of current background data.

The Structure of the Industry

ECONOMIC FUNCTION AND LOCATION

In economic terminology the textile industry, in general, could be described as follows.[3] It is a light, semidurable consumer-goods industry selling in a highly price-elastic market. (For our purposes industrial producer-goods textiles and fancy handicraft-type products are excluded.) It generally involves little weight loss between the raw material and the finished product and a relatively high added value. On this basis a location near its consumer market rather than near the source of its raw material, or at a transportation junction, is indicated.

LEVEL OF MECHANIZATION

Technologically, the textile industry is in a state of arrested mechanization due to the semidurable, price-elastic, and above all stylistic nature of its products. The same is even more clearly true in the garment industry, where automation is almost prohibited by the vagaries of consumer tastes (or designers' machinations). This is especially striking because technologically it would be a relatively simple matter to construct an automated, completely integrated (cleaning, spin-

---

Labor Productivity of the Cotton Textile Industry in Five Latin American Countries (E/CN.12/219, New York: 1951). United States, International Cooperation Administration, *Notas sobre la industria textil en el Perú* (Lima: 1956). Peru, Ministerio de Trabajo y Asuntos Indígenas, *Informe preliminar sobre las fábricas textiles del Cuzco* (Lima: Septiembre 1956). Peru, Ministerio de Trabajo y Asuntos Indigenas, *La industria textil en el Perú* (Lima: 1957).

[3] Morton R. Solomon, "The Structure of the Market in Underdeveloped Economies," *Quarterly Journal of Economics*, LXII (August 1948), 525.

ning, weaving, and finishing) textile factory if only long enough runs of one type of cloth could be sold. Fibers, like chemicals, are amenable to flow processing. But consumer tastes intervene, limiting textile production to the assembling of batches of products at different stages of processing, which are then mixed by hand for the next stage of processing. The flow process breaks down completely in the weaving sheds to be partially restored in the finishing stage.

Added to the generally arrested stage of mechanization in textile technology, there is, in Peru's case, the factor that her industry was beginning at a time when England's textile industry had already started to decline economically and stabilize technologically. Therefore, Peruvian mills, until very recently, often began operations with second-hand or outdated labor-intensive machinery. This was appropriate originally because of the shortage of capital and the surplus of apparently cheap labor.[4] Today most students of the textile industry bemoan this lack of concern with labor productivity and suggest the utilization of the latest labor-saving machinery, in spite of the surplus of cheap labor, in order to avoid the problem of excessive labor costs later as wages rise but workloads and the labor force tend to remain frozen.[5] In general, it seems that those most distant from the problem recommend an "Indian" (Asian) style maintenance of labor-intensive production,[6] whereas on-the-spot managers and United Nations technicians prefer greater labor efficiency.

LABOR INTENSITY

The textile industry in general is labor intensive. Thus, its "normal" tendency to locate near its customers is offset

---

[4] Latin American Economic Institute, *The Cotton Textile Industry in Latin America*, Pamphlet Series No. 6 (New York: 1942), p. 5.

[5] United Nations, Department of Economic and Social Affairs, *The Industrial Development of Peru* (E/CN.12/493) (Mexico City: 1959), p. 39.

[6] Cyril S. Belshaw, "Adaptation of Personnel Policies in Social Context," in Wilbert E. Moore and Arnold S. Feldman (eds.), *Labor Commitment and Social Change in Developing Areas* (New York: Social Science Research Council, 1960), p. 104.

(except for the garment industry) by the desire to obtain cheap labor. Also, its labor intensity tends to increase as finer grades of cloth or yarn are desired at any one level of mechanization. This characteristic of the textile industry gives the newly developing poorer countries an international advantage. Currently this great disparity in labor costs has been largely offset in most countries by protective tariffs, but in Peru's case, at least, this protection was not made really effective until the 1950's. Both before and after World War II, Japan's even lower labor costs had demoralized Peru's internal market. Thus, Peru's textile industry had been through almost a life cycle of standard historical experiences even before the other branches of manufacturing had begun to develop.

SKILL LEVEL AND LOCATION

The arrested stage of textile technology makes the level of mechanical skills of the work force of some importance, especially in the case of weavers. There are many "machine-tender" jobs in textile mills, but the majority of workers are in relatively highly skilled occupations involving considerable variation and initiative within the context of the range of skills demanded in factories from the least mechanized to those at automated levels of development. Thus, flight to areas lacking an industrialized labor force in an effort to secure cheap labor is self-defeating. Several factories in Peru seem to demonstrate this assertion. (The flight to the South in the United States, it should be noted, has been not to the most backward, depressed, "preindustrial" areas, but to communities which have long had a textile industry, i.e., North Carolina and southern Virginia. In the same manner the only successful post-1945 textile mills established outside of Lima are in Arequipa. It is Peru's second largest city and one with several prewar textile factories already in operation.) Solomon's statement that textiles lead in industrialization because they can use the unskilled type of labor which is in such oversupply,[7]

[7] Solomon, *op.cit.*, p. 525.

would seem to be overstated if not in error. He also notes that textile plants usually locate in urban areas because the industry is consumer-oriented and labor, in general, is immobile. The immobility of labor in industrializing areas would seem, on the basis of recent studies, to be a mistaken interpretation of the facts. Except for uninhabited or isolated rural areas, labor in quantity has been available to most of the earliest urban manufacturing industries in most societies; it is the quality of the labor which has been the primary problem.[8] Textile factories in Peru located in urban areas partly because they could not effectively utilize the cheapest type of rural labor available. A fuller discussion of the matter of labor quality and plant location is at the heart of the analysis in the following chapter.

SEX STEREOTYPING

The textile industry is considered a "light" industry partly because it is more important for the workers to have dexterity than brawn. Historically and contemporaneously, the textile industry throughout the world has used both sexes at a wide range of ages in virtually all positions. There is no universal pattern of sex or age stereotyping on a technological basis such as is found in mining, metal working, and other heavy industries. In India most textile workers are male; in Japan they are female; and in England, a mixed "Lancashire system" exists.

This pattern has varied throughout the development of the British cotton textile industry, with women in general moving into jobs that have become mechanized. When the "putting-out" system was in vogue, most weavers were male and spinners were female.[9] Later, as power looms were developed and the early spinning machines required a "walking" action

---

[8] Clark Kerr, John T. Dunlop, Frederick Harbison, and Charles R. Myers, *Industrialism and Industrial Man* (Cambridge: Harvard University Press, 1960), p. 8.

[9] Neil J. Smelser, *Social Change in the Industrial Revolution* (Chicago: University of Chicago Press, 1959), p. 184.

on the part of the operator, the opposite sex stereotyping existed.[10] Women, as in Peru, took over "heavy" handweaving during its economic decline, thus demonstrating the absence of a "real" sex limitation even here.

By the time Peru's cotton textile industry was developing, after 1900, and British textiles had begun to decline, there was a reversion to widespread female and child employment in the British industry. This pattern of job stereotyping was the immediate model for Peru in part because so many skilled male workers in England were displaced and hence available for employment abroad as foremen.

"The Lancashire system." A consequence of the on-the-job type of training which most of the British managers and technicians have had is their allegiance to "the Lancashire system." This system in England is neither as consistent nor as traditional as the British foremen in Peru think, but for purposes of explaining their job assignment policies, it might as well be. In England it allegedly involves the following features:

1. An extensive degree of corporate and plant specialization.

2. A highly developed *gemeinschaft* among middle-level foremen and technicians which counteracts the effects of the above specialization. Much business is undertaken and a fairly free exchange of technical "know-how" within different levels of management occurs in nearby pubs.

3. A long and narrowing system of apprenticeship, which allows some skilled blue-collar workers to advance to lower-level managerial and technical positions.

None of the above aspects of this "system" was carried over to Peru. Peruvian textile plants are almost all fully integrated, and in the almost paranoid climate of Peru's business relationships, any communication between managements in competing firms was, until recently, cause for dismissal. British ex-foremen are, therefore, generally ill-prepared to direct the

---

10 *Ibid.*, p. 182.

production of these mills. In particular, they arrive in Peru with such backgrounds as that of specialization in weaving bath towels and are expected to direct the entire process from opening cotton bales to the increasingly complicated finishing process.

The two areas in which they can express their traditional beliefs are in job assignments and employment practices, especially with respect to sex. Thus, having a degree of unsureness about their other problems, they tend to be especially dogmatic in this area.

Another feature of the "Lancashire system" imported to Peru is an extremely complex system of piece-rate wages. The willingness of Peruvian labor leaders to accept this system of payment is explained by the following factors: (1) As mestizos with a *cholo* rank-and-file membership, they admit, "Peruvian workers are lazy and would not work on time rates"; (2) the nature of textile machinery and the extreme variability in yarn and design mixes do in fact make workers relatively responsible for their own work, especially the weavers. Thus, the existence of a piece-rate system per se is not viewed as an arbitrary British particularism. Nevertheless, the particular "theories" about what types of looms or weavers or counts of yarn are "harder to work," are matters of great controversy among even the experts, and in these cases nontechnical types of authority are often decisive.

A Short History

FOUNDING ERA 1896–1914

During the first brief era of relative political stability after Peru was given independence, two Spaniards attempted in 1848 to establish a cotton textile mill in the, by then, run-down town house of a famous viceroy's mistress, la Casa de Pericholi. It shortly failed, and no further attempts were made to manufacture cotton textiles until about 1900. In 1861, a now very picturesque woolen mill was packed into

Cuzco on llama back to be erected on the hacienda of a recent immigrant from Catalonia in Spain. (Known as the only part of Spain exhibiting the "Protestant ethic," it is currently the center of Spanish industry.) The first urban and still the largest woolen mill was founded in 1896 in Lima by recent Italian immigrants who arrived with the necessary capital and experience. This firm still recruits its technical and managerial staff directly from Italy or from within its by-now-widespread "clan" of native-born relatives.

The first major period of textile mill establishment was from 1896 to 1914.[11] During the United States Civil War, England turned to Peru, among other alternative sources, for raw cotton for her own textile industry. By 1900 a few of the English exporting houses in Peru decided to divert some of their raw material into the domestic production of the cheapest grade of cotton goods.

The significant aspects of this early period were the following.

Absence of tariff protection. In the terms used to describe the early eighteenth-century United States, this period in Peru's industrial history was an era of "salutary neglect." In the opinion of the United Nations report on Peru's cotton textile industry, it was the absence of any substantial protection until after World War II that explains the greater efficiency of Peru's textile industry in comparison with those of other Latin American countries.[12]

Full integration. Each of the firms began as a fully integrated processing operation from the cleaning of raw materials to the sale of "finished" bolts of cloth. In the beginning such an organizational pattern seemed necessary because of the absence of other textile firms specialized in complementary activities. As a result, most Peruvian mills possess individual

[11] See Appendix A for individual histories of the textile mills in our sample.

[12] United Nations, Department of Economic and Social Affairs, *Labor Productivity of the Cotton Textile Industry in Five Latin American Countries*, p. 4.

machines and whole divisions which have never been able to operate efficiently owing either to their excessive size relative to their consumer demand or more generally to their lack of smoothly flowing integration with other processing stages in the same mill.

In this respect it should be noted that Peru did not follow the Lancashire model. In England, regional and stage-of-processing specialization by firms was well organized.[13] Also, Peru by-passed the domestic putting-out or subcontracting system which was so notorious a part of English textile history.[14] There was no need or opportunity for the differing spurts of progress in perfecting first looms, then spindles, and again weaving. The chronic production maladjustments in Peruvian mills arise from the fact that, with a small-scale integrated mill, it is impractical, if not impossible, to schedule a wide variety of quantities and types of cloth and yarn and at the same time keep all sections of the mill in full-time coordination.[15] Yet,

[13] Sydney J. Chapman, *The Lancashire Cotton Industry* (Manchester: Manchester University Press, 1904), p. 148.

[14] In Guatemala during World War II, McBryde found an entirely different situation. There a highly developed "putting-out" system had grown up, especially for the weaving of the now famous Guatemalan cotton skirts. The weavers, mostly *ladinos* (*cholos* or mestizos in Peru), used the Spanish treadle-style manual looms on commission from urban merchants. Whole families and areas specialized in certain types of weaving and design. This comparison will be especially relevant to our discussion in view of Nash's later study of the Cantel textile mill, which is located in the same area. This, the only textile mill in Guatemala, was apparently supplying the coarse, white cotton yarn for most of the country and had thus virtually eliminated hand-spinning of cotton. As in Peru, Indian textile production is limited largely to wool spinning and weaving in the traditional manner. (Felix Webster McBryde, "Cultural and Historical Geography of Southern Guatemala," Publication No. 4 [Washington: Smithsonian Institution, Institute of Social Anthropology, 1945]. Manning Nash, *Machine Age Maya* [Glencoe, Ill.: The Free Press, 1960].)

[15] There are perhaps three basic ways to coordinate human economic actions: (1) *gemeinschaft* or community consensus; (2) contract and minimal consensus through a market mechanism; (3) direct administrative control. In modern large-scale producer goods industries, considerable technological efficiency seems possible through administrative coordina-

in Peru, textile production occurs largely through administrative control over fully integrated plants rather than through
the market as in the "West." This is especially irrational since
factory administration is a slowly developing art in Peru.

Displacement of handweavers. Peru's urban weavers, as was
mentioned earlier, had long since been put out of work by
years of tariff-free importation of English goods.[16] In 1900,
to be sure, probably two thirds of all Peruvians still spun or
wove their own clothes, but this segment of Peru's population
remained a world apart. Urbanites had long since rejected
domestic handmade cloth. When the Peruvian weaving guilds
disappeared, unlike the case in England, they were replaced,
not by individual artisans producing for the same urban
market through the domestic "putting-out" system, but by
imported materials. In Peru weaving in isolated areas has
partially "degenerated" from a full-time male profession to
a part-time female occupation. Today one finds Indian women
hand-spinning and weaving on primitive looms, while those
Indian men who still weave do so on Indian versions of the
medieval Spanish loom as a part-time occupation.[17]

The social origin of the entrepreneurs. The textile entrepreneurs were largely foreign immigrants who arrived with
the money and training to carry out their function. They
were "strangers" but not marginal in the manner of Jews in
Europe, or Indians and Chinese in Asia. They were "elite
strangers" from cultures highly valued in Peru, enjoying vir-

---

tion, although the tendency toward the oligopolistic manipulation of the
price mechanism obscures the question of their financial efficiency. The
main industry, apparently least amenable to such control even in fully
socialist economies, is the stylistic consumer-oriented semidurable type
such as textiles. If it is to be controlled primarily by administrative
coordination, then public taste must likewise be regimented. Such personal habits and tastes would seem to be minimal universals beyond the
scope of the police power of the state, at least in an urban industrial
society.

[16] Alejandro Garland, *Reseña industrial del Perú* (Lima: 1905), p. 113.

[17] William W. Stein, *Hualcan: Life in the Highlands of Peru* (Ithaca,
N.Y.: Cornell University Press, 1961), p. 87.

tually the same status that the English businessmen in India enjoyed when it was an English colony. (England owned a controlling share of the Peruvian economy from 1895 to 1930.)

A few creole Peruvian merchants subscribed part of the capital in some cases, but the inevitable co-owner disagreements, along with opportunities for more secure and profitable ventures in urban real estate and government-subsidized deals, tended to limit Peruvian financial participation. Today the larger textile firms are still almost entirely owned and managed by foreigners. Some of them are Peruvian citizens but not fully Peruvian in a cultural sense. Their legal status had led to the impression that the textile industry is "national." It is true, and important, that a smaller percentage of profits from textile firms are exported than from oil or mining industries. However, the wealthier Peruvian businessmen reputedly deposit money abroad as readily as do foreigners working in Peru.

The essential fact at this point is that there were virtually no Peruvian (Spanish- or Indian-descended individuals of several generations' residence in Peru) entrepreneurs, managers, or engineers in the Peruvian textile industry.[18] Only today are foreign-citizen-owned firms hiring a few Peruvian engineers and managers in this field, and at lower wages than their foreign predecessors received, because of pressure from the government to "nationalize" their labor force and management. Ironically, it is the ostensibly "national" firms who eagerly "pirate" away the foreign technicians from the explicitly foreign-owned companies.

DEVELOPMENTAL PERIOD 1914–1950

Effects of the First World War. World War I dramatically exposed Peru's degree of integration in the world market as

[18] "Virtually every important material enterprise [in Peru] has been inaugurated and developed by foreign capital and foreign promoters." Clayton S. Cooper, *Latin America: Men and Markets* (Boston: Ginn & Co., 1927), p. 72. "The highest percentage of foreign owned mills [in Latin America] are found in Peru." Latin American Economic Institute, *op.cit.*, p. 7.

a raw-material supplier by simultaneously creating a local depression and inflation.[19] Needed imports could not be obtained or readily substituted for exports now vital to Peru's
economy. The textile industry, however, prospered since it relied largely on domestic raw materials for a domestic consumer's market. The general climate of unrest gave rise to
the first welfare legislation and unionization, and in both
cases textiles was the obvious industry to be controlled.

The Great Depression. The Depression of the thirties co-
incided with two events of consequence for the textile industry: (1) the aggressive competition of Japanese textile imports, which gave rise to the first protective, but still low,
tariffs, and to a number of other promising but never fully
realized steps, e.g., an Industrial Development Bank;[20] (2) the
influx of European refugees, primarily Jews. Many, especially
from Eastern Europe, developed small garment shops and
knitting mills, some of which served as the basis for postwar
growth into spinning and weaving mills, usually rayon.

No new mills began operation during the Depression, but
a number were reorganized, in most cases passing from the
hands of original entrepreneurs into the hands of the two
largest foreign firms or local banking or commercial interests.

The Second World War. World War II was a period of even
greater prosperity for the textile industry, net profits of 28
to 33 percent being normal.[21] Unfortunately, during the war
machinery was overworked and poorly maintained (only in
part due to the shortage of replacements) and profits drained
off for other investments. As a result, the industry was poorly

[19] See L. S. Rowe, *Early Effects of the War upon the Finance, Commerce and Industry of Peru* (New York: Carnegie Endowment for International Peace, Oxford University Press, 1920).

[20] This bank was chartered in 1936 and is still in existence. It did
make some loans to textile firms but primarily to those with political
connections. Most either were defaulted or resulted in the Bank or
rather one of its directors taking over the firm concerned.

[21] Latin American Economic Institute, *op.cit.,* p. 18.

prepared to face the postwar resumption of the prewar depression in textiles.

The Industry's Current Problems

By 1950 the Peruvian government was forced to assist an industry in chronic trouble. The sources of its many problems as described by the various studies referred to and as noticed by personal observation are discussed in the following sections.

PRODUCTION

Excessive integration. Most firms are still entirely integrated, not specialized by plant and firm as in developed economies. Thus, in view of their small scale (many having less than 500 looms and 1,000 spindles), they cannot employ all of their equipment or labor to maximum advantage. Generally, one department is ahead of the others. In addition, much of the equipment used in preparation and finishing operations requires a far larger minimum level of production to be financially efficient. Already Peruvian mills altogether have seven large modern "combined" German finishing machines when five would take care of the entire industry's potential capacity. Moreover, all of the larger firms which do not yet possess one of these machines now have one on order. A shortsighted commercial outlook seems to be largely responsible. The mills that now have these machines charge so much for taking in finishing work from their competitors that it is necessary for each of the competitors to buy its own machine in self-defense. By charging somewhat less, the present finishing-machine owners could make such a defensive investment by their competitors uneconomic and could at the same time ensure themselves enough production to justify their own investment. A compromise solution proposed by a United Nations textile expert would involve the establishment of independent finishing firms to be run in a "professionally" independent businesslike manner, even if they are still owned by one of the established mills.

The disruption of the labor force is the aspect of this problem that is of greatest interest to this study. One of the important sources for the apparently worker-caused "instability" of the labor force is the frequency of short-term layoffs due to poor production planning.

Outmoded machinery. Even before the depreciation of the *sol* and the recent arguments in favor of labor-intensive types of industrial development, many Peruvian textile mills started operations with second-hand European or American machinery. Its cheapness and availability, due to a decline in production or to modernization in the exporting countries, were a sufficient advantage. Recently, however, the government, on the advice of United Nations textile experts and those local factory owners who have purchased new equipment, has strictly forbidden this practice.

High labor costs and low productivity. In order to enlarge our perspective on Peru's comparative position in this respect, we will cite some excellent cross-cultural material. Shortly after the study of labor productivity in Peru's cotton textile industry was completed in 1950, the International Labor Office made a comparative study of textile wages in 25 countries.[22] Their findings with respect to Peru's position are the following: (1) As expected, Peru fell in the lowest of the four groups distinguished by the study, i.e., those with wages under $0.20 per hour. The United States average at that time (1948) was $1.31 per hour. (2) Peru was the only country which consistently showed no official sex differentiation in wages for the same work. This type of discrimination is legally declining all over the world and has been rather effectively eliminated in Peru during the immediate postwar years due to the unprecedented political influence of the Textile Workers Federation through the ascendency of the APRA from 1945 to 1948. (3) Typical of the newly developing nations, especially in Latin America, textile wages in Peru were

[22] International Labor Office, *Textile Wages* (Geneva: 1952) p. 10.

among the highest within manufacturing. This is due to the fact that the usually higher-paying steel, electrical, and chemical producers' goods industries had just begun to develop. (A sign of industrial development then would be the relative decline of textile wages.) (4) In Peru, as in the rest of the world, textile wages rose faster than the average industrial wage in the immediate postwar era from 1945 to 1950. The International Labor Office report attributes this to a rise in production, presumably to make up for postponed wartime demand and thus to a resulting shortage of textile labor. In this respect I feel the report is somewhat mistaken. In general, I.L.O. analyses tend to play down the role of government intervention, perhaps because today such action is so often based on a facile application of I.L.O. recommendations. This report also exhibits a preference for classical economic assumptions about supply and demand as the basic wage-determining factors in precisely those countries and sectors where such factors are least operational.

Their observation that Peru's real textile wages as of 1948 had risen more than those of any other country since 1938 calls for further explanation. (Peru's textile wages increased by 139 percent, followed by Chile, 108 percent; Mexico, 104 percent; and several other Latin American countries.) [23]

Various factors accounted for this dramatic rise in wages. During World War II the textile industries of each of the Latin American countries had its national markets to itself and so enjoyed a boom. Government efforts to fix wages in Peru during the brief period of real textile labor shortage were to no avail. Labor and management connived to let wages "creep upward" as they did in the cost-plus war industries in the United States. Price controls did not function either, since the wartime textile market was largely a seller's market. When the war ended, the sale of locally manufactured goods fell off rapidly as buyers ordered imported cloth years ahead. Although overall sales did rise during the immediate

[23] *Ibid.*, p. 19.

postwar period it was due not to higher production by the established Peruvian mills but to imports, especially Japanese and Chinese, and secondarily to the establishment of new rayon mills. From a position in 1945 where it was supplying 98 percent of the national market, the cotton textile industry slipped to 80 percent by 1951 and recovered to 90 percent by 1956 only with the help of much higher tariffs.[24]

Therefore, a part of the rise, but only a minor part, was based on a wartime labor shortage. The important aspect of the immediate postwar Lima labor market is that it was grossly oversupplied. The great wave of migration to Lima, which had begun in 1940, had provided so many extra workers by 1945 that textile wages should have dropped rather than risen. In addition, the third and even second shifts used in wartime were stopped, thus throwing additional, and experienced, textile workers into the market. Nevertheless, real wages climbed even more steeply between 1945 and 1948.

The basic reason for this sharp postwar increase in textile wages was the ascendency to power, for the first time in its history, of the APRA, whose strongest labor support had always come from the Textile Workers Federation. The subsequent government-decreed pay increases and other special benefits, many limited exclusively to textile workers, were the pay-off for years of loyal support. What was actually more important, however, was the first real enforcement in the textile industry of the generous laws already on the books, i.e., an escalator clause tied to a cost-of-living index for textile workers only and a special 10 percent bonus again limited to textile workers, as well as the general labor laws.[25]

Other factors in the increased level of textile wages have been (1) equalization of pay by sex (and hence the subsequent reduction in female employment); (2) the disappearance of woolen mills paying some of the lowest wages, to-

[24] Perú, Ministerio de Trabajo y Asuntos Indígenas, *La Industria Textil en el Perú*, p. 67.
[25] *Ibid.*, p. 110.

gether with the establishment of new rayon and woolen mills paying above-average wages.

The I.L.O. finds this increase in textile wages peculiar, since Peruvian textile labor productivity did not increase between 1943 and 1949.[26] Apparently the close linking of wages to labor productivity belongs to another moral order. In the United States textile wages are high in relation to productivity, according to the International Labor Office, while in Japan they are very low in relation to the productivity of the largely female Japanese labor force.[27]

The I.L.O. report concluded with a summary statement about Latin American textile efficiency as capable of a five-fold increase if (1) modern equipment were installed; (2) the plants were of such a size as to enjoy economies of scale; (3) the plants were administered efficiently (the latter presumably involving an administratively less integrated process) .[28]

We cannot leave the subject of Peruvian textile labor productivity without noting that in cotton goods, at least, it is relatively high in comparison with the four other Latin American countries (Brazil, Mexico,[29] Chile, Ecuador) studied. This is explained as follows:

[26] International Labor Office, *op.cit.*, p. 55. A recent study by Christopher Clague ("Economic Efficiency in Peru and the United States" [unpublished Ph.D. dissertation in economics, Harvard University, 1966]), lists Peruvian textiles as the least efficient branch of manufacturing, compared to shirt-making, shoes, leather-tanning, hosiery, glass containers, tires, and cement. The latter cases are recent and more efficient (and more capital-intensive) industries, while the various garment and tanning shops face a highly competitive market. Textile factories, however, sell in reputedly the most cartelized market in Peru.

[27] International Labor Office, *op.cit.*, p. 63.   [28] *Ibid.*, p. 70.

[29] The lower productivity of the Mexican textile industry could, in part, be explained by the following factors: (1) It was well established by 1843 with 57 mills in operation. (2) The entrepreneurs were French and Spanish merchants rather than English textile technicians. Today many mills are owned by Mexico City department stores, hence are even more vertically integrated than many of Peru's mills. "The entrepreneurs in the Mexican cotton textile industry have always been cautious and

Though the textile industry in Peru also developed most intensely during the early part of the century, it reveals certain contrasts with the majority of the Latin American textile industries founded in about the same era, in that it has progressed relatively further, not only as regards the increase of its capacity, but also in the degree of modernization of its installations. From 1925 until the present date, Peru's textile production capacity has been increased by 68 percent, whereas that of Brazil and Mexico increased 40 percent and 18 percent respectively. During the same period, Peru has modernized about 30 percent of its equipment, whereas Brazil and Mexico have only 7 and 10 percent of modern equipment, respectively. Unlike the other countries, this degree of modernization of equipment in Peru has been achieved mainly by the gradual replacement of the machines in the old establishments; in other countries, this has been predominantly achieved by the building of new mills. Thus, often within the mills themselves, one finds a great variety of different types of machinery in Peru, whereas in other countries, on the whole, one may draw a fairly clear distinction between the old and modern mills. The production of Peruvian industry is featured by relatively high standards of quality, as compared with those of other Latin American countries. This may be largely attributed to the excellent quality of the cotton grown in Peru. It is possible, however, that the fact that Peruvian industry has been protected to a relatively smaller extent than other Latin American countries may also have exercised considerable influence, since the Peruvian industry has had to compete constantly against the quality of foreign production.[30]

---

conservative . . . [and] extremely shortsighted." (3) Heavy tariff protection was available from the earliest days of this industry's operations. See Sanford A. Mosk, *Industrial Revolution in Mexico* (Berkeley: University of California Press, 1950), p. 129.

[30] United Nations, Department of Economic and Social Affairs, *Labor Productivity*, p. 10.

The maintenance of the machinery, the quality of the products and other conditions indicating effective administration, are better in Peru than in the majority of the old mills of other countries. . . . These mills were originally installed with less labour; most of the technicians were brought from more industrialized countries [United States and England] and labour organization was patterned on that adopted by regions where wages are high and machinery cheap.[31]

The strong English influence in Peruvian textile operations was revealed in the following observation: "It is curious to note that one of the mills had recently installed new English looms of the ordinary type (non-automatic); this probably reflects the influence of the English belief that automatic looms do not produce the best quality."[32] In any case it would appear that on-the-job-trained English foremen feel most comfortable working on the equipment with which they grew up.

Thus, while Peruvian industrial labor relations has been governed largely by "political" factors, the textile firms up to the early 1950's have had to compete in quality and price with imported goods in a relatively open market. It could be argued also that the "artificial" raising of their labor costs, while they were simultaneously exposed to normal retail competition, has been a favorable combination of pressures. Faced with cheaper labor or less competition, Peruvian mills would now be no better off than the Mexican or Brazilian mills. The industry's pre-1950 situation may thus be referred to as a fruitful combination of salutary neglect and strategic pressure.

The competitiveness of the wholesale textile goods market is not, however, an established fact. According to a reputable Peruvian source, "textiles are the most cartelized industry in Peru." This might be an exaggeration, but various specific

---

[31] *Ibid.*, p. 105.   [32] *Ibid.*, p. 111.

agreements in restraint of trade were observed in operation in 1959.

MARKET

Raw material problems. Peru's cotton mills use the very high quality, native-grown long-staple fiber for their largely low-quality goods because it is so readily available and the price is controlled below the export level by the government. As far as the economy as a whole is concerned, it would be far more profitable to export most of this valuable raw product and import a lower grade of cotton from neighboring soft-currency countries.[33]

The woolen mills pay an extravagant price for raw wool, a price which is higher than for the equivalent quality of imported wool. In addition, it is a mixture of all grades and types, generally of low quality, and it must be bought in carload lots. As a result, those mills not tied commercially to a wool hacienda belonging to the mill owner must buy as much as twice what they need in order to get the necessary quality and quantity. This is only one of the major reasons explaining the near bankruptcy of all the older provincial woolen mills.[34]

The artificial-fiber mills (only rayon in Peru) have concentrated largely on cut fibers rather than continuous fiber because the raw material producing plant erected in Lima by members of the current commercial "oligarchy" is so heavily protected by tariffs that its product costs two to three times that of cut fiber.[35]

At this point it should be noted that one of the major problems facing the cotton and woolen mills is the inroads artificial fibers and cloth are making into their markets. Most of the comments made in this section about the problems facing the textile industry apply primarily to these two older

[33] Roger Haour, *Informe preliminar sobre la industria textil peruana* (Lima: United Nations Program of Technical Assistance, 1958), p. 77.

[34] Perú, Ministerio de Trabajo y Asuntos Indígenas, *Informe preliminar sobre las fábricas textiles del Cuzco*, p. 4.

[35] Haour, *op.cit.*, p. 78.

types of mills. Most of the rayon mills were started after 1945 with the latest machinery and under more competent management than is generally found in cotton or woolen mills. The only factor which prevents the rapid displacement of cotton and a greater adulteration of the wool content in woolen goods is that, in spite of the fact that rayon yarn costs half as much as cotton, it is still sold in Peru, by common agreement, for more than cotton.

Product sales obstacles. Unlike the woolen mills, the cotton mills sell 80 percent of their products wholesale, but to a group of retail merchants who have collusively fixed their prices so high that they are beyond the reach of at least a third of the Peruvian population.[36] In general, Peruvian textiles, due to the cost-increasing factors discussed, are greatly overpriced in terms of their quality and the size of their market.

The woolen mills retail almost all of their production through their own specialized shops, thus adding to their troubles by concentrating all of the possible commercial risks under one corporate roof. The rayon mills wholesale all of their production and thus obtain the widest distribution.

[36] The following are two estimates of the size of the Peruvian consumer market for industrial goods. Note that neither assumes that as much as a half of Peru's population are regular consumers of manufactured textiles.

A. Textile Markets	1956 population	Annually salable pieces of cloth*
Urban Spanish	3,000,000	982,000
Rural mestizo	1,000,000	120,000
Urban *cholo*	1,000,000	70,000
Rural *cholo*	3,000,000	80,000
Jungle	1,000,000	?

* 24-47 feet long by 28-40 inches wide.

Robert S. Ray, *Notas sobre la industria textil en el Perú* (Lima: International Cooperation Administration, 1956), p. 15.

B. "From 25 to 40 percent of Peruvians, living largely on the coast and in larger urban areas, are normal consumers of textiles." Roger Haour, *Estudio sobre la modernización de la industria textil en el Perú* (Lima: United Nations, 1959), p. 13.

Shortage of capital. As is typical of all underdeveloped countries, liquid capital for initial investment and for operation is "usuriously" expensive for manufacturing enterprises. This situation is due to the maximum concentration of commercial risk plus the relatively long time required for a return on manufacturing investments. In the case of Peruvian textile firms, there is the additional factor that the owners of many of the mills are not primarily "industrialists" but merchants who generally have other nonindustrial enterprises (usually also not so "public"). Thus it is profitable for them to bleed as much capital as possible out of an industrial concern into a real estate company, an hacienda, or other concerns which, for a variety of reasons, are not as subject to government control as are the manufacturing plants. One usual device is to have the owner's various nonindustrial concerns do business at exorbitant rates with the textile firms. The high costs often complained of are thus, in part, fraudulent. Such devices, however, are often not necessary in an institutional context of extensive bribery of government officials.

Other more substantial reasons for this shortage of capital are the lack of a real capital market or stock exchange and both the insufficiency of funds and an improper lending policy on the part of the Banco Industrial del Perú. There is also in Peruvian life, in general, and most strikingly in business activities, a *desconfianza*, a lack of public confidence, which, among other things, immobilizes or diverts much of what capital is available. Fraudulent bankruptcies are the rule, with public creditors obtaining the last rather than the first call on the available assets.

INSTITUTIONAL ENVIRONMENT

Industrial organization. Within the Sociedad Nacional de Industria (National Industrial Society) there is a textile committee which in form could serve as the voice of "modern management" as opposed to the interests of government, labor unions, and merchants, which are in some respects at odds with those of textile manufacturers. But, in fact, the Society as a whole and especially the Textile Committee has failed until quite recently to fill this or any effective role for the following reasons: (1) It has been dominated by the representatives of wholesale and retail commercial interests, who are not much concerned with problems of productivity, quality controls, extending the market, etc. (2) Most of the owners of textile mills have many other interests. Except for occasional verbal agreements on higher tariffs or antiunion tactics, little general consensus exists within the ranks of textile owners and managers. (3) In addition, the social backgrounds of the various owners differ very widely, from the recently arrived Eastern European Jews to the third-generation Italian Peruvians to the short-term employees of the largest United States–owned firm.

The cult of business secrecy is, therefore, highly developed. One of the reasons for the failure of the Textile Research Institute at the Engineering University (established by the United States Government at the request of the United States–owned textile firm) is that most of the mill owners will not let the Institute's experts into their mills. If they seek help at all they prefer to bring bits of cloth to the Institute, hoping to obtain advice without endangering their security. It would seem, however, that most of the owners fear unfavorable comparisons and the pirating away of their best men rather than the loss of any valuable trade secrets. The owners and managers fear pirating because everyone is playing the same game. The smaller locally owned firms do not have the access to the international labor market for managers or technicians which the three or four largest firms enjoy. So there is a leakage "downward" of foreign personnel aided currently by governmental pressure on the larger, more obviously foreign-owned firms to "nationalize" their administrations. These larger firms obtained a law prohibiting such contract breaking, but to little avail. This pirating, it would seem, is actually desirable in that it has raised the salaries in these vital occupations and has disseminated the required capacities in a more effective manner.[37]

Ownership and control. In the light of the above-mentioned facts, the type of control exercised over the Peruvian textile industry at the present time could economically and ideologically be called mercantile and financial. Many of the firms are owned by men whose primary concerns are retail and wholesale selling or banking.

With only two exceptions—and these are the two largest concerns—all these firms are family-owned and usually family-managed. The family as a social institution has played and is continuing to play this role in Peru because only the family was sufficiently independent of the Church and the state (on the assumption that these two institutions in Peru were incapable of functioning effectively as industrial entrepreneurs), and it alone enjoyed enough control over men and resources to carry out this function.

Parsons, however, predicts that in currently underdeveloped countries the family will not rise to the occasion; hence industrial development will have to await a transformation of the government that will allow it to take responsibility for industrialization.[38]

It can be argued that this is an overstatement with respect to Peru. Here we have a country which has not yet experienced a basic social upheaval in the style of the Cuban and Mexican revolutions. No Peruvian governments to date have conformed in action to the nationalist-socialist philosophy apparently inevitable in most developing countries today. Consequently, it could be said that in Peru the family was the appropriate or at least the only feasible institution to control early manufacturing ventures.

Labor organization and labor laws. As a result of the political power of the textile unions, the very extensive social

[37] Haour, *op.cit.*, p. 44.
[38] Talcott Parsons, *Structure and Process in Modern Societies* (Glencoe, Ill.: The Free Press 1960), p. 110.

welfare and labor laws are rather rigidly enforced in this industry. Historically the textile unions were the earliest and generally the strongest industry-wide union. The Textile Workers Federation was founded in 1919 with unions in eight factories covering 1,200 workers. By 1961 it had grown to 82 locals with an estimated 21,000 workers, thus making it second only to the mining federation in membership.[39] It served as the primary union base for the APRA and has enjoyed outstanding success in protecting its workers. ". . . textile workers, who in the United States have experienced great difficulty in raising their wages, are among the best paid blue-collar workers in Peru."[40] In addition, they have obtained a number of laws favoring textile workers, the *bonificación textil*, the textile bonus of 10 percent, and the only escalator clause in Peru.

The most important consequences of the application of these laws have been (1) the primacy of seniority as the criterion for promotion and (2) the virtual inability of a firm to fire or lay off a worker after 90 days of employment or to close down an unprofitable plant without resorting to extensive fraud and bribery. Aside from paying the agents from the Ministry of Labor and some union officials regularly and heavily, the most popular current technique to offset union power is the erection of a new plant adjacent to the old one but under a new name with functional independence. Through this apparently shallow ruse, the many advantages of a new operation can be gained, the primary one being more demanding work loads. On automatic looms, 60 of which one American or English worker would ordinarily oversee, the customary work load in Peru is 14. The usual policy is to pay the best of the workers from the old mill 10 to 20 percent more if they will work in the new mill on twice as many machines. Needless to say, such corporate structures look peculiar if one's only information is the data reported in

[39] James L. Payne, *Labor and Politics in Peru* (New Haven: Yale University Press, 1965), p. 19.

[40] *Ibid.*, pp. 35, 175.

the government statistics. The old plant continues to run and is the one exhibited to visiting congressmen concerned with the industry's problems.

In summary, this study deals with a branch of manufacturing industry, in an underdeveloped country, that is overdeveloped relative to the apparent size of its market and prematurely stereotyped in its technical and labor organization. Its costs and prices are too high and labor efficiency too low, and it faces a generally hostile environment in terms of relevant institutions: the government, labor, and commercial organizations.

CHAPTER 5

Textile Labor Recruitment

In this chapter the process of worker recruitment to the Lima–Callao area will be analyzed in terms of migrant–non-migrant origins, current and previous occupation, historical changes in ages on employment, kinship ties, and union policies. Throughout this and the two following chapters, the primary variables to be considered are sex, seniority, occupation, birthplace, age on employment, and plant location.

Before taking up the analysis of the data on the 13 mills in this and the two following chapters, the sample will be described. It was designed to cover most of the largest of Peru's textile mills on the grounds that the largest could be expected to come closer to embodying a modern industrial organization. The sample therefore does not represent the entire industry as to the distribution of plants by size. However, it is representative in that it includes cotton, rayon, and woolen mills. It also covers not only the Lima–Callao area, but also Arequipa and Cuzco.

The definition of a textile mill, for inclusion in the sample, involves only spinning, weaving, and finishing operations. Textile operations covered by the Peruvian census definition, but not included in this sample, include rope and string spinning, fishing net weaving, knitting mills, and garment shops. All of these are smaller plants than the ones studied. The actual coverage of the sample is discussed in detail in Appendix B.

In Appendix A, there are short vignettes of each plant and firm. The plants have been renamed to maintain as much as is feasible the degree of anonymity promised the owners and managers who were interviewed.

The Textile Plant Sample

Santa Maria. Avenida Garibaldi, an Italian-run, fully integrated woolen mill, is the oldest Lima plant still in operation under the same management. It was founded around 1900, near the center of Lima.

The Avenida La Plata woolen plant of the same firm was gradually put into operation during the early 1940's in the new industrial section between Lima and Callao, at first as a spinning mill but gradually as a fully integrated replacement for the Garibaldi mill. The latter, however, continues in operation.

MacGregor & Sons. El Futuro, a downtown, fully integrated cotton mill, is also being slowly phased out of existence in favor of several very modern plants in one of Lima's slum suburbs.

La Junta is a nearby cotton mill belonging to the same English firm, which is being renovated instead of being replaced.

El Misti in Arequipa is this firm's only provincial mill. It is a renovated, fully integrated cotton mill in a self-contained factory town outside the city of Arequipa.

Blessing Co. El Indio, an old integrated cotton mill, was purchased from its original owners by a United States mercantile house. Textile mills have always been a reluctant venture on the part of this company, in part because they are a minor but politically bothersome branch of their overall operations. This firm is the largest single employer of textile factory workers in Peru.

El Cholo is a post-1940 addition to El Indio which for a variety of reasons is treated as a separate entity.

La Perfecta. This is a small but otherwise modern and efficient integrated rayon mill established in 1936.

Lustrada. This is a cotton spinning mill established by some Syrian textile merchants from Bolivia. It went into bankruptcy subsequent to the 1959 survey.

117

El Fideo. This is a marginal spinning plant established in 1938. It is run as a separate corporation and in a semiclandestine manner. Through close kinship ties to a large, Italian-owned, integrated mill, it actually functions as part of a larger complex.

Aguilar. This plant in Arequipa is a small, fully integrated woolen rug-weaving plant gradually put into operation after World War II. It had originally been a manual weaving operation, and still does not use looms to weave the fancier styles of rugs. It is the only instance in our sample of Peruvian (creole) ownership and management. The technicians, however, are all Europeans.

La Inglesa. This is Arequipa's newest although not most efficient textile mill. It is an integrated woolen mill specializing in alpaca, vicuña, and other "exotic" woolen fibers.

Oropesa. This is Peru's oldest operational textile mill, having been established in 1861 on a plantation about 20 miles outside the city of Cuzco. It is a fully integrated woolen mill producing a variety of traditional fabrics for local Indian preferences. It operates only during those months when the nearby stream is full enough to provide power. In this and other respects it is an outstandingly picturesque enterprise.

Origins

One of the central themes of this study has been the rural as opposed to urban location of factories in terms of the literature on cultural obstacles to industrial labor force recruitment in underdeveloped areas. My case in favor of the location of factories in the largest possible urban center is based on the central assumption that there the unfavorable effects of indigenous pre- or anti-industrial traditions can be much more easily counteracted.[1] The countervailing force of the urban

[1] The usually unfavorable implications of such rural locations are described in the United Nations study of labor productivity. "Since the majority of factories [in Brazil] are very large and have been established at some distance from the towns, they now form important communities

milieu does not depend, however, only on locally born residents. In the booming capital cities of Latin America, about half of the total population and a larger proportion of the workers will be migrants.

While such people will bring some traditional rural customs with them, there are countervailing factors which favor cultural change. Migrants are not normally a representative sample of rural areas, but rather younger, better educated, and more ambitious than the average, assuming a voluntary migratory flow. Therefore, to exploit the advantage of an urban locale, a factory manager need not hire only locally born workers.

It will thus be interesting to see what relationship the origins of Lima's textile workers have to those of the total population in the Lima–Callao area, as well as to those of the population in slum sections of the city that were covered by two surveys.

Given the salient gap between Peru's rural sector and the Lima–Callao area, most factory managers have quite explicit ideas as to the preferability of local or migrant workers. (It should be noted that the use of the term "migrant" does not imply the continuous movement of the migratory farm workers that exists in the United States. Peru is experiencing an "excessive" amount of rural-to-urban migration, but once workers are established in the city there is little intraurban mobility, either residential or occupational, owing to the shortage of both housing and employment at the lower class level.) There

---

which depend both economically and socially on the mills. The owners, who are fully convinced of the importance of labor–management relationships, have for many years sought to surround their employees with all the social benefits which develop a sentiment of attachment to the factory. . . . The offspring of the workers from an early age are trained for factory work. . . . This is especially noticeable in the case of female labor whose ability to find work outside this community is naturally more restricted." (United Nations, Department of Economic Affairs, *Labor Productivity of the Cotton Textile Industry in Five Latin American Countries* [New York: 1951], p. 18.)

was not, however, much relationship observed between the actual pattern of worker origins and expressed managerial preferences, with several exceptions. The manager of Garibaldi did succeed in holding down the number of non-*Limeños* in his employ. In several other plants there were rule-of-thumb preferences for particular departments or provinces, with Ancash the favorite in two cases. The arguments pro and con were as follows: That in favor of *Limeños* emphasized their greater freedom from paternalistic expectations and their presumed higher level of education and skill. Some employers also warned against the creolized *serrano* as even worse than the *Limeño*: "they are easier to handle at first, but once they pick up a bit of city sophistication they are impossible—and by then you are stuck with them." One rather mistaken idea many managers entertained was that provincial migrants were generally "Indians," although, as will be seen from Tables 2 and 3, the heavily Indian departments were underrepresented even in general migration and more so among the textile workers. It can be said that in Lima there were virtually no Indians among the male migrants and none at all among the females in the textile factory sample. In Arequipa the situation is quite different, as the description of the workers in Aguilar reveals (see Appendix A). At Oropesa near Cuzco many workers did not even speak Spanish or wear shoes, two outstanding signs of Indianness.

Those (the majority) preferring migrant labor in Lima made the following points: (1) they tend to be more docile and (2) skill and training are not significant problems.

Before examining the migration patterns of the textile workers it will be helpful to look at the behavior of the entire Peruvian labor force in this respect. In Table 1 it can be seen that the manufacturing sector is second only to agriculture in high level of labor force stability. Only half of the economically active males and little more than a quarter of the females in manufacturing have moved away from the departments of their birth.

TABLE 1

MIGRATION OF ECONOMICALLY ACTIVE PERUVIANS AS OF 1961*

	Distribution by economic sector of all workers	Migrants, of all economically active	Distribution by sector of migrants			
			1951 or before	1952-1956	1957-1961	No information
Total population		37.6%	40.8%	15.7%	39.9%	3.7%
Male—Total	100.0%	37.5	41.4	15.5	39.3	3.7
Agriculture	54.8	21.1	37.7	14.4	43.2	4.7
Manufacturing	12.1	51.8	49.4	18.3	29.8	2.5
Transportation	3.7	54.6	54.9	13.0	27.9	4.2
Commerce	8.3	56.9	49.3	16.1	31.2	3.4
Construction	4.2	58.6	44.2	16.4	36.7	2.6
Public utilities	0.3	65.4	48.7	20.7	27.6	2.9
Mining	2.6	66.9	21.8	18.4	57.0	2.8
Services	9.9	68.9	35.1	14.1	47.0	3.7
Unknown	4.0	42.7	39.4	15.3	40.3	4.9
Female—Total	100.0	37.9	38.7	16.3	41.5	3.4
Agriculture	31.7	14.4	34.4	14.2	46.4	5.0
Manufacturing	17.1	27.3	55.5	17.2	23.8	3.4
Transportation	0.7	38.7	57.1	13.9	25.5	3.4
Commerce	11.6	47.7	58.3	16.3	22.6	2.7
Public utilities	0.1	50.9	49.5	12.4	30.7	7.4
Construction	0.1	51.3	47.1	16.6	34.9	1.4
Mining	0.3	54.4	25.3	13.9	56.0	4.8
Services	34.5	61.4	30.3	16.6	49.8	3.3
Unknown	3.9	36.1	42.2	16.6	37.1	4.1

* Data from Dirección Nacional de Estadística y Censos, *Censo nacional de población, 1961*, Vol. i, Tomo II, p. xviii.

One of the least stable sectors is mining, which illustrates my point about the recruitment and commitment problems of rurally based industry. The agricultural sector also has a highly mobile element—the seasonal workers on some of the coastal haciendas. However, in recent years the Peruvian sugar industry has stabilized its labor needs through mechanization. Seasonal agricultural labor, of course, is also common in the sierra, but it often does not require a change of residence.

The most mobile group—services—includes the largely migrant domestic servants who constitute a significant proportion of this sector, especially in the case of females. In the province of Lima, 11.4 percent of all of the economically active are domestic servants, and of these, 86 percent are female. For the nation as a whole, 5.6 percent (considerably underenumerated) of the labor force are domestics, 82 percent of whom are female. Domestic service proliferates in the larger cities, and is relatively more a female occupation there than in rural areas.[2] (In the United States in 1950, 2.6 percent of the labor force was made up of domestics, 95 percent of whom were women.[3])

Those of both sexes in service occupations are also second in the recency of their migration to the most mobile sector, mining. This latter type of employment is unstable for reasons of both demand and supply. The workers tend to be uncommitted, because of their proximity to home areas and distance from any attractive city, and because of the fluctuations in international ore prices which makes labor demand change frequently.

Manufacturing, on the other hand, has not only not grown relative to its 1940 proportion of the labor force, but it also has one of the lowest percentages of those who have moved within the past five years. The percentage of females is even lower than that of males, again a reflection of the reduction in their overall employment in this sector. As we shall see, relatively fewer migrant women are employed in textiles than migrant men.

[2] Dirección Nacional de Estadística y Censos, *Resultados finales de primera prioridad, sexto censo nacional de población, 1961* (Lima: 1964), Table 14, pp. 244-245 and 250-251.

[3] Special Report P-E No. 1B, *Occupational Characteristics, United States Census of Population, 1950*, pp. 1B-27.

TABLE 2

Patterns of Internal Migration to Lima–Callao

Population unit	Migrants M	Migrants F				

HISTORICAL DEVELOPMENT

Percent of Migrants by Era of Arrival and Sex, of All Migrants in Lima in 1961‡

Population unit	M	F		Total	1951 or before	1952-56	1957-61
Garibaldi	31%	17%					
El Futuro	61	54					
La Junta	66	53	Males	100.00%	48.5%	19.1%	32.4%
El Indio	55	51	Females	100.00	48.8	19.0	32.2
El Cholo	61	64					
La Plata	76	79					
La Perfecta	53	75					
Lustrada	65	65		*Percent of Migrants per Era Employed, of All Workers Ever Hired*			
El Fideo	65	83					

AVENIDA GARIBALDI

Era hired

	M	F		1900-1920	1921-1940	1941-1945	1946-1950	1951+
Total, 1959 (9 plants)	60	51						
			Male	36%	36%	30%	56%	27%
Lima–Callao, 1940	30	40*	Female	30	13	22	12	50
Lima–Callao, 1961	44	44†	Percent females of all hired	29	33	53	30	12
Lima only	45	45						
Callao only	37	33						

LA PLATA

Era hired

	1942-45	1946-50	1951+
Male	68%	85%	76%
Female	47	0	80
Percent females of all hired	55	2	6

* The 1940 data on migration in Peru is of little use for present purposes. It consists only of one table giving the department of current residence for both sexes combined. (See República del Perú, *Censo nacional de población y ocupación de 1940*, Vol. I, Table 145, p. 462.) Therefore no direct evidence is available on migration by sex to the city of Lima. Migrants to the department of Lima and the province of Callao combined, minus

the migration between them and those born abroad, constitute 28 percent of their tot*
population. However, in Volume I of the introductory text of the 1940 Census, the fo*
lowing figures were mentioned (p. clxiv): 49 percent of all the economically active in th
department and 62.5 percent of the economically active in the province of Lima (vi*
tually equal in population to the city) were not born in the department of Lima. (B*
some born in the department are also, of course, migrants to the city of Lima.) Howeve*
this figure leaves out Callao, which, although Lima's nearby (8 kms.) port city,
legally a separate "constitutional province" functionally equivalent to a department. It i*
however, solely a city, so its 28 percent migrant population probably comes closer t
Lima's true figure. However, in the entire department of Lima, the internal migratio*
rate is also 28 percent. Consequently, the combined Lima department–Callao percer*
migrant is 28 percent. Presumably the rate of migration to the city of Lima is somewh*
higher than that to Callao.

† The 1961 percentages as presented here exclude all persons born abroad, bot*
Peruvian and foreign—and those who moved between the cities of Lima and Calla*
This intraurban movement accounts for 3 percent of Lima's male migrants and 22 percer*
of its female migrants. In the case of Callao, the effect of removing this type of mov*
ment is to reduce its migrant population as follows: males 50 to 37 percent, females 4*
to 33 percent. This correction should be made in all studies of rural-to-urban migratio*
to Peru's capital area. The frequent failure to account for this "intraurban-intradepar*
mental" movement has resulted in an overestimation of 1940 migration to the Lima*
Callao area.

‡ In this case it was not possible to eliminate *Chalacos* (natives of Callao) who move*
to Lima, or vice versa. Therefore *only* the Lima figures are presented, as being le*
affected by this problem. (See Dirección Nacional de Estadística y Censos, *Censo nacion*
de población [Lima: 1965] Vol. I, Tomo II, Table 25.)

In Table 2 is presented a comparison of the percent the
migrants constitute of the various population units. Overall,
a larger percentage of the textile factory workers are migrants
than of the general Lima–Callao population. However, a more
relevant comparison would be with the percent migrant
among those economically active. This information is not
available for the province of Lima. For the country as a whole
in 1961, 37.5 percent of all economically active males and 37.9
percent of all economically active females are migrants. However, this average of extremes is not very instructive in this case.
One would normally expect the economically active to be
more mobile than children by virtue of having more time in
which to have moved. In Table 3, it can be seen that in comparison with the total population of *barriada* dwellers, only
slightly more of the textile workers are locally born. However,

if the more relevant "heads of families" is used as a basis of comparison, the adult factory workers turn out to be more often local in origin. Therefore it can be said that migrants constitute a smaller proportion of the textile factory workers than they do of Lima's comparable adult population.

The figures on the historical development of migration to Lima in Table 2 reveal that although about half of all migrants arrived in Lima over 10 years before the 1961 census, the rate of arrival in the subsequent decade was increasing. This, however, refers to the absolute number of migrants. A comparison of the 1940 and 1961 censuses demonstrates that the proportion of migrants had not risen significantly during the interval. The high fertility level of recent arrivals soon offsets the numerical effects of the parents' arrival by the addition of more citizens to the base population on which these figures are calculated.

Consequently, during the interval 1940 to 1961, Lima's factory owners have faced a labor market with increasing numbers, if not a rising percentage, of migrant workers. Therefore, it will be of interest to see how they responded, deliberately or spontaneously, to this situation. For two factories, data on all workers ever employed were available, thus permitting some examination of this question. (The current workers in the other plants could have been arranged according to year of hiring, but without comparable data on those separated from these plants who were hired at the same time as those still employed, we have no assurance that each surviving "cohort" [or "still-employed fellow arrivals grouped by year employed"] is similar in background to all hired in the year in question.)

In Avenida Garibaldi we have a fairly representative picture of the history of Lima's textile plant labor recruitment. The other plants revealed the same differentials (except that without the Garibaldi evidence their pattern could well be misleading as noted above), namely (1) a higher percent of male migrants in most eras; (2) a declining percentage of females after 1945 (only three women were hired after 1951); and (3) a rise in the percentage of females during the World War II labor shortage comparable to the extension of the labor market which occurred in the United States in this period. Both plants exhibit the same response to the increased availability of migrants in the postwar period, although in the case of Garibaldi a deliberate effort was subsequently made to cut down on their employment.

La Plata's level of migrant employment is higher than that of any other plant. It began operation just as the flow of migration to Lima assumed flood proportions. It is also located out of the center of Lima, along a highway clotted with squatter slums. None of the other plants in this sample was as close to these burgeoning peripheral lower-class areas. Most of the plants are located nearer the center of Lima. The same higher level of migrant employment can be seen in comparing El Indio with El Cholo. They belong to the same firm and are located only a block apart but are run independently as far as employment is concerned. El Indio began in 1905, while El Cholo opened in 1940 and hence has a larger percentage of migrants. In both cases, the age of the firm need not have had this effect; the managements could easily have made selections counter to the pattern of background of the available supply.

The significance of a migrant background is examined more thoroughly in Table 3. A comparison of the origins of the factory workers and the 1940 and 1961 total population reveals that the coastal mestizo departments contributed proportionately more and the sierra Indian departments less to the worker migrants to Lima–Callao (leaving aside the mixed departments and the jungle area). This is especially true of the two major Indian departments of Cuzco and Puno. This contrast is even greater if we compare both the total (43.7 percent) and worker (57.2 percent) migration to Lima–Callao

TABLE 3

PROPORTIONATE CONTRIBUTIONS OF PERU'S POPULATION TO THE CITY OF LIMA-CALLAO, AS A PERCENT OF ALL RESIDENTS OF LIMA-CALLAO BY CATEGORY

Birthplace*	Population type*	Textile workers (1959) Male	Textile workers (1959) Female	Origin of 1940 Lima-Callao population† (M + F)	Origin of textile workers (1959) (M + F)	Origin of 1961 Lima-Callao population‡ (M + F)	Distribution of 1961 population by residence (M + F)	1956 Barriada census†† Male	1956 Barriada census†† Female	Heads of families	San Cosme‡‡ census (1953)
Lima–Callao	M	39.5%	48.8%	70.6%	40.8%	56.3%	18.5%	37.4%	44.7%	11.3%	44.4%
Ancash	M	11.3	8.7	5.2	10.9	4.7	5.8	7.8	7.6	11.7	0.4
Provinces of Lima**	M	7.8	4.2	a	7.2	4.1	4.0	13.0	11.5	10.0	a
Arequipa	M	6.5	9.2	2.9	6.9	3.7	3.9	3.4	3.1	5.4	2.3
La Libertad	C	4.0	6.0	2.9	4.3	3.7	5.9	5.3	4.8	7.8	3.2
Ica	C	4.1	4.7	3.1	4.2	2.8	2.6	3.1	2.5	4.8	1.7
Apurimac	S	4.2	0.6	0.6	3.5	2.1	2.9	3.8	3.2	5.7	2.1
Junín	S	3.2	2.8	4.1	3.1	3.4	5.3	3.8	3.5	6.0	9.7
Cajamarca	M	3.1	3.0	1.4	3.0	2.2	7.5	3.2	2.9	5.3	2.7
Piura	C	3.1	2.0	1.2	2.8	2.5	6.8	2.3	2.0	3.3	0.4
Ayacucho	S	3.3	0.4	2.3	2.8	4.0	4.1	6.1	4.9	10.4	21.1
Lambayeque	C	2.7	3.0	1.3	2.7	2.1	3.5	2.0	1.8	2.8	0
Huánuco	S	1.7	1.2	0.9	1.6	1.4	3.3	1.8	1.7	2.9	1.2
Huancavelica	S	1.6	1.4	0.9	1.5	1.4	3.1	2.1	1.5	3.4	4.2

Continued

TABLE 3
(continued)

Birth-place*	Popu-lation type*	Textile workers (1959)		Origin of 1940 Lima-Callao population† (M+F)	Origin of textile workers (1959) (M+F)	Origin of 1961 Lima-Callao population‡ (M+F)	Distribution of 1961 population by residence (M+F)	1956 Barriada census††			San Cosmet‡‡ census (1953)
		Male	Female					Male	Female	Heads of families	
Pasco	S	0.8	0.4	b	0.7	0.8	1.4	1.0	1.0	1.7	0.8
Cuzco	S	0.8	0.6	0.7	0.7	1.5	6.2	1.4	1.1	2.2	0.6
Moquegua	M	0.5	1.0	0.3	0.6	0.2	0.5	0.1	0.1	0.3	0.1
Tacna	C	0.5	0.6	0.4	0.5	0.3	0.7	0.2	0.1	0.4	0.2
Puno	S	0.4	0	0.3	0.3	0.8	6.9	0.8	0.4	1.1	0.3
Amazonas	J	0.3	0.2	0.2	0.3	0.4	1.2	0.4	0.5	0.6	0.05
Tumbes	C	0.2	0.2	0.2	0.2	0.2	0.6	0.2	0.1	0.2	0
Loreto	J	0.1	0.2	0.4	0.1	1.0	3.4	0.3	0.3	0.5	0.02
San Martin	J	0.03	0.2	0.1	0.06	0.4	1.6	0.2	0.2	0.3	0.2
Madre de Dios	J	0	0	0.02	0	0.04	0.2	0.03	0.07	0.03	0.02
Foreign		0.3	0.6	c	0.3	c	c	c	c	c	c
Total %		100	100	100	100	100	100	100	100	100	100
No.		(2550)	(493)								

a, included in Lima-Callao; b, included in Junín; c =excluded.

NOTES TO TABLE 3

* Ranked according to each area's contribution to the combined worker sample in column 4. The population designation refers to the location and culture of the bulk of the population: C = coastal mestizo or "mixed" Spanish speaking; S = sierra, predominantly Indian; M = a department which has a mixture of both C and S types; J = jungle.

† Dirección Nacional de Estadística, *Censo nacional de población y ocupación, 1940*, Vol. I, Cuadro 145, pp. 462-465. In 1940 migration data is available only for the entire department of Lima. Consequently, Lima–Callao's 70.6 percent figure is too high. Probably 5 to 10 percent should be assigned to the provinces of Lima.

‡ Dirección Nacional de Estadística y Censos, *VI Censo nacional de población*, Vol. I, Tomo II, Cuadro 25, p. 6. The 1961 data covers migration to the *province* of Lima (the greater Lima metropolitan area) and Callao.

** Includes all of the provinces in the department of Lima outside the province (city) of Lima itself.

†† Based on unpublished data from José Matos Mar's 1956 census of Lima's barriadas. See José Matos Mar, "Migration and Urbanization," in Philip Hauser (ed.), *Urbanization in Latin America* (New York: UNESCO, 1961), Chap. VI, for some published findings from this data.

‡‡ J. P. Cole, *Estudio geográfico de la gran Lima*, Section IV, p. 12 (Lima: Oficina Nacional de Planeamiento y Urbanismo, July 1957). Includes 4.3 percent of unknown origin.

with the proportion the residents of these departments constitute (18.5 percent) of the population of Peru in 1961.

A countervailing factor, of course, is proximity. When all the departments of Peru were ranked according to (1) the distance of their capital cities from Lima and (2) their relative contribution to Lima–Callao's migrant population, a high correlation coefficient of 0.75 was obtained, that is, the nearest departments tended to send more migrants. Thus we find the departments of Ancash and Lima (the balance of the department outside of the city) at the head of the list. Arequipa, which is both coastal and sierra, is a disproportionately heavy textile-worker contributor, owing to the fact that it has the second largest city in Peru and is the terminus for one of the two major rail lines (the other ends in Lima and goes through Junin, a purely sierra department).

In most cases, as expected, women constitute a smaller proportion of the migrants. The exceptions (Table 3) are limited solely to coastal departments and Arequipa.

This crude but sufficiently reliable measurement of origins has demonstrated that among Lima's (adult) textile workers there are relatively more migrants than among the general population. However, the proportion of migrants among the textile workers is significantly lower than among the heads of families in the slums which have grown up since 1940 on the north and west sides of Lima. Moreover, those who are migrants are disproportionately from coastal, non-Indian areas, whether compared to the origins of all the migrants to Lima or to the relative sizes of their departments of birth.

Occupational Distribution by Sex and Origin

If Lima's textile workers are categorized by occupation and then these occupations are ranked according to level of skill, the following distribution of origins within each occupation appears.

Occupation	Distribution of migrants		Percent female in each occupation
	Male	Female	
Loom mechanic	50%	0%	—
Weaver	54	48	15.5
Operatives	59	54	17.8
Operative's helper	62	35	4.5
Light manual worker	59	50	53.5
Peon	61	34	1.9
Average percent	60	51	16.2
Total Lima workers	(2550)	(493)	

Among the male workers there is a fairly consistent increase in the proportion of migrants as skill level decreases. In the case of the female workers there are two different groups— weavers in jobs where women will not be replaced by women when the current group leaves through normal attrition, and light manual workers, which includes the "unchangeably" stereotyped female jobs such as inspecting finished cloth.

Previous Employment

The utility of previous industrial experience to employers is not a settled issue in terms of our perspective of the rationality of the labor market and of employment practices. Employers in underdeveloped countries bemoan the shortage of skilled, efficient workers. For many authorities, the educational deficiency is the prime obstacle to economic development. Yet many employers refuse to hire experienced workers, largely, it would seem, because they are harder to discipline. Some also complain that such workers would have to unlearn bad habits and that it is easier to train fresh recruits.[4]

[4] Guillermo Briones and José Mejía Valera, *El obrero industrial: aspectos sociales del desarrollo económico en el Perú* (Lima: Universidad Nacional Mayor de San Marcos, 1964), p. 67. There was no appreciable relationship

Before World War II, and for some time thereafter, it was generally assumed that the acquisition of technical skills was a major labor problem in underdeveloped areas. More recent studies indicate that there are few people, whether Bedouins or jungle cannibals, who cannot learn how to operate machinery, if staying at the job is made rewarding in their terms.[5] Consequently, however suspect the expressed preference of some Peruvian managers for "green" workers may be, such a policy probably would not, per se, lower efficiency, given the well-established custom of hiring in at the bottom. This apprenticeship system does, of course, so stereotype work habits that subsequent efforts to change work loads and practices, even at higher pay levels, are usually resisted. There is certainly a loss of flexibility in terms of both the employer's ability to hire and fire and in his ability to reorganize. Only for a brief period while new plants are being established does management enjoy a "full" prerogative in structuring the organization of production.

In fact, it appears that the most difficult period in the structuring of the Peruvian urban industrial labor force is not when workers first enter industrial employment but at a later period when management tries to restructure the organization of production to meet changing market conditions, due to either a rise in labor costs or an increase in competition from domestic or foreign producers. As Morris found in his study of the Bombay cotton textile industry, the period of greatest labor–management conflict was during the cost-cutting stage of the 1920's when Japanese competition first began to hurt the Indian domestic market.[6]

---

between either size of firm or wage level and the workers' education noted in this survey of Lima factory workers.

[5] Clark Kerr *et al.*, *Industrialism and Industrial Man* (Cambridge, Mass.: Harvard University Press, 1960), pp. 8, 178, and 186; and Walter Galenson, *Labor and Economic Development* (New York: John Wiley & Sons, 1959), p. 4.

[6] Morris David Morris, *The Emergence of an Industrial Labor Force*

It appears, then, that one cannot use the employment of experienced workers, if available, as a criterion for establishing the modernity or rationality of management. On the other hand, a categorical refusal to hire experienced workers would probably tend to increase the level of labor turnover. In Peru the present high level of labor stability is an unfavorable element in terms of the development of a modern industrial structure. It appears that a somewhat higher level of labor turnover would make the reorganization of these mills considerably easier.[7] On the other hand, it must also be remembered that the categorical exclusion of groups of qualified workers does not per se constitute a fatal defect in an industrial labor market, if among those considered for employment there are sufficient workers in terms of both quality and quantity.

It must also be remembered that one possible consequence of extending the number of "available" workers in any labor market is that management thus increases its labor supply and can therefore cut wages. As discussed above, given the great surplus of labor in Peru, such a policy could drive wages so low that the development of domestic manufacturing industry would be inhibited. This has not occurred, however,

---

in India, A Study of the Bombay Cotton Mills, 1854-1947 (Berkeley and Los Angeles: University of California Press, 1965), pp. 202, 205.

[7] In the United States most established occupations (new ones often go through a phase of sex indeterminacy) tend to be relatively sex-stereotyped even though many could as well be performed by the opposite sex, and are in other societies. The crucial point is this: Among those workers considered, are there enough to fill a firm's or society's requirements? The somewhat higher level of efficiency which might be achieved by considering *anyone* physically capable of doing a job is presumably offset, at least in the case of sex (but not race), by the maintenance of a "necessary" division of labor in other areas of life on the basis of this characteristic. (This argument is not intended as an ideological rationalization of sex "prejudice" in employment, but rather is designed to explain how an industrial society cannot, and perhaps must not, attempt to achieve a completely extensive labor market in which anyone is considered available for any job at any time as long as they have the relevant ability.)

due primarily to government actions rather than a managerial policy of excluding workers from consideration.

In the case of the two factories for which nearly complete information on previous employment is available, considerable use was made of workers with previous industrial experience. Both started operation in Lima in the early 1940's. They could thus draw upon a body of 10 to 15 thousand other nearby textile factory workers if they wished—although the war years brought about a temporary shortage for all of these mills as they added to their labor force in order to meet the increased local demand for domestic production.

In Table 4 it can be seen that 42 percent of the males born in Lima and 33 percent of the migrant males had worked in factories or manufacturing shops before being hired by one of the two textile factories. The most outstanding of the four groups of workers, however, are the female migrants, 54 percent of whom have had such a background. It is clear that female textile workers are a very select group today, quite untypical of all lower-class Limenian females. The recent policy of reducing female employment has meant cutting down to the most skilled women on the most immovably stereotyped female jobs, namely some types of spindle banks and manual finishing operations. Migrant females are especially untypical since, for the most part, their previous factory experience has been not in Lima but in one of the three centers of provincial textile production: Cuzco, Arequipa, and Huancayo. This group is also untypical of migrant females in that none admits to ever having been a domestic servant, the primary transitional occupation for newly arrived lower-class *serranas*. Of course, as the discussion of migration revealed, Lima's textile workers have not come from the Indian areas of the country in the same proportions as the general migration to Lima, nor in particular do they resemble the distribution by origin of the slum population now developing on Lima's outskirts.

TABLE 4

PREVIOUS OCCUPATIONS BY SEX AND ORIGIN IN TWO LIMA FACTORIES

	Total* workers	Previous occupation†									
		Textile factory	Other factory	Small manu-facturing shop	White collar	Mechanic & artisan	Military	Domestic service	Urban manual	Rural manual	Home or school
Lima Male	197	100%	21%	14%	7%	2%	17%	3%	0.5%	16%	3%	17%
Migrant Male	363	100	17	12	5	1	16	6	1	25	10	7
Lima Female	12	100	8	8	9					25		50
Migrant Female	24	100	38	13	13					8		28
Total Male	560	100	18	13	6	1	16	4	1	22	8	11
Total Female	36	100	28	11	11					14		36

* This is the total number of workers in the two plants for which previous occupation data were generally and reliably available, namely, El Cholo and La Plata. The data have been combined since these plants were established in 1940 and 1943 respectively and have both been growing steadily since. They are also similar in modernity of managerial practices. In all, data on previous occupations were unavailable for 5.4 percent of the males and 8 percent of the females. The missing cases were distributed proportionately by origin so the omissions were not deemed to be significant in view of the analysis being attempted.

† "Mechanics and artisans" include only "modern" skilled occupations, such as plumbers, carpenters, and electricians, not solely traditional crafts such as hand weavers (there were none of these). "Urban manual" includes such jobs as street vendors, construction workers, waiters, truck drivers' helpers—all low-skilled occupations.

This pattern of prior provincial factory experience begins at "the end of the line" in Fabrica Oropesa outside Cuzco. It is the oldest, most isolated, and least efficient mill in Peru. Yet its owner wryly boasts that he runs the "textile school for all Peru," since so many of his workers leave for mills in the city of Cuzco or Arequipa. His (1959) observation was confirmed by a subsequent visit in 1965 to the city of Cuzco's two plants, where it turned out that 30 percent of the workers had previously worked in Oropesa. It was also the case that many of the workers in La Inglesa and Aguilar, in the city of Arequipa, had come from the other Cuzco area mills, some of which had gone bankrupt just before the 1959 survey.

The least experienced group, and one drawn on less, relative both to the size of the other three groups employed and to the size and nearness of its population of origin, is that of locally born females, half of whom had never worked before.

The male migrants are interesting in that only 10 percent of them had ever worked in agriculture. A quarter had previously worked in unskilled manual jobs in Lima. Twice as many migrant as local males had previously been drafted into military service. It is the policy of the army to do relatively more of its recruiting in rural areas. (For all workers the most effective protection against being called up unwillingly is an influential employer.) The male migrants are also the group with the most previous employment experience, reflected in their higher age on employment (see the following section on the pattern of ages on employment).

In view of the literature on the degradation of traditional artisan crafts during industrialization, it is interesting that no worker reported that he or she had even been a hand-weaver, although many similar traditional crafts were listed. As mentioned above, this craft had been effectively driven out of urban areas by years of duty-free textile imports during the nineteenth century.

Another way in which previous occupations can be examined is in terms of the worker's current position, seniority, and age on employment, as in Table 5. Although textile factory work was one of the major previous sources of employment, it was not proportionately represented in the background of the weavers, the chief high-prestige occupation in the mills. (The most skilled workers were the handful of maintenance mechanics.) Whereas 19 percent of all male workers were previously employed in textile mills, only 10 percent of the weavers had had this background. This arises from the fact that advancement to the weaver level is normally strictly controlled by seniority; hence those entering on their first job at an earlier age are more likely to advance to this position. Actually no single previous job stands out

TABLE 5

AGE ON EMPLOYMENT AND SENIORITY OF WEAVERS, BY PREVIOUS
EMPLOYMENT*

	All weavers		Previous occupation			
			Textile factory		First job	
eavers	Age	Seniority	Age	Seniority	Age	Seniority
ma–Callao						
ale	19	18	27	6.5	18	19
male	20	14	25	7	0	0
igrant						
ale	22	8	32	6	18	12
male	23	16	37	7	0	0

* Throughout this study all averages are medians unless otherwise indicated.

for either migrant or local males as being related to attaining a weaver's position. Only the maintenance mechanics revealed a strong association between previous related jobs and current positions. They were also the only group to enter "late"—on the average at 28—some as late as the 50's, and still succeed. The other major group of late arrivers ended up disproportionately in low-level dead-end yard and clean-up jobs (*pampa peones*) whether *Limeños* or migrants.

Other verbal evidence was offered, during the 1959 survey, of selective "pirating" of skilled workers, especially for such crucial jobs as dyeing and operating the finishing machine. Such mobility, however, followed a pattern. It rarely occurred among the smaller so-called "Peruvian" firms within one city. In Arequipa, for example, the four mills had an agreement not to employ each other's workers. It did occur (1) *from* the larger foreign-owned firms, especially from La Junta, *to* the Peruvian firms or (2) between "national" firms in *different* cities or areas. In the former case there was an explicit willingness to pay for special talent whereas in the latter case the Limenian or Arequipan mills were taking advantage of poorer working conditions in provincial mills; hence no premium reward had to be paid. All these workers needed was the assurance of the job.

In conclusion, it should be noted that these factories, although consciously preferring young workers, still obtained a considerable proportion with previous "industrial" experience. However, only in a few jobs was it a basis for selection.

The Secular Change in the Ages on Employment

In considering this crucial index of extensity, it is relevant first to discuss the general subject of absolute and relative ages. One of the classic Western misperceptions of "native peoples" arises in the case of guessing the age of those already physically mature. They either seem ageless or prematurely aged, depending on racial characteristics, diet, and health conditions. In addition, it should be recalled that in a society in which the average life expectancy—30 to 35 years—is less than half that in the United States and in which formal education, if enjoyed at all, is generally terminated before the age of 12, a 20-year-old is 30 to 40 years old in terms of social expectations in the United States. To be sure, the welfare laws, which are patterned on Western models, establish 30 to 35 years as a normal career period, but this serves primarily to prevent an extraordinary drain on the pension system.

Consequently, even the younger ages on employment observed in the worker population are those of adults and not adolescents. Furthermore, it could be argued that the perception of time in this society differs from that in the United States. Our "hustle" and their reputed *mañana* philosophy notwithstanding, Peruvian workers live more from day to day, whereas North Americans, at least those with elements of "the Protestant ethic," postpone some pleasures and make many long-range plans in the justified expectation of a much longer life. Thus, the difference between 20 and 25 is greater in Peru than in the United States, and the statistical significance of the sometimes apparently small age differences discussed cannot be established precisely by the usual tests of significance.[8]

Bearing in mind the additional problems involved in reconstructing trends from contemporary data, discussed in Appendix B, such as the "snapshot problem,"[9] it seems clear that there is a significant difference between the ages on employment of *Limeños* and provincials. For *Limeños* the age on employment has risen for both sexes in all the older plants fairly regularly except for a temporary decline in the case of females during World War II. Migrants, on the other hand, have exhibited a declining age on employment which "met" that of the Limenian between 1940 and 1950 in the Lima mills.

As a result, the ages on employment were fairly far apart during the pre-1940 period. The evidence available on previous employment suggests that the higher age on employment of the migrants arises not from a "late" arrival in Lima but from having changed jobs more frequently before settling

[8] It should be noted here that our data on workers do not rest on samples from their plants but, in all cases except one (La Inglesa in Arequipa), on complete counts of all workers employed in 1959.

[9] See Appendix B on the "snapshot" problem.

down.[10] The explanation of this differential must of necessity be hypothetical. In the case of the *Limeños*, their rising age seems to conform to the general "Western" pattern. It is a response to prolonged education and legislation prohibiting the employment of children. In addition, a possible decrease in domestic authoritarian control over children may have persuaded some managers that they were a bad bargain.

In the case of the provincial decline in the age on employment, some other factors are involved. One, suggested already in much of the literature on the recruitment of industrial labor,[11] is the necessity for a testing period even in fully industrialized societies before a career pattern is stabilized, at least on the blue-collar level, where vocational skills are largely learned at work. The same necessity, however, presumably faces the Lima-born, but perhaps in this case their relatively greater preparation for factory work, plus their awareness of the shortage of employment opportunities, keeps them at their first factory jobs. In addition, they do not have the village alternative to fall back on.

In order to compare the ages on employment of different groups of workers, seniority must also be considered because of the alternative trends mentioned above. The current age of both sexes, for instance, differs greatly in most of the older mills, women being older than men. The phasing out of women has not only increased the seniority of the survivors relative to men, but it has also tended to disfavor female migrants even in plants where migrant males are increasingly preferred. This recent decrease in the percentage of women employed has also resulted in a decided rise in the age on employment in the last period (1951–1959).

In Table 6 it can be seen that seniority for Lima's males

10 See Chapter 2 and the earlier discussion of previous employment.
11 See S. M. Lipset and F. Theodore Malm, "First Jobs and Career Patterns," *American Journal of Economics and Sociology*, XIV (1955), 247-261.

varies inversely with age on employment if the plants are listed as follows:

TABLE 6

COMPARISON OF THE AGE ON EMPLOYMENT AND SENIORITY, BY PERIODS OF EMPLOYMENT FOR LIMA'S FOUR OLDEST MILLS

Origin	Sex	Mill*	Age on employ.	Sen.	1900-1920	1921-1940	1941-1945	1946-1950	1951-1959
Lima–	M	a	18	22	15	17	19	21	21
Callao		b	21	12	17	20	32	22	24
		c	21	11	26	19	21	23	22
		d	20	14	13.5	17	19	20	24
Lima–	F	a	19.5	17	17.5	19	18.5	21.5	19
Callao		b	20	16	20	18	20	20	21/32
		c	19	14		18	17.5	22	23
		d	22	13	12.5		17.5	22.5	25
Provinces	M	a	25	14	20	26	24.5	25	25
		b	23	9	17	25	25	23	24
		c	23	7		23.5	23	22	24
		d	25	9	16.5	21	19.5	23	28
Provinces	F	a	26	20	19	28	25	27	
		b	22	16	20	19	27	21	19.5
		c	20	11		22	19	18	24
		d	21	13	14	15	21	20	23

* a—Santa María: Avenida Garibaldi   c—MacGregor & Sons: La Junta
b—MacGregor & Sons: El Futuro   d—Blessing: El Indio

Mill	Median age	Median seniority
Avenida Garibaldi	18	22
El Indio	20	14
El Futuro	21	12
La Junta	21	11

This pattern is the basis for our first-observed trend—the secular rise in the age on employment for workers born in

Lima–Callao. In the case of the females, only Garibaldi upsets this generalization. Its largely Lima-born female workers (over twice the percentage from Lima than in any other integrated mill) exhibit a relatively high age on employment in view of their seniority.

In the case of both sexes from provincial areas, the age on employment varies directly with seniority, especially for females, that is, the age on employment has declined among the more recent recruits.

	Males			*Females*		
Mill	Age	Seniority		Mill	Age	Seniority
Avenida				Avenida		
Garibaldi	25	14		Garibaldi	26	20
El Indio	25	9		El Futuro	22	16
El Futuro	23	9		El Indio	21	13
La Junta	23	7		La Junta	20	11

Kinship

Another factor affecting the recruitment of workers is kinship. In El Futuro, where data on this characteristic were available, it was found that there were no significant differences by origin in the percentage of "related" workers. However, both migrant and local females tended to have more relatives in the firm than males. There are also marked differences by occupational status, the weavers having proportionately more relatives than those in any of the lower-prestige jobs, especially in the case of the female weavers. These kinship ties in no recorded case went beyond the immediate family, nor did they ever include a mother-daughter combination.

In advance two alternative hypotheses had been considered: (1) that *Limeños*, by virtue of greater numbers of available relatives, would have more relatives in the same mill than migrants; and (2) that migrants, from current need and traditional practice, would prefer to continue relying on relatives more than the more urbane *Limeños*. Both may be considered rejected in one sense or supported. Oscar Lewis argues that urbanization in Latin America can occur without breakdown.[12] What he, I believe, should be saying is that Mexico City, and certainly Lima, are far from being the epitome of urban industrial culture. If migrants can maintain traditional rural customs even in such a big city, this proves not that urbanization need not destroy rural traditions, but rather that a sufficiently heavy wave of rural migrants, especially in a society marginally Western, can ruralize the city faster than the city can urbanize the migrants.

It should also be noted, however, that in United States literature on urban sociology there has been a reaction away from Louis Wirth's "classic" characterization of the city.[13] This has taken the form of a search for persistent traditional rural *gemeinschaft* institutions which are interpreted as not mere survivals but functioning parts of modern urban life.[14] Since Lima is not yet an "industrial" city, and since there is much evidence of cultural and personal breakdown, the above hypotheses either are not upheld or are irrelevant.

The management at El Futuro and some other mills used to favor kinship ties on the grounds that they could control the newcomers better by shaming their established relatives into taking on the task of disciplining the neophytes. This manipulation of kinship has apparently ceased to work. Currently, El Futuro's managers find that fathers disclaim responsibility for their sons' behavior and show their paternal concern only by resenting any managerial discipline of their sons

[12] See Oscar Lewis, "Urbanization without Breakdown," *The Scientific Monthly*, LXXV (July 1952), 31-41; and Oscar Lewis, "Further Observations on the Folk-Urban Continuum and Urbanization with Reference to Mexico City," *Proceedings of The Rural–Urban Migration Conference, May 11-12, 1964* (Bethesda, Md.: National Institute of Mental Health, 1964).

[13] Louis Wirth, "Urbanism as a Way of Life," *American Journal of Sociology*, XLIV (July 1938), 1-24.

[14] See especially Eugene Litwak, "Occupational Mobility and Family Cohesion," *American Sociological Review*, XXV (February 1960), 19-20.

as a personal affront. As a result, it is now official policy to avoid relatives and no longer to allow the "inheritance" of particular machines. Since this change of heart is well known to the workers, it has been partially circumvented by a collective worker conspiracy to hide the relatedness of any new recruits.

In connection with the role of the family as a factor in labor recruitment, it should be mentioned that the Peruvian family is far from being a clan in the strict sense of the term. In urban areas kinship ties differ from those in the United States more in the strength of the bonds than in the size of the meaningful unit. Trusting and mutually helpful relationships are rare outside the family and the *compadrazgo* ties. The basis for this situation is a type of "amoral familism."[15] As Fried observed, "Households are so jealously inner directed that extended social obligations of any kind do not have any priority. . . . What has priority . . . is the constant struggle to maintain and extend security."[16] Stein notes: "The important goal is the self-sufficiency, the survival of the household unit. This reliance on the family, an inward turning limitation on inter-personal investments, is perhaps the product of centuries of political castration."[17]

An additional factor favoring the chain of relatives is the matter of timing. The casual applicant today is more likely than not to find no opening or only temporary clean-up or construction work at a factory. Only those on the inside know when jobs are available, and they can advise their relatives.

Union Policy

The preferences of most of the Textile Workers Federation

[15] Edward C. Banfield, *The Moral Basis of a Backward Society* (Glencoe, Ill.: The Free Press, 1958), p. 85.

[16] Jacob Fried, "Acculturation and Mental Health among Indian Migrants in Peru," in Marvin K. Opler (ed.), *Culture and Mental Health* (New York: Macmillan, 1959), p. 126.

[17] William W. Stein, *Hualcan: Life in the Highlands of Peru* (Ithaca, N.Y.: Cornell University Press, 1961), p. 336.

leaders for rank-and-file members are fairly consistent. They feel that they can work better with male *Limeños*, excluding all females and male migrants. With the exception of their own relatives, whom they feel they can control, they prefer to avoid whole families of workers in the same plant since this so often leads to "pointless" grievances which divert union members from "central issues." Most Aprista union leaders are not, however, in a position to have any direct influence on labor recruitment.

The few Communist union leaders in Cuzco have an entirely different policy. Forgoing immediate economic gains and thus any strikes against their firms, they are exchanging labor peace for a controlling hand in the hiring, firing, and promotion of workers. Their preferences are the opposite of the Aprista leaders since they want to utilize the potential power of the Indian masses in the south. The mills in the city of Cuzco thus had a largely Indian labor force, one third of whom were women. In contrast to this pattern, and to that in Lima, the very isolated Oropesa mill outside the city of Cuzco had no union and an almost entirely male and non-Spanish-speaking labor force.

In concluding this chapter on labor recruitment, it is interesting to point out that the textile workers in the Lima–Callao area exhibited the same pattern of backgrounds as that observed by Bradfield in his survey of Chimbote. This coastal boom town has grown largely through migration from 4,234 in 1940 to 64,000 in 1961 to the point where only 5 percent of the heads of households in 1961 were born locally. However, among the migrants, although 75 percent had been born in "rural areas," only 17 percent had been working in agriculture and only 39 percent said their fathers had been farmers.[18] They came largely from small towns rather than truly rural areas and had already engaged in nonagricultural occupations.

[18] Stillman Bradfield, "Some Occupational Aspects of Migration," *Economic Development and Cultural Change*, XIV, No. 1 (October 1965), 69.

CHAPTER 6

The Issue of Labor Stability

The earliest stage of industrial labor recruitment is reputedly plagued by high rates of turnover and absenteeism owing to cultural obstacles to worker "commitment" to the demands of an industrial society. It now appears that this phenomenon has been overrated and misunderstood. In the first place, the pre-World War II literature which was so concerned with this problem was dealing largely with rural plantation and mine labor. Peru's textile industry, on the other hand, has grown slowly and largely in Lima, the only other significant development being near the cities of Arequipa and Cuzco. More serious is the misinterpretation of much of what labor instability does exist even in urban areas. It is usually assumed, more or less explicitly, that the workers are primarily responsible for this problem since management, implicitly, is more advanced by virtue of being more educated and having undertaken an industrial enterprise. A reading of Chapter 4 and the plant histories in Appendix A should indicate that Peru's textile owners and managers are not paragons of industrial virtue. However, one need not argue that they are "irrational" by virtue of traditionalism or technical incompetence. The overall context in which they must operate is equally to blame.

A high level of labor turnover, it appears, has not characterized the development of Peru's textile mills. Evidence for this assertion consists of (1) verbal reports from current owners and managers, which, however, sometimes refer to events 30 to 100 years ago; (2) the absence of references to this problem in the urban textile industry in any historical sources; (3) data on all ever employed in two plants and on separated workers since 1941 in a third; (4) the pattern of median seniority in terms of the age of each firm; (5) confirmation by a more recent survey of Lima factory workers.

Patterns of Turnover

Let us take up this evidence starting with the strongest data—those on all ever employed in two plants. This unusual find was available in one of the oldest factories in Peru, the Santa María–Avenida Garibaldi plant, and in a newer mill, La Plata, belonging to the same firm.[1] It includes in the first case the cause and year of separation, thus allowing a plausibility check on the given causes as well as an indication of the level of turnover during the firm's crucial earlier days. This firm is clearly an extreme case, as the plant history in Appendix A points out. It grew very slowly near the heart of the old, once-fashionable downtown section of Lima. Nevertheless, the pattern of turnover rates should be noted for comparison with data on the two other plants (see Table 7). As is inevitable with such an index, the first period yields a high rate owing to the large proportion of arrivals. From then on the rates decline, until, as in the case of the other plants, they climb in the early 1950's when the anti-APRA Odría dictatorship made large-scale layoffs possible.

The La Plata plant reveals a higher level of turnover than the Garibaldi mill. Until 1956, La Plata managed to get away with keeping about 40 percent of its employees in the "temporary" category, to which only construction workers are supposed to belong. They could thus discharge them at will. More recently they have been expanding rapidly, hence again have a higher rate of turnover. In this plant, of the 274 workers ever employed, 66, or 24 percent, have left since its founding in 1942. At this rate, it would have a higher rate of separation at its sixtieth anniversary than has Avenida Garibaldi.

Finally, the data on La Junta on all separated voluntarily

[1] See Appendix A.

TABLE 7

TURNOVER INDICES*

PERU—THREE TEXILE MILLS					
		Average annual rate			
Avenida Garibaldi		La Plata		La Junta	
1889-1910	10.7	1942-46	12.5	1941-45	4.3
1911-1920	6.8	1947-51	3.7	1946-50	3.4
1921-1930	3.6	1952-58	6.9	1951-59	4.6
1931-1940	2.5				
1941-1950	5.1				
1951-1958	1.0				

UNITED STATES—ALL MANUFACTURING†				
Ten-year *annual averages*			*Five-year* *annual averages*	
1924-33	49.3		1924-28	45.7
1934-43	55.9		1929-33	52.9
1944-53	60.2		1934-38	48.0
1954-63	44.4		1939-43	63.8
			1944-48	71.0
			1949-53	49.4
			1954-58	40.2
			1959-63	48.6

* See Appendix B for a discussion of turnover index methodology. This index is calculated as follows:

$$TI = \frac{accessions + separations}{\text{size of plant at start of period} + \text{size of plant at end of period}} \times 100$$

† These rates were recalculated from the Bureau of Labor Statistics figures to conform with the TI formula.

or laid off (but not died or retired) since 1941 also indicates a low level of turnover. The missing groups of separatees, however, would raise La Junta's rates closer to those of La Plata. The La Junta data are of more interest for purposes of analyzing the causes of separation.

Before passing on to the other evidence on the low level of turnover and the causes of separation, the above figures should be placed in the context of industrial turnover data from other countries. In Table 7 *annual* turnover indices for all manufacturing workers in the United States are presented. There are a number of minor factors reducing comparability, but for present purposes the much higher United States level establishes the objective of this presentation.[2] As Parnes notes, "on the basis of fragmentary evidence . . . the amount of job movement in the United States is considerably greater than in most European countries, and . . . this is a product not only of a larger volume of voluntary movement here than abroad, but also of a greater incidence of layoffs."[3] In a study of 111 Italian industrial firms with an average of 2,290 employees each, the average annual rate of turnover was only 7 percent.[4]

In a review of British blue-collar turnover experience Silcock observes the following patterns:[5] (1) annual rates vary widely between firms, from 5 to 133 percent; (2) the majority

[2] In order to achieve an adequate level of comparability between the Bureau of Labor Statistics data and the Peruvian turnover indices, the BLS accession and separation rates were added together and divided by 2. This procedure would yield the same figure as produced by the Hartshorne turnover index (if the raw figures on which the BLS indices were based were available) only in the case that accessions equalled separations. If a firm either increased or decreased in size, halving the combined turnover figures would yield too low a turnover index. It is recognized that in fact the odds are that very few firms remained stable. However, since the direction of error would work against the hypothesis at hand—namely that Peruvian rates are much lower than North American—it was deemed proper to allow this bias to stand. The point is that even with underestimated United States rates the Peruvian rates still are very much lower. See Jeanette G. Siegel, "The Measurement of Labor Turnover," *Monthly Labor Review*, LXXVI (May 1953), 519-522, for a discussion of the Bureau of Labor Statistics series of turnover indices.

[3] Herbert Parnes, "The Labor Force and the Labor Market," in H. G. Heneman, Jr. (ed.), *Employment Relations Research* (New York: Harper & Bros., 1960), p. 19.

[4] M. Gardner Clark, "Government Restrictions to Labor Mobility in Italy," *Industrial and Labor Relations Review*, VIII (October 1954), 4.

[5] H. S. Silcock, "The Phenomenon of Labour Turnover," *Journal of the Royal Statistical Society*, Part IV, Vol. XVII (1954), 429-440.

of separations are at the request of the employee (contrary to the situation in Peru) ; (3) turnover lessens with an increase in the worker's seniority, age, and skill; (4) turnover is higher among women than men, especially married women; (5) turnover fluctuates seasonally and according to business cycles; (6) factories located near alternative sources of comparable employment suffer a higher rate of "wastage" than isolated plants.

In Peru, the opposite appears to be the case, as rural factories suffer a high rate of turnover because of commitment problems, harvesting and family obligations, etc. In urban areas, on the other hand, the alternative opportunity factor is offset by the stabilizing forces discussed in this section. Silcock's own research verified the general observation that in periods of unemployment labor turnover is low since (1) those laid off are generally those with the least seniority, hence, otherwise also less stable; (2) the few taken in can be highly selected; and (3) few would care to leave voluntarily. Peru's labor market is, of course, not directly comparable to either end of a business cycle in a developed economy. It is depressed in the sense that there is urban unemployment, but this condition can long co-exist with a relatively high level of prosperity for the employers and the employed workers. Lima, however, does have labor market conditions closer to a slump than a boom in a developed society, at least for the lower level of blue-collar workers.

Causes of Separation

In the cases of Avenida Garibaldi and La Junta, the causes of separation were also available (see Tables 8 and 9). My focus on worker-initiated turnover leads me to pay more attention to the voluntary leavers than to those fired or laid off. In the case of Garibaldi, the former group is slightly larger, but two features of its membership should be noted. The discharged male workers far outnumbered the voluntary leavers

TABLE 8

SEPARATED AVENIDA GARIBALDI WORKERS, BY CAUSE, SEX, ORIGIN, AGE ON EMPLOYMENT, SENIORITY, AGE ON SEPARATION, COMPARED TO CURRENTLY EMPLOYED WORKERS

Origin	Current workers %	Separated workers %	Separated workers No.	Quit voluntarily No.	Quit voluntarily %	Age retirement No.	Age retirement %	Died No.	Died %	Discharged No.	Discharged %
Lima–Callao											
M	69	49	67	16	35	14	54	14	64	23	53
F	83	78	49	21	81	8	62	8	80	12	86
Provinces											
M	27	30	41	4	9	11	42	6	27	20	47
F	14	20	13	4	15	5	38	2	20	2	14
Europe											
M	4	21	29	26	56	1	4	2	9		
F	3	2	1	1	4						
Total											
M	100	100	137	46	100	26	100	22	100	43	100
F	100	100	63	26	100	13	100	10	100	14	100
Distribution by cause and sex											
M	100	100			34		19		16		31
F	100	100			41		21		16		22

Continued

TABLE 8
(continued)

Origin	Current workers	Quit voluntarily	Age retirement	Died	Discharged
			MEDIAN AGE ON EMPLOYMENT		
Lima–Callao					
M	18	19.5	26	17.5	20
F	19.5	17	16.5	17.5	16
Provinces					
M	25	19.5	27	30	25
F	26	16.5	18	21	26
Europe					
M	30	36	30	33	
			SENIORITY		
Lima–Callao					
M	22	18	35	33.5	25
F	17	12	39	29	12
Provinces					
M	14	14	37	28	26
F	20	25	32	38	19.5
Europe					
M	4	5	32	18	

TABLE 8
(concluded)

Origin	Quit voluntarily	Age retirement	Separated workers		
			Died	Discharged
	MEDIAN AGE ON SEPARATION			
Lima–Callao				
M	37	66	56	42
F	32	58	54	29
Provinces				
M	37	66	60	51
F	40	55	59	53
Europe				
M	40	52	51	

except for the 30 Europeans (Italians). This unique group (no other European immigrants showed up in any other factory sample among those currently employed) spent an average (median) of only five years in the plant before moving on, presumably to better jobs. They were employed, on the average, at age 36 and were in this and other respects an atypical group. This plant's Italian management was willing to serve as a way station for immigrants from their "home" country. The female voluntary quitters (only one of whom was Italian) are predictably more numerous than those in all other categories. One of the few universals such manpower studies have been able to establish is the greater employment instability of women, a phenomenon which has both biological and cultural roots.

Excluding the Italians, we find that 26 percent of the separated workers quit, while 33 percent were fired or laid off. Of equal interest are the figures on the median seniority of the quitters, which, while generally lower than that of other groups of separated workers and those currently employed, is still substantial, especially in view of the short life expectancy of workers during the earlier decades of this century (estimated to be 35 to 50 years).

The data on those who died or were retired due to age reveal that 35 percent constituted this minimum level of turnover. The median seniority of over 30 years indicates that they had spent a full working career in this plant.

Also of interest in Table 8 is the lower median age on employment of voluntarily separated migrants to Lima[6] compared to currently employed migrants. This suggests that migrants entering at an older age are more likely to want to stay. If reliable educational data were available, it might be that the leavers were more educated than those who remained.

[6] Throughout the discussion of birthplaces and migration, Lima or Limeños will be used as a shorthand for the Lima–Callao urban complex. Callao is Lima's nearby (8 km.) port city which happens to have been incorporated as a separate constitutional province.

On the other hand, the seniority level of this group is similar to that of currently employed migrants. A more likely explanation is that in this plant, among the currently employed, migrants are found disproportionately in lower-level positions even when the crucial matter of seniority is taken into account. Male migrants are 27 percent and female migrants 14 percent of the current labor force in Garibaldi, but only 17 percent of the male and none of the female migrants are weavers, while 86 percent of the peons are migrant males. Migrants, especially from the sierra, according to explicit managerial design, tend to be shunted off into low-level dead-end *pampa* (yard) jobs. The higher age on employment of migrants of both sexes than of *Limeños* is also an unfavorable factor, since for all workers a late, i.e., past 21, age on employment is highly associated with limited promotion possibilities. This migrant handicap is only partially due to the greater chance a younger entrant has to accumulate the necessary seniority. Controlling for both age on employment and seniority still reveals that *Limeños* have a greater chance of promotion. Hence the voluntary separation of these migrants in view of the length of their seniority, suggests that they are not a group unable to adjust to factory life but are, rather, reacting to promotion obstacles. However, these migrants are few in number as compared, in the case of males, to migrants who were fired. In this respect they are similar to male *Limeños* in that the most important single cause of separation is being fired or laid off.

The discharged group also reveal some interesting traits. They are not the youngest workers or those with the least seniority. On the contrary, except for females from Lima, their seniority was as great as or greater than that of current workers. It would be more to the point to mention that recently Peruvian managements have been very anxious to get rid of older workers before normal retirement in order to lessen separation and pension costs.[7] Those efforts have resulted in a game between labor legislators and dishonest or devious employers, in which the latter try to circumvent the law and the former make crude legalistic efforts to plug loopholes.

In the case of La Junta (Table 9), data are available on four types of separatees since 1941: those fired during the trial period, those fired after 90 days, those who quit voluntarily, and those transferred as valued workers to one of the firm's newest plants. If one reckoned that the same proportion of workers retired or died at La Junta as at Garibaldi (La Junta was founded in 1918), another 40 separated workers would have to be added for these latter causes. This would still yield a cumulative separation figure of 26 percent, on a base of the 1959 employment of 430 workers, which again suggests a high level of stability.

The small number of separated women conforms to their low proportion among those still employed in 1959: 9 percent (40 women). They are still relatively more mobile than the men, with 23 percent as compared to 17 percent for males, especially in view of the sex differential in the voluntary quitting category.

Unlike the Garibaldi management, La Junta prefers selected migrants over *Limeños*, as can be seen by comparing the male differentials by origin in the "discharged-after-90-days" column with the "transferred" column in Table 9. Women in general are being removed from the labor force here as in other textile factories. Only one was transferred to the new plant.

The "discharged-under-90-days" column was set up separately in order to shed some light on those in this group to

---

[7] The Lima worker survey (1962) revealed (p. 36) that the workers who were fired had a bimodal age distribution, those under 19 and those between 50 and 59 being discharged disproportionately. See Guillermo Briones and José Mejía Valera, *El obrero industrial* (Lima: Instituto de Investigaciones Sociologicas, Universidad Nacional Mayor de San Marcos, 1964).

see if they were significantly different from either those retained or those separated in other ways. The male origins of the under-90-days group are virtually identical with those retained. On the other hand, their age on employment is significantly under that of those still employed. However, they were mostly released during the same 1954–1956 market slump and dictator-supported managerial-prerogative period in which most of those employed over 90 days were discharged. So while some selective weeding out may have occurred, the similar dates of discharge and managerial memory reveals that they were released in batches.

There is an interesting differential in the voluntary separatees by origin. *Limeños* left sooner, and younger, again reflecting a managerial preference for migrants as well as the generally higher age on employment of migrants.

Among those who left voluntarily, the peak period of departure for *Limeños* was during World War II, while migrants left in considerable numbers during the slump period of 1954 to 1956, suggesting that prosperity increases urban-born workers' interfirm mobility as it draws migrants into the city, while a recession reduces urbanite interfirm mobility and perhaps sends the migrant home. In general, the Limenians entered younger and stayed a shorter time than the provincials as well as apparently leaving under different conditions. Also, Limenians left voluntarily over an "individualistic" widely scattered pattern of years, while provincial migrants left in groups.

In a complementary pattern, of the nine workers transferred to the new plants, none of the eight males was from Lima. On the average they had entered employment at a slightly older age than all provincial males and had nine to ten years of experience in La Junta before being "promoted" to the newly established plants. These new plants, incidentally, were constructed outside Lima near the rapidly growing *barriadas* into which the newly arrived migrants first come.

TABLE 9

SEPARATED LA JUNTA WORKERS, BY CAUSE, SEX, ORIGIN, AGE ON EMPLOYMENT, SENIORITY, AND AGE ON SEPARATION, COMPARED TO CURRENTLY EMPLOYED WORKERS

| | Current workers | Separated workers | | *Separated workers* | | | | | | | |
| | | | | Discharged under 90 days | | Discharged after 90 days | | Quit voluntarily | | Transferred to new plant | |
Origin	%	%	No.	No.	%	No.	%	No.	%	No.	%
Lima–Callao											
M	34	34	22	8	33	3	43	11	42		
F	47	56	5	1	100	1	50	2	40	1	100
Provinces											
M	66	66	43	16	67	4	57	15	58	8	100
F	53	44	4			1	50	3	60	8	100
Total											
M	100	100	65	24	100	7	100	26	100	8	100
F	100	100	9	1	100	2	100	5	100	1	100
Distribution by cause of separation											
M		100			37		12		40		12
F		100			11		22		56		11

TABLE 9
(continued)

| | | Separated workers | | | |
Origin	Current workers*	Discharged under 90 days	Discharged after 90 days	Quit voluntarily	Transferred to new plant
		MEDIAN AGE ON EMPLOYMENT			
Lima–Callao					
M	22	20	26	20	
F	23	17	24	17	19
Provinces					
M	24	21.5	21	21	
F	18		18	22	24.5
			SENIORITY		
		days	years	years	years
Lima–Callao					
M	11	—90	2	2	
F	14	—90	3	1.5	7
Provinces					
M	7	—90	2	3	
F	11	—90	1	7	9.5
			MEDIAN AGE ON SEPARATION		
Lima–Callao					
M		20	30	23	
F		17	27	18.5	
Provinces					
M		21.5	24.5	24	
F			19	27	

* Hired during the post-1940 period in which all of the separated workers were employed. Earlier eras of employment yielded a different pattern of ages on employment.

The major points about turnover revealed by the data in Table 9 are the following: (1) Less than half (43 percent) of the separated workers left voluntarily. This figure would be even lower if retired workers and those dying while still employed had been included. (2) The overall level of stability is apparently very high in spite of this firm's efforts to decrease it.

We have again observed an apparently low level of labor force turnover, and of what turnover there is, more than half is the result of managerial initiative. Also, for the second and third causes of separation, those fired after 90 days and those leaving voluntarily, the provincial males are relatively more stable than the *Limeños*.

The Level of Seniority

In Table 10 the median seniority by sex, origin, and firm is presented. Seven of the firms were over 35 years old and hence had existed long enough for a worker to have spent a full worklife there. A stability index is then presented for all firms, defined as the percentage which the seniority of the group in question is either of 35 years or of the age of the firm, whichever is less. This would be an extremely crude estimate, since different firms could have had widely different histories and still yield the same index. However, all but two firms have increased their employment erratically but continuously. Only La Junta and Garibaldi have experienced a reduction in their 1959 employment from their historical peak. Therefore, since growth in size tends to pull down the level of seniority, this index will underestimate the level of stability, except, of course, for the two firms with a declining employment. Even in these cases, if the decline occurred solely through age attrition, the level of stability would be correctly estimated, whereas if it were accomplished largely by discharging short-term employees, the resulting high level of seniority of the remaining workers would overestimate the degree of sta-

TABLE 10

STABILITY INDEX AND SENIORITY, BY SEX, ORIGIN, AND FIRM,
COMPARED TO THE AGE OF THE FIRM

		Seniority				Stability index			
		Locally born		Migrant		Age of firm	Locally born		Migrant	
Group		M	F	M	F		M	F	M	F
	Lima									
	Garibaldi	22	17	14	20	63	63%	49%	40%	57%
A	El Futuro	12	16	9	16	58	34	46	26	46
	El Indio	14	13	9	13	54	40	37	26	37
	La Junta	11	14	7	11	41	31	40	20	31
	La Perfecta	5	21.5	7	17	23	22	93	30	73
	El Fideo	16	17.5	14	13.5	21	76	83	67	64
B	El Cholo	9	4	9	4	19	47	21	47	21
	La Plata	6	7	6	8	16	38	44	38	50
	Lustrada	5	5	4.5	5	9	56	56	50	56
	Arequipa									
	El Misti	9	23	13	21	64	26	66	37	60
	La Inglesa	10	9	8	5	12	83	75	66	42
	Aguilar	4	3	5	5	6	67	50	83	83
	Cuzco									
	Oropesa	14	5	19	—	98	40	14	54	—
	Average, Group A						42	43	28	43
	Average, Group B						48	59	46	53
	Average of all 13 mills						48	52	45	52

bility. Given Peruvian legal and political conditions, the former tends to be the case.

Overall, female workers reveal a slightly higher level of seniority than males, yet we have already observed that among the leavers women have a lower level of seniority and are more likely to leave voluntarily. This apparent contradiction can be resolved by observing that there are two sharply different groups of female employees: the larger number of short-term workers and the much smaller number of careerists. This was also revealed by the bimodal age distribution of women, indicating the same double-entry tendency observed in the United States, i.e., before and after children.

The general level of stability appears to be high; on the average workers have been employed either 17.5 years or half of the possible time period given the age of their firms. Since most of the firms are growing or stable, average seniority could not be much higher.[8]

Groups A and B in Table 10 were differentiated to determine the effect of the plant's age and the effect of using the arbitrary 35-year career figure. (The legal requirements for pensions and retirement have been changed several times over the past 20 years.) Since only 39 of the approximately 500 workers ever hired since 1900 at Garibaldi were pensioned off at the end of a 30-, 35-, or 40-year career or at age 60 to 70, this 35-year career figure is high and therefore reduces the apparent level of stability below that of the younger firms. Recalculating Group A on the basis of the

[8] To clarify this point, consider several hypothetical cases.

CASE A: Complete stability—100 percent. All workers were hired when the plant opened and are still employed.

CASE B: 10 percent growth for 10 years, starting with 100 workers. If no workers leave, in the tenth year the median seniority would be 8 years or 80 percent. If turnover were highest among the most recent workers this figure would even increase; if proportionate to the year employed there would be no change; and if the longer-term workers left disproportionately, the level of seniority would decrease.

In the case of our "average" firm a sufficient number of workers with middle and high levels of seniority were separated, for various reasons, to bring this rate down to about 50 percent. For instance, in Case B, if half of each of the first 5-year cohorts and about a quarter of the second 5-year group had left by the tenth year, the median seniority would be 5 years or 50 percent. This method of reaching the 50 percent level, however, is more likely to occur in firms approaching 35 years of age so that an increasing number of older leavers separate by dying or retiring. Younger firms normally would tend to lose more workers with relatively lower levels of seniority.

1962 legal change to a 30-year career brings the two groups closer but only the Lima males overtake their counterparts in Group B as the most stable group.

	Lima		Migrant	
	M	**F**	**M**	**F**
Group A—average (recalculated on 30 years)	49	50	33	50
Group B—average	48	59	46	53

In conclusion, the pattern of levels of median seniority by firm, sex, and origin add to our evidence in favor of a high level of personnel stability. Again it must be stated that seniority levels reflect stability only under conditions of growth *and* if other evidence on a lower level of turnover among short-term workers is available.

Other Evidence on Labor Turnover

The only other published data on Lima's industrial workers which bear on this question are from a survey carried out in 1962 on 1,092 workers.[9] The authors begin by considering the general problem of migrant-worker adjustment to both the urban and factory settings in the light of Moore and Feldman's pessimistic expectations.[10] Briones and Mejía Valera conclude that migrants have not found this adjustment very difficult. In fact, of the two milieus of adjustment, the urban per se is more difficult than that of the factory.[11] At work, as Briones and Mejía Valera see it, the "shock of incorporation" is softened by relatively high wages and the novelty of industrial work and of new friends and experiences. Also migrants enter employment at relatively undemanding low-skilled posi-

9 Briones and Mejía Valera, *op.cit.*

10 Wilbert E. Moore and Arnold Feldman, *Labor Commitment and Social Change in Developing Areas* (New York: Social Science Research Council, 1960), p. 49.

11 Briones and Mejía Valera, *op.cit.*, p. 21.

tions. This study revealed that the major difficulty in adjustment to city life was the problem of finding work. The authors imply, however, that one reason for the relatively conflict-free adjustment of these workers is that they have succeeded to some extent in making over their new world according to traditional expectations,[12] i.e., the city has been somewhat ruralized by mass migration. It should also be added that we ought not to be guilty of technological determinism. Although many of these factories are filled with fairly modern machinery, they do not thereby inevitably require full conformity to the "ideal type" norms of industrialism. Thus perhaps both the city and the factory have met the worker halfway.

Another reason for the ease of adjustment is the fact that disproportionately few of the migrants (23.6 percent) were previously employed in agriculture.[13] Migrants are rarely representative of their areas of origin. They are almost universally younger, better educated, and less agricultural than the average in their home areas. They are not only a favorably selected group for adjustment but have also probably experienced some "anticipatory socialization" through education and mass media.

The authors of the Lima worker survey then directly measured the level of worker job mobility (Table 11) by ranking workers as high (more than 5 moves per decade), medium (2 to 4.9 moves), low (0 to 1.9 moves). These results were explicitly interpreted as refuting the common idea that there is a high level of turnover in such labor markets. (It should be noted that this study focused on worker mobility, not personnel turnover per firm. The latter is higher, since a minority of workers account for a major portion of the moves.) As in our sample this study also shows the higher turnover of women.

In addition this study demonstrated the universal tendency for the young to be more mobile.[14] The authors also observed, in a subsample of 290 workers in metallurgical and chemical

---

[12] *Ibid.*, p. 25.   [13] *Ibid.*, p. 29.   [14] *Ibid.*, p. 34.

TABLE 11
Mobility Rates between Jobs, by Sex*

Mobility	Men	Women	Total
High	19.0%	33.9%	23.9%
Medium	41.5	35.7	40.0
Low	39.5	30.4	37.1
Total percent	100.0	100.0	100.0
Number of workers	(774)	(277)	(1051)

* Briones and Mejía Valera, *op.cit.*, p. 33.

mills, that 68 percent had spent at least 80 percent of their entire working careers in their present jobs. (These firms pay the highest wages in Peru.) [15] Another measure they offer is that only 13.6 percent of their entire sample had worked less than a year for their present employer. This study also cites a Chilean source[16] as revealing that in 1959, 29.1 percent of the blue-collar workers in manufacturing and construction in Santiago had had no more than 1.9 different employers in the previous decade.

The primary factors giving rise to the low turnover suggested by the Briones and Mejía Valera study and my own research are the following:

1. The great surplus of workers relative to the demand for their labor.

2. The relatively high wages and good working conditions in Lima's larger factories. Textile workers in particular have long been the elite of Lima's proletariat thanks to their early and relatively effective unionization.

3. The fact that the strict seniority provisions insisted on by the unions, and generally adhered to by management, make

[15] *Ibid.*, p. 32.
[16] Instituto de Economía, *Movilidad de la mano de obra* (Santiago: 1960), p. 8 (mimeographed).

165

new starts disadvantageous for workers. Moreover, in view of the long-standing preference of most employers for young, inexperienced workers for all but a few mechanical maintenance jobs, the job-seeker over 25 may have trouble even beginning at the bottom in a factory.

4. The additional problem that there is a chronic housing shortage in all the rapidly growing capitals of underdeveloped countries. As a result, most workers are confined to jobs within walking distance of their homes unless they happen to be near one of the cheap bus lines. The major bus lines in Lima have two drawbacks from the point of view of worker transportation: their greater cost and the "shame" the workers feel being mixed in with well-dressed people. The slum route buses are radically different from the crosstown lines. The former are usually very rundown, cast-off school buses from the United States, while the major lines have upholstered Mercedes-Benz coaches.

Evidence of the limited tolerance of workers for distance comes also from the La Plata mill, which was established in a then underdeveloped stretch of land halfway between Lima and Callao during World War II. Their initial cadre, many of whom are still there, were largely experienced workers from Callao whose former employers had gone bankrupt during the Depression.[17] Even today a disproportionately small percentage of this plant's workers are from the city of Lima.

The reasons given by those who have changed jobs were the following: 50.7 percent quit voluntarily and 22.1 percent were discharged; the balance gave miscellaneous reasons or no answers (these figures required a recoding of the data offered in the Lima worker survey).[18] This higher rate of voluntary separations than that observed in my sample of data by employer may be explained by the following factors: (1) Workers

[17] One was Peru's only linen mill and the others were some garment shops.

[18] Briones and Mejía Valera, *op.cit.*, p. 36.

prefer to state that they have left of their own volition rather than admit that they have been fired. (Their data came from worker responses to a questionnaire while mine were obtained from personnel files.) (2) Not all those discharged are fairly represented in their sample since only currently employed workers were included. Probably a voluntarily separated worker is more likely to find new employment than a discharged one, especially since considerable use is made of references from previous employers.

Absenteeism

Reliable evidence was not readily available in enough firms to investigate the problem of absenteeism. Verbal reports by managers, however, agreed on the fact that most factories had to carry a 20 to 30 percent overload of workers before the *salario dominical* went into effect in order to be able to man their equipment on a regular basis.[19]

As of 1959 none of the 13 managements felt male absenteeism to be a major personnel problem. Female workers had always been absent more than male and, since they have come to be more expensive as well, there is now a policy of cutting down on their employment.

[19] The *salario dominical,* or Sunday wage, is a bonus of a seventh day's wage if a worker shows up regularly throughout the week. It was proclaimed January 1, 1949, under the dictatorship of General Odría, and has reportedly cut absenteeism in half.

CHAPTER 7

The Structure of the Manufacturing Labor Force

In Chapters 5 and 6 the focus was primarily on labor mobility of various types. In this chapter the current structure of the textile industry will be placed in the context of the entire Peruvian labor force, especially that of other manufacturing establishments. The national labor force is of interest in itself, even apart from the position within it of the textile industry.

Between 1940 and 1961, the dates of Peru's only reliable national censuses, the relative importance of textiles decreased. It is still a major branch of industrial manufacturing, second only to food processing in the total number of workers, but it now has lower rankings with respect to its wage level, efficiency, average size of plant, and other characteristics that reveal its degree of industrial development. Historically it can be said that while Peruvian textiles originally had the advantage over the Mexican industry, as described in Chapter 4, of a later start and a more alien group of entrepreneurs, they have now exhausted this lead and have prematurely jelled at a low level of efficiency. They are protected by high tariffs and operate in a very cartelized domestic market.

A Comparison of 1940 with 1961

From the only censuses taken in the twentieth century, it can be seen that the Peruvian labor force is still predominantly agricultural. The principal sector in which there has been growth between 1940 and 1961 has been not manufacturing but services (see Table 12). A high figure for the latter has

TABLE 12

The Peruvian Labor Force 1940*–1961†

	Percent male in each sector		Percent of all workers in each sector				Total	
	1940	1961	1940	1961			1940	1961
Agriculture	68.5%	86.2%	62.4%	49.7%	} Primary sector		64.4%	51.8%
Extractive	97.3	97.3	1.8	2.2				
Manufacturing	43.5	71.8	15.4	13.1	} Secondary		17.2	16.6
Construction	98.0	99.0	1.9	3.3				
Commerce	67.8	72.1	4.6	9.1	} Tertiary		16.8	27.2
Transportation and communication	95.3	95.1	2.1	3.0				
Services	50.9	50.8	10.2	15.2				
Other	80.1	78.4	1.6	4.4			1.6	4.4
Total of all economically active	64.6	78.2	100	100			100	100

THE LABOR/WORK FORCE‡

(The percent the economically active are of various base populations)

	1940 Total	1961 Total	Urban	Rural
Economically active				
Total	39.9%	31.5%	33.0%	30.1%
Male	52.1	49.6	49.5	49.7
Female	27.9	13.6	16.7	10.8

* Dirección Nacional de Estadística, *Censo nacional de población y ocupación, 1940* (Lima: 1944), Vol. I, pp. 360, 606-607, 69.

†Dirección Nacional de Estadística y Censos, *Sexto censo nacional de población—resultados finales de primera prioridad, 1961* (Lima: 1964), p. 230, Table 11.

‡ *Ibid.*, pp. 220-221, Table 10.

been associated with industrial societies. However, as Bauer and Yamey found in West Africa, the early transitional stage of industrialization exhibits a fractionalization of the unskilled labor market through the proliferation of personal services and petty vending.[1] Properly counted, trading occupations and personal services are apparently at a peak during the period in which most official statistics still show the population to be overwhelmingly agricultural. Of course, many of these activities are not regarded as "occupations," but merely as sources of income. Apparently the early transitional stage of industrialization is marked occupationally by multiple job-holding, while the specialization of one income-producing, status-defining occupation per worker is a feature of a more "mature" industrial society.

The most productive sector, extraction, unfortunately cannot provide much employment opportunity for the expanding labor force, owing to the rapid mechanization taking place in this industry as well as in coastal agriculture. Only services and the transformation of raw materials could expand rapidly enough to absorb the increase in population.[2]

The most striking shift between 1940 and 1961 is the decline in the proportion of the economically active (Table 12), in spite of the fact that the movement of some rural workers into the commercial labor market should "normally" create an artificial increase in paid employment during this stage of industrialization. In 1940, 39.9 percent of the total population was "working," while by 1961 only 31.5 percent fell into this category.

Let us first consider artificial explanations:

1. A change in definition with respect to major categories of workers, especially unpaid family workers. However, in both

[1] P. T. Bauer and B. S. Yamey, "Economic Progress and Occupational Distribution," *The Economic Journal*, LXI, No. 244 (December 1951), 741.

[2] Clark Kerr *et al.*, *Industrialism and Industrial Man* (Cambridge, Mass.: Harvard University Press, 1960), p. 183.

United Nations, Department of Economic and Social Affairs, *Analysis and Projections of Economic Development. VI, The Industrial Development of Peru* (Mexico D.F.: December 1959), pp. xxiii to xxvi.

cases unpaid family workers were counted and they had the following weights:

	Unpaid family workers as a percentage of all workers by sex	
	1940	1961
Male	8.5%	8.0%
Female	22.7	12.8

This category is largely a rural one. The decline in unpaid female family work could be accounted for by a change in definition, but it could also result from the likely trend to neolocality in Peruvian family structure (that is, couples residentially independent of their respective parents). This change seems to be linked to the process of industrialization and would shift women, according to the 1940 census definition, from economically active unpaid family workers to economically inactive housewives (this possibility cannot yet be checked from available 1961 data).

2. An increase in the "dependency burden"—those under 14 and over 60. The opposite trend is revealed by the figures in Table 13. The working-age population has increased con-

TABLE 13

THE DEPENDENCY BURDEN 1940–1961

Age	1940	1961
0-14 (dependents)	58.0%	43.3%
14-59 (working age population)	35.6	50.8
60+ (dependents)	6.4	5.9
Total population	100	100

siderably during this period; thus the increased proportion of inactives are probably coming from the 15 to 60 working-age group. This shrinking in age and sex limits constitutes a narrowing in the extensity of the labor market. Its significance, however, is not self-evident. The largest "retiring" group is made up of women in rural areas, although in relative terms the decline in female employment in manufacturing (still largely a handicraft category as defined by the census) is greater. Here two factors are at work: the increasingly greater proportion of male factory employment, and perhaps the exclusion of women from factory work. With the data available no further explanation can be offered than the neolocality trend mentioned above and the legal disadvantages to employing women we have already discussed. Given the assumed surplus of labor, it "makes sense" that one category of potential competitors has been partially retired. But it is not clear how these women are being supported. It also has yet to be determined how far beyond the textile industry this effect extends.

The smaller proportion of those working can thus not be accounted for by an increasingly unfavorable dependency burden, nor is it clearly a case of changed definitions. In any case, relatively more people are not "working."[3] This could

[3] In this respect I must take exception to the argument presented in *Características económicas*, in *Sexto censo nacional de población, 1961* (Lima: 1966), Vol. i, Tomo IV, p. vii. The author contends that this apparent decrease in the percentage of the economically active (or of the employed) is false because (1) the 1940 figures are "too high" since they were as high as those of industrialized nations; and (2) there has been much economic development since 1940; therefore surely even more people should be employed than before. The first point does not present a positive argument against the 1940 census. In fact, it is perfectly possible for nations of different levels of economic development to have roughly the same percentage of their populations economically active. Moreover, the commercialization of labor normally creates an artificial increase in the so-called labor force as previously unpaid workers in subsistence agriculture take on paid labor. Such a false growth factor should have operated between 1940 and 1961 in Peru. Hence the decrease is all the more striking.

The second argument seems naive at best. To be sure, there has been an absolute increase in production since 1940, but the population has grown even faster. As the text noted on page xi, since 1940 the population has grown almost 60 percent while the labor force has grown only 29 percent. It seems clear that Peru's population is growing faster than

indicate that the economy has become more efficient, thus making this reduction possible as well as desirable in a still leisure-oriented society. It is more likely, however, that the population is growing so fast that the economy cannot employ all of the working-age population even in the irrationally specialized petty commerce and personal service sector. As some of the evidence discussed in Chapter 1 under "The distribution of income and wealth" suggests, it is possible that a significant bottom section of the population is absolutely as well as relatively worse off.

It should also be noted that while a smaller proportion of the population is working, and, moreover, relatively fewer of all workers are women, more women are working in urban than in rural areas. Urbanization per se tends to increase female labor force participation. However, Peru is still predominantly a rural country. Therefore the decline in rural female labor is occurring faster than urban opportunities are opening up.

The National Distribution of Manufacturing Establishments

Besides the censuses of 1940 and 1961, other less reliable as well as less valid sources of data are the annual registers of manufacturing firms conducted by various agencies (see Ap-

---

her rate of economic development and that the true rate of unemployment in 1961 would be not 0.9 percent but a rate much higher. In a country which provides no unemployment compensation, there is no point in defining oneself as "unemployed."

A source of support for my contention that women have been the major group removed from the labor force are the figures on page vi of this volume of the census, which reveal that 47.6 percent of economically active women are illiterate while only 28.7 percent of men are in this category. Peru's sex-segregated system of education has not dealt equally with both sexes. Therefore, as industrialization proceeds and a minimum level of literacy becomes a requirement for employment, women will be disadvantaged, with, of course, a 15 to 20 year lag after improvements in the education of current children.

pendix B). In the case of the entire manufacturing sector in all of Peru, the Ministry of Finance[4] reports an average of 140 *obreros* per plant on the basis of a sample of 818 plants, while the Ministry of Development[5] covers 2,606 plants with 39 *obreros* each. In the Lima–Callao area their figures are, surprisingly, lower. (The Ministry of Finance lists 112 workers per plant in 434 plants, and the Ministry of Development reports 30 workers per plant in 2,097 plants.) Apparently either the greater coverage of plants in Lima results in the inclusion of a larger proportion of small plants, thus creating the impression that there are more small plants in the city—or in fact this is really so. If the average manufacturing plant in the city of Lima–Callao is in fact smaller than the few small-town and rural plants, a plausible explanation would be that the economies of scale are such that only a large plant could function in areas where the entrepreneur must often supply his own overhead utilities, such as water, power, and sewerage.

Another conclusion suggested by these differing figures is that the more inclusive the enumeration is, the smaller is the size of firm covered. The same differential appears if we contrast this 1954 data with the 1963 Census of Manufacturing covering 162,820 workers in 4,151 plants (39 workers per plant) [6] whereas the 1954 figures of 101,003 workers in 2,606 plants results in 45 workers per plant.

Undoubtedly there has been real absolute growth in manufacturing during this period (even if not in proportion to the rest of the labor force), but it is possible that much of this growth has been through the proliferation of smaller plants (largely in Lima–Callao) rather than a relative increase of employment in the larger plants.

There are a number of reasons for this hypothetical possi-

[4] Ministerio de Hacienda y Comercio, *Anuario estadístico del Perú, 1954* (Lima: 1957), p. 487.

[5] Ministerio de Fomento y Obras Públicas, *Estadística industrial año 1954 y padrón de industrias manufactureras* (Lima: 1956), pp. 52 and 66.

[6] Dirección Nacional de Estadística y Censos, *Resultados preliminares primer censo nacional económico, 1963* (Lima: 1965).

bility (the given evidence cannot test it). There is a tendency for the family-owned firms not to grow beyond a size directly controllable by close relatives of the owners. Also, for financial-legal reasons, many sections of essentially one productive operation are separately incorporated in order to avoid the various "penalties" of "political visibility." While some real growth in manufacturing has occurred between 1954 and 1963, I believe a major portion of the difference between these figures can be explained by the various factors listed above.[7]

The Lima–Callao Labor Force[8]

Turning to the Lima–Callao area, where the bulk of the textile factory sample was obtained, it can be seen in Table 14 that manufacturing ranked second to services as a source

TABLE 14
THE LIMA–CALLAO LABOR FORCE IN 1961*

	National		Lima–Callao	
	TOTAL	% MALE†	TOTAL	% MALE†
Agriculture	49.7%	86.2%	6.0%	87.4%
Extractive	2.2	97.3	.6	90.4
Manufacturing	13.1	71.8	22.9	79.7
Construction	3.3	99.0	6.7	98.9
Commerce	9.1	72.1	18.7	68.9
Transportation				
and communication	3.0	95.1	6.1	94.9
Services	15.2	50.8	31.7	51.7
Unknown	4.4	78.4	7.3	72.4
Total	100	78.2	100	72.2

* Dirección Nacional d Estadística y Censos, *Características económicas* (Lima: 1966), Vol. I, Tomo IV, Table 92.

† Percent in each sector who are males.

[7] For a discussion of the problems involved in using the Annual Manufacturing Registry data, see Appendix B.

[8] Dirección Nacional de Estadística y Censos, *Características económicas* (Lima: 1966), Vol. I, Tomo IV, Table 92.

of employment in 1961. Manufacturing has a higher percentage of males in the city, since artisan shops, which employ many women, are more common in small towns and rural areas. Commerce, on the other hand, offers women more opportunities in the city than in the rest of the country.

In 1963 the manufacturing census listed 23,308 plants with 193,427 workers throughout Peru.[9] Of these, 82 percent had less than five workers. Of the 4,151 plants with five or more workers, 67 percent were in Lima, with 64 percent of all the workers in this category.[10] This high degree of centralization is deplored even in the introductory text of this census. An industrial promotion law exists which attempts to encourage a dispersion of factory locations, but it has not enjoyed much success in the face of the overwhelming disadvantages facing most types of manufacturing outside of Lima–Callao.

Bearing in mind the limitations of the 1963 manufacturing census discussed in Appendix B, some hypothetical conclusions may be drawn from Table 15. Plant size, defined in terms of the number of *obreros,* varies inversely with the ratio of *empleados* to *obreros,* that is, the larger plants have relatively fewer *empleados* (rank order correlation of —0.85). This is so in spite of the fact that there are more *empleados* per plant in the larger plants (+ 0.84). The point is that the number

[9] Dirección Nacional de Estadística y Censos, *Resultados preliminares primer censo nacional económico, 1963* (Lima: 1965), Table 3. For this analysis the 20 of the 58 specific types of industries which employed over 40 *obreros* were selected (with the exception of the government-run monopoly tobacco factory). They are ranked according to the number of *obreros* employed. The median-sized industry employed 27 *obreros.*

[10] Dirección Nacional de Estadística y Censos, *Resultados preliminares primer censo nacional económico, 1963.*

The 1961 census (*Características económicas,* Vol. I, Tomo IV, Table 83) lists 410,980 workers as being employed in the manufacturing sector. The additional 200,000 workers beyond those enumerated in the 1963 census of manufacturing establishments with 5 or more workers, are presumably in shops of 4 or less. However, the 1963 census presumes to cover these as well and lists only 30,607 in this category. The 200,000 balance come from "household" industry according to the 1963 census (page vi), and hence many are probably something less than full-time artisan craft occupations.

TABLE 15

THE 1963 DISTRIBUTION OF MANUFACTURING ESTABLISHMENTS*

Industry	Empleados per plant	Obreros per plant	Empleados per 100 obreros	Mean salary of empleados (soles)	Mean wage of obreros (soles)	Ratio salaries to wages	Number of plants
	A	B	C	D	E	F	G
Nonferrous metals	423	1398	30	[data not available]			3
Breweries	89	324	28	98,637	36,841	2.7	7
Airplane construction	52	260	20	45,358	22,106	2.0	4
Sugar mills	44	183	24	53,746	15,806	3.4	29
Railroad shops	13	177	7	63,620	38,476	1.6	6
Paper pulp	34	163	20	71,960	22,469	3.2	8
Cement	51	150	34	108,075	47,498	2.3	6
Textiles	15	97	14	54,857	24,674	2.2	189
Iron and steel	29	96	29	65,321	34,167	1.9	17
Fish canning	12	91	13	45,732	10,998	4.1	29
Glass	12	81	14	55,918	22,410	2.5	27
Fish flour	15	80	19	52,485	17,235	3.0	132
Candy	15	71	20	53,055	15,512	3.4	23
Rope and net weaving	6	50	10	136,311	6,873	19.8	10
Dockyards	10	50	20	46,088	30,701	1.5	36
Leather except shoes	12	46	25	30,525	17,168	1.8	85
Miscellaneous food processing	10	45	22	52,644	24,146	2.1	98
Dairies	11	42	26	48,773	19,042	2.5	42
Paint and varnish	27	41	66	68,188	22,601	3.0	10
Fruit and vegetable canning	10	41	24	30,594	8,246	3.7	7
Average all manufacturing plants	8	31	27	46,598	19,517	2.4	4,151
Top 20 branches	17	86	20	51,163†	22,186†	2.3†	768

* Dirección Nacional de Estadística y Censos, *Resultados preliminares primer censo nacional económico, 1963* (Lima: 1965), Table 3.
† Except nonferrous metals.

of *empleados* per plant does not increase at the same rate as the number of *obreros*.

This pattern, if correct, is somewhat contrary to expectations if we assume that larger plants are more modern or more mechanized. Mechanization (that is, a shift to capital-intensive production) or an increase in size, or both, tends generally to give rise to a larger number of administrative, technical, and clerical personnel in industrialized countries. Why not then in Peru? A clue can perhaps be found in the inverse relationship between the ratio of *empleados* to *obreros* (Column C) and the pay gap between them (Column F). The higher the ratio of *empleados* to *obreros* is, the lower is their income differential (—0.88). It is also the case that the larger the plant, in terms of the number of *obreros*, the lower is the pay gap (—0.87).

It is not, however, the case that the larger plants have both a low *empleado–obrero* ratio and a low pay gap. Of the 20 types of industry listed, only textiles, of those branches that are incontrovertibly factories, fits this pattern. (The other two in this category are airplane construction or repair and railroad yards.) When size, *empleado—obrero* ratio, and pay gap are considered simultaneously, this sample breaks down into four groups:

1. Small plants with a high ratio of *empleados* to *obreros* and a large pay gap, which is the opposite of textiles. In this group are found fruit canning, paint factories, and dairies.

2. Small plants with a low ratio and a low gap; in this category we find only dockyards, a marginal type of manufacturing.

3. Large plants with a high ratio and a large pay gap. Here there are only two groups, breweries and sugar mills. These operations are incontrovertibly factories and are well above the average size of Peruvian factories. These two cases conform to the above-mentioned expectations that in such countries there must be a large pay gap between scarce skilled labor and overabundant unskilled workers. Although reliable efficiency data are not available for these two industries, there

is reason to believe they are probably among the most efficient plants in Peru.

4. Finally, we have the case of the textile mills, with a relatively low ratio of *empleados* to *obreros* and a low pay gap between them.

In place of a forced rationalization of the exceptional case of textiles, more obvious explanation is available. Textile plants have above-average levels of employment per plant. They are also parts of larger companies which generally house some of their clerical and administrative staff in physically separate establishments that could well have escaped listing in the manufacturing census altogether. Most of the textile firms with two or more physically separated plants have a downtown office housing higher administrative clerical and sales personnel. If these workers were properly categorized by industry, the ratio of *empleados* to *obreros* would rise considerably. The industrial sectors with smaller plants, especially where each firm owns only one plant, are more likely to house all their personnel together. This is also suggested by the high ratio (27) of *empleados* to *obreros* in all 58 branches of manufacturing. This latter figure, of course, includes the majority of plants which employ less than 40 *obreros*.

As for the question of the low textile pay gap, it should be noted that the wages of the textile *obreros* rank sixth, while salaries of textile *empleados* are ninth out of the 19 largest plants for which pay data are available. Both categories of workers are unionized, but it is the *obrero* federation which has the greater power (by law they must join separate unions). The *empleados* are, of course, not all unionized; only the lower clerks and reclassified manual workers would normally join an *empleado* union.

The low salary–wage ratio in textiles is probably to be explained by the fact that in these largely family-run firms the top administrators do not draw a substantial *visible* salary but prefer to take most of their income in dividends and diverted services as explained in Appendix B. In the few larger firms in the textile industry run by professional managers this is not the case.

This explanation of the deviant case of textiles in having both a low *empleado–obrero* ratio and a low pay gap could, of course, apply to other industries. But in order to check this hypothesis, one would have to identify the actual ownership and management in each firm. This would be a formidable task in the environment of secrecy and *desconfianza* described above and in Appendix A.

Pending such a study, it can only be concluded that textiles may be a deviant case in comparison to the other large-plant branches of manufacturing, most of which are newer and probably more efficient.

Returning to the observation that there is a high ratio of *empleados* to *obreros* in the smaller plants, the explanation may be that in the smaller plants a number of workers have been shifted from the *obrero* to *empleado* category as a matter of a job reclassification rather than that these plants actually employ more highly educated white-collar workers. As mentioned in Chapter 4, there has been much reclassification of what is still blue-collar manual work into the *empleado* category in recent years. Sometimes this is done by governmental decree, but often it is done on the initiative of management. It can be an effective strategy to divide the manual workers into a proletarian elite and a lower mass. It also constitutes a psychic reward (as well as entry into the better-appointed *empleado* governmental medical facilities) in place of a pay raise.

There are still other possibilities which could account for top-heavy smaller plants. Just as Peru's service sector, in general, is far ahead of Peru's level of industrial development, so too, on a small scale, is the employment of clerical and administrative personnel in smaller firms out of phase. Nepotism and an even lower level of labor efficiency in clerical and administrative work than in manufacturing operations are possible explanations for this situation.

If these possibilities exist, perhaps there is an evolutionary sequence to be expected as industrialization progresses. At the beginning there will be an excessive number of white-collar workers, for the reasons given. Subsequently a tightening-up phase follows as the size of employment per plant rises faster than the switch from labor- to capital-intensive production occurs. Finally, a return to a higher proportion of white-collar workers occurs as labor costs rise and capital goods become relatively cheaper. The tightening-up phase is being postponed in Peru by the high level of population growth, and hence that of the labor supply, as well as by the other factors tending to hold down the size of employment per plant.

In addition, there is a low but positive correlation $(+ 0.44)$ between the average pay of *empleados* and that of *obreros*, that is, it is not the case that the higher the *empleado* salary is, the lower will be the *obrero* wage. It has already been noted that larger firms have less of a pay gap. If one could extrapolate a static differential through time, this would indicate that as the size of plants increases the pay differential would decrease. This would conform to North American expectations, but, of course, cross-sectional differentials often do not permit temporal extrapolation. However, it is also true that the larger plants pay *obreros* more and that the correlation is a bit higher $(+0.40)$ than that for the increase of *empleado* salaries with the size of the plant $(+0.35)$.

The above findings, it should be reiterated, can only be treated as hypothetical relationships in view of the questionable nature of the raw data. However, the strength of the correlations and the plausibility of the explanatory rationale make them deserving of further investigation.

The National Textile Labor Force

Turning now to the textile labor force, in 1940 the census listed 190,910 workers in the "textile industry." However, this category, even more so than other manufacturing categories, was made up largely of manual artisans, especially dressmakers and garment workers. Moreover, it is impossible to sort out the factory workers (see Appendix B on the use of the 1940 and 1961 censuses). In 1940 employment in the textile industry was 50 percent of the entire manufacturing category, while by 1963 it had dropped to 7.8 percent. Its 83 percent female sex composition in 1940 marked it as overwhelmingly a domestic industry. Only in the department of Lima (covering the city as well as a large rural area) did a preponderantly male textile labor force appear (66 percent), revealing that even in 1940 the textile mills employed a far smaller proportion of females than was the case in the United States (50 percent).[11]

The 1961 census comes closer to explicitly listing factory workers as such, but there is still considerable doubt as to the size of the universe from which our 13-plant sample was drawn. It appears on the basis of 1961 data that at least 25 percent of all the workers in the Lima–Callao area were included in the sample (see Appendix B on the coverage of the sample). The total textile category in 1961 was still 73 percent female and hence largely artisan.

Some of the 71,194 employed textile workers in Peru in 1961 were explicitly identified as artisans and some as factory workers,[12] but a third group was undefined in this respect.

	Number of workers	Percent female
Clearly factory workers	9,065	23
Apparently artisans	52,124	74
Doubtful	10,005	24
Total textile workers	71,194	73

[11] Janet M. Hooks, *Women's Occupations Through Seven Decades*, Women's Bureau Bulletin No. 218 (Washington: United States Department of Labor, 1947), p. 23.

[12] Dirección Nacional de Estadística y Censos, *Sexto censo nacional de población, 1961*, Vol. I, Tomo IV, Table 80, p. 44.

The 1963 census of manufacturing establishments listed 189 textile spinning, weaving, and/or finishing mills with 21,054 workers, 18,327 of whom were *obreros*. (Unfortunately no data on sex were presented.)

Although textile plants, in 1963, were still the most numerous of those employing over an average of 40 *obreros,* and although they still employ the second largest percentage of *obreros* of any of the 58 branches of manufacturing, they are no longer first or even near the top on any other of the characteristics listed.

The Characteristics of the Lima Textile Sample

At this point, having drawn as much from published data on the whole industry as seems feasible, we will turn to the nine Lima plants in the sample.

WHITE-COLLAR OCCUPATIONS

As explained in Chapter 3, the long-standing, Latin caste-like line between manual and nonmanual occupations had been reinforced in Peru by labor legislation until 1961, when some modifications were introduced, as explained above. Even without this reinforcement, the differences between urban factory workers and white-collar employees would still persist, owing to the extreme middle-class distaste for manual work. An additional factor tending to separate these employee categories is the current Indianization of the blue-collar labor force through migration.

One of the primary differences between *obreros* and *empleados* is that the rate of turnover of both male and female *empleados,* from the lowest clerks up to plant managers (unless they are closely related to the owners), is much higher than that of *obreros.* This accounts for the fact that, although the average age on employment of office employees is higher than that of plant workers, their average seniority is much lower.

The reasons for this higher level of mobility would seem to be the following:

183

1. The blockage to promotion existing in most companies due to a preference for foreigners, as much in small as in large firms, or a preference for relatives, a situation usually limited to smaller firms. Just as factory workers face an educational barrier to promotion across the line to white-collar work, employees face an ascribed blockage based on nationality and kinship.

2. The faster growth of educational opportunities than of occupational opportunities adds an increasingly excessive number of candidates for these positions. As a result, the salary level of the lower male clerks has already dropped below that of the average textile factory worker.

3. In addition to the increase of educated male applicants, women are now moving into white-collar work, thus further broadening this market.

The reaction of white-collar employees to the "over-rational" state of their labor market is in itself irrational. They do not respond to the higher pay in skilled manual work by moving "down." Their reaction to the "premature" proletarianization of white-collar work (that is, occurring long before office automation would have brought about this effect) has been unionization, in some instances more radical and vigorous than in the case of any blue-collar occupations, e.g., the Bank Clerks Union. Those employees who do organize apparently exhibit a lower rate of turnover (on the basis of impressionistic evidence and discussions with union leaders).

In general, employees react individualistically by moving to improve their situation rather than "staying put" and resisting collectively. An alternative which further depresses the salary scale is the very common practice of taking on additional jobs, some of which might even be of a manual nature if not highly visible, e.g., driving their cars at night as *colectivos*[13] or as

---

[13] *Colectivos* are taxis which parasitically follow bus routes but stop anywhere and pick up passengers until the car is full. They tend to be faster than buses and a bit more expensive.

regular taxis. The best-paid *empleados* below the managerial level tend to be those who have a regular job in a strategically located government office, such as the Ministry of Labor or Finance, and who also have other jobs with private firms which desire "influence" in this bureau but lack "connections" at a higher level.

This high rate of mobility of *empleados* lowers salaries in at least two ways: (1) it brings the force of the total and excessive labor supply to bear on demand, and (2) it keeps the level of seniority low, a factor which tends to vary closely with the level of salaries. To the extent that on-the-job experience increases the value of an employee to a firm, this value is lost.

Another difference of equal importance between the blue- and white-collar textile labor force is that, while women are moving out of the plant, they are moving into the office. However, these are not the same women. The unacceptability of ex-factory females for white-collar work is based not so much on their being older than the usual beginning employee, as on their darker skin and lack of education. It was noted that racial segregation does not exist in Peru in the same form as in the United States. In general, social discrimination in Peru is "cultural" rather than racial. But in this case the tone of a girl's skin and especially the color of her hair, as well as her beauty, are of great importance for at least "modern front office" jobs.

In Peru today we find several types of offices with respect to their deliberate stereotyping on a racial and sexual basis:

1. Traditional offices, whether front or back, are all male, headed by a creole or foreigner, and staffed by moderately dark mestizos.

2. Transitional offices, the front office leading the change, will have some young light-skinned secretaries working beside older darker men.

3. Modern offices employ largely "fair" females.

Type 3 is found largely in "front" offices in the public's eye and in the downtown sales departments of textile firms. The plant office, if physically well segregated from the mill, tends to be transitional (a high degree of segregation is crucial if "attractive" light-skinned females are to be obtained). If the plant office is virtually "on the floor," the office staff tends to be all male. Some of these latter offices have provided the only known opportunities for crossing the *obrero–empleado* barrier for *obreros* already educationally qualified for clerical work. In no cases were these men able to continue up within the firm's employee hierarchy. A move to another firm was a prerequisite for further promotion.

Another aspect of the entry of middle-class women into clerical work is that they are less expensive than either males or factory females. Their ability to undersell male workers arises from the fact that in Peru virtually all middle- and upper-class females are dependents of some family. It is not the custom for members of either sex, no matter how old, to leave the home of their parents until marriage. In addition, female clerks are likely to be less expensive to their employers in terms of maternity benefits, since the percentage of married women or unmarried mothers is much lower among *empleadas* than among *obreras*. This is partially a result of the age preferences of employers, but in larger part it is due to the still strong dislike middle- and upper-class Peruvian women have for being seen pregnant in public.

Another characteristic of the *empleado* labor market which especially affects textile mills is the "pirating" away from the larger foreign-owned firms of their foreign technicians. The firms to which these men go are primarily the middle-sized, ostensibly national mills. The owners of this group, although generally Peruvian citizens, are of immediate and conscious European extraction, for the most part Italians, Jews, and *Turcos* (an inclusive term for non-Jewish Levantines).

The dispersion of this stream of technicians has not entirely blocked the advancement of Peruvians, since the Blessing complex has decided to "nationalize" its administration. Therefore, a Peruvian engineer stands a better chance for promotion in a politically visible North American firm than in a so-called national one.

There is a major difference in this respect between British and North American managers. British managers do not follow the American pattern of working themselves out of a job. The reasons for this are, first, that as largely factory-educated men, they are ill-equipped as well as unwilling to teach their skills. Furthermore, and perhaps more decisive, for a British worker or foreman displaced at home, a country like Peru offers a relative, if not an absolute, improvement in life situation. Few care to return to England except to retire. Consequently, they tend to guard their craft secrets from their immediate Peruvian subordinates (which often requires them to take on certain manual tasks normally not performed by administrators of their rank). For most North Americans, on the other hand, given the relatively better conditions in the North American textile industry, a job abroad is generally regarded as an adventuresome tour of duty calling for some sort of hardship allowance and leading, it is assumed, to a better position on return to the United States. Consequently, they tend to be willing to work themselves out of a job by training "native" subordinates. Peruvian skilled workers, clerks, and engineers are very conscious of this particular difference and predictably tend to prefer the North American as a superior. But the rank-and-file workers, on the other hand, find the English administrator more agreeable, since the latter has made more of a life commitment to Peru than has the usual North American and thus has learned to "handle" his *obreros* more in the traditional Peruvian manner.

THE EMPLOYMENT OF WOMEN

General pattern. Perhaps the most clear-cut difference between the labor market in the United States and that in Peru arises in the case of female employment. In the United States, the proportion of employed women has risen from one sixth of the labor force to one third since 1900.[14] The increasing percentage of married women has been even more impressive. The labor force participation of this latter group has increased 200 percent since the turn of the century. The structural reasons for this are well understood: (1) Reduction in the "heaviness" of most jobs, thus removing one traditional basis for male stereotyped jobs. (2) A generally increasing demand for white-collar labor accelerated during World War II and the Korean War by extreme labor shortages.

The motivations for this shift would appear to be only partially economic, and presumably less "rational" in this sense than the work motivation of men, thus making classical economic models even less applicable to female workers than to male workers. Mahoney found that income was decreasingly relevant past age 29 for married women. Furthermore, women with large families were less likely than married women in general to work when the children were under six, and more likely to work thereafter.[15] The double-entry participation of married women—women working before children arrive and again after they have matured[16]—was also observed.

In Peru, on the other hand, the proportion of women dropped from approximately a third of the labor force in 1940 to about a fifth by 1961. This reverse trend is occurring in spite of the fact that urbanization normally increases the participation of women in the labor force. In 1961, 16.7 percent of urban women worked, while only 10.8 percent of rural women were being paid for their labor. In other words, the total reduction of female employment is so great that it more than offsets the effect of urbanization.

From Table 12, comparing the 1940 labor force with that of 1961, it can be seen that the largest proportional reduction has occurred in manufacturing, with agriculture second. Com-

---

[14] Thomas A. Mahoney, "Factors Determining the Labor Force Participation of Married Women," *Industrial and Labor Relations Review*, IV (July 1961), 563.

[15] *Ibid.*, p. 576.　　　　　　　　　[16] *Ibid.*, p. 568.

merce, which could be expected to have taken up some of the slack, has not done so.

One should not expect the development of the Peruvian labor market to parallel that of the United States in view of Peru's chronic labor surplus, since the United States during the nineteenth century experienced a relative labor shortage. In Peru the widening or emancipating effect of a shortage is not available to favor increasing female participation. Women are, of course, drawn into the labor market under quite different conditions as well. During the low end of business cycles many businesses cut labor costs by shifting to cheaper female employees as preferable to closing down altogether.

In Peru, however, labor and social welfare legislation, at least in urban areas and in larger unionized firms, has succeeded in making the employment of women at the blue-collar level more expensive than the employment of men. Their wages are legally equal to those of men, but their work loads tend to be lower and the variety of fringe benefits, especially for mothers, much higher.

Unions, for their part, have never made a real effort to protect women per se, except for requiring the full payment of the above benefits. The leadership of the textile unions is well aware of the decline in female membership and privately expresses no regrets. Their primary dissatisfaction with female members is that they are harder to get out for meetings and demonstrations and, in general, are harder to control. Some still express the fear that the wage scale is undercut by cheaper female labor. This is true in many nontextile factories and in the marginal knitting mills whose unions are a part of the Textile Workers Federation. It is not true at all in the majority of Lima's and Arequipa's spinning and weaving plants.

This decline in female employment is probably not a general feature of the Lima labor market, but rather of the strongly organized blue-collar sector. In *empleado* occupations, women are still in the process of breaking down the traditional male predominance in clerical positions. Nationally, 30 percent of all *empleados* and 10 percent of all *obreros* are women. The situation in the Lima–Callao area is virtually the same, with *empleados* 30.5 percent and *obreros* 12.4 percent female.

In the case of Peru's textile workers, we find an unusually low participation of females and one that is due to decline even further. In 1940, 35 percent of the national labor force was female. In 1954, according to the *Anuario estadístico*, only 9 percent of all workers in registered manufacturing establishments as shown in Table 16[17] was female. The usefulness of this count, however, is limited since it primarily covers the larger firms. Nevertheless, the 1954 differentials are significant. The highest percentage of females in any category was in knitting mills, with food processing and textile mills next. The proportion employed in Lima–Callao (14 percent) is much higher than in provincial areas (5 percent), but the national figure of 9 percent is still extremely low. This would seem to indicate what random observations also suggest, that in general women are limited largely to marginal industries and domestic service.

Our sample revealed that most of the larger mills had reduced their female employment to 16 percent by 1959. Nevertheless, we would not suggest extrapolating this curve to zero by 1970. On the contrary, it seems already that most modern mills have stabilized their use of women at no more than 10 percent in a few stereotyped jobs, primarily manual finishing operations. In the future, the number of women the mills employ will probably depend on the requirements of these jobs, which could rise somewhat, given a more elaborate variety of styles and products.

A resurvey of El Cholo in 1965 revealed that no women had been hired for the previous eight years—that is, none since

[17] This registration included 818 firms and 114,744 workers, and thus is, at best, a purposive sample of all firms, i.e., including most of the larger companies especially in Lima–Callao, and perhaps 20 to 30 percent of the actual labor force.

TABLE 16

OCCUPATIONAL DISTRIBUTION BY SEX IN 1954*

| | Total Peru | | | | Lima–Callao | | | |
| | % Female | | % Branch is of total labor force | | % Female | | % Branch is of total labor force | |
Economic category	Sector	Branch	Sector	Branch	Sector	Branch	Sector	Branch
I. Agriculture	4		27		18		4	
II. Manufacturing	21		32		20		58	
Textile mills		21		10		23		17
Knitting mills		81		1		80		2
Bottling plants		7		2		6		3
Rubber factories		6		0.4		6		1
Food processing		23		6		13		9
III. Commerce	3		3		4		7	
IV. Construction	0		2		0		5	
V. Transportation & communication	0.0001		9		0.001		11	
VI. Public utilities	0		0		0		4	
VII. Services	19		2		19		5	
VIII. Mining	1		25		0.7		6	
Total labor force %	9		100	1	14		100	
No.			(114,744)				(48,583)	

* Ministerio de Hacienda y Comercio. *Anuario estadístico del Perú, 1954* (Lima: 1957), pp. 471-494.

1957. The percentage of women remaining in this plant in 1965 was 4.5 percent (down from 5.8 percent in 1959). In this group of 27 women, only one was a weaver; 10 still held positions on spinning machines (a female job in many countries), while the rest held "hard-core" female jobs in the finishing room inspecting cloth visually for flaws. There were also three women in the day nursery as required by law.

Table 16, therefore, does not give us much encouragement about the future prospects of women in manufacturing operations. Already the very modern rubber factories and the food processing plants employ relatively fewer women than do the textile firms, largely because, if our reasoning is correct, they were founded more recently.

Variations. The differentials in the employment of women by occupation, origin, age on employment, and previous employment are generally worked out as part of the analysis of the other variables. At this point, however, it is relevant to mention a pervasive differentiation by origin. Provincial females are, by virtue of their mobility, predictably less representative of their birthplaces than are the *Limeñas.* This is clearest in the fact that they have had much more previous work experience than have the Lima-born women, even holding constant the age on employment. Unfortunately, it was rarely possible to obtain the age on arrival in Lima or family status in transit as a means of separating the probably few voluntary female migrants from the majority who were brought by their families or by employers as domestic servants.

Historical pattern. The economic pressure against the employment of women in industry is particularly striking because Peru's chief manufacturing sector is still predominantly light, semidurable consumer goods, i.e., textiles and processed food, a sector ordinarily employing women.[18]

According to Collver and Langlois the general pattern of

[18] Mary M. Cannon, *Women Workers in Peru,* Women's Bureau Bulletin No. 213 (Washington, D.C.: U.S. Department of Labor, 1943).

female labor force participation develops as follows:[19] (1) In the early stages of industrialization, the shrinkage of available nondomestic work, especially in cities, may exceed the opening up of new opportunities, thus resulting in minimal female participation. (2) From this point on the participation rate rises, as women shift out of domestic service, first into industry and later into commerce.

There need not be, however, a significant universal correlation between economic development and female participation, since differing family norms and labor market conditions often counteract what would "normally" be a regular increase.

In sequence, Peruvian women's first entry into the modern urban labor market was in light manufacturing. Thus, in this "fashion cycle" the lower class led, contrary to the usual relationship of class and innovation among women. This occurred about 1900 in Lima, and even earlier in the woolen mills near Cuzco. Then during World War I a handful of women were employed in white-collar positions in some of the foreign firms in Lima. During the Depression of the thirties, the middle-class barrier to female employment was finally broken.

A premature stereotyping or foreclosure of lower-class female economic and thus social opportunities seems to be occurring. James has noted the same systematic elimination of female workers in the Bombay cotton textile industry.[20] There, too, women have become more expensive to employ than men, due to the "early" application of generous welfare laws.

As a consequence, Peruvian women are being squeezed out of this sector of the blue-collar market. While other opportunities are now opening for some women at the white-collar level, they are not, of course, for the same people. Lower-class fe-

[19] See Andrew Collver and Eleanor Langlois, "The Female Labor Force in Metropolitan Areas: An International Comparison," *Economic Development and Cultural Change*, x (July 1962), 367-385.

[20] Ralph C. James, "Discrimination Against Women in Bombay Textiles," *Industrial and Labor Relations Review*, xi (January 1962), 209-210.

males are thus being pushed back to marginal employment such as domestic service, street vending, prostitution, and back-alley garment shops where these laws are not enforced.

This exclusion of women represents a narrowing of the extension of a part of the labor market, a process which seems inevitable if labor is relatively cheap and plentiful. Labor markets are normally extended when labor is in short supply and new categories of workers are then pulled in, as during World War II in the United States.

Speculatively, this case suggests a pattern of female labor-market participation at the blue-collar manufacturing level. In the earliest stages of industrialization a high percentage of women will be employed as a carry-over from their full-time participation in the preindustrial work force. This carry-over is amplified in manufacturing by the fact that most early factories process agricultural raw material, tasks long relegated to women.

Later on, as manufacturing is increasingly mechanized, a higher percentage of blue-collar jobs are reserved for men, and women either retreat to domestic employment or go into clerical or service occupations in conformity with structural changes in the economy. In the former case the retreat to domesticity of blue-collar women is made possible by the rising income of their husbands, and made necessary by the absence of relatives to care for children.

This model fits United States as well as Peruvian history, but the latter phase has questionable relevance wherever the start and perhaps the whole process of industrialization is to be burdened by an enormous surplus of labor. The blue-collar women not enjoying factory wages in Lima are not, in general, the wives of well-paid workers, but more likely unmarried mothers forced to resort to inadequate means of supporting their children. The recently observed proportion of abortions (15 percent of all pregnancies) among a sample of

232 lower-class Lima women suggests that radical measures are being taken to meet this situation.[21]

In reference to fertility and employment, Collver and Langlois take the position that a constantly increasing participation by women in the labor force is desirable in order to reduce the birth rate, on the assumption that working women have fewer children.[22] It can be argued that the authors' apparent goal of the limitless rationalization of human economic effort constitutes the fallacy of reification on a policy level. It does not follow that if some increase in the participation of women is desirable for overall labor productivity that more of an increase is better yet, unless labor productivity per se is an ultimate goal.

Also, while the depressing effect of employment on fertility seems generally irrefutable, the generous maternity benefits in Peru awarded, in practice, primarily to workers in factories could partially counter this effect among those who remain employed. This effect probably accounts for Stycos'[23] observation that there is, among "currently mated women in Lima (1960-61) no clear-cut relation between fertility and employment status. The present analysis gives little comfort to Peruvians who are hoping for increased entry of females into the labor force as a solution to high birth rates."

COMPADRAZGO

Another institutional factor influencing the structure of the industrial labor force is that of *compadrazgo*. As was noted above, this institution flourishes more in Latin America than in Europe, and apparently more in situations of social striving

[21] Françoise Hall, "Birth Control in Lima, Peru—Attitudes and Practices," *Milbank Memorial Fund Quarterly*, XLIII (October 1965), 419.

[22] Andrew Collver and Eleanor Langlois, *op.cit.* pp. 384-385.

[23] J. Mayone Stycos, "Female Employment and Fertility in Lima, Peru," *Milbank Memorial Fund Quarterly*, XLIII (January 1965), 53-54. Carleton also observed in Puerto Rico that employment did not decrease fertility. Robert O. Carleton, "Labor Force Participation: a Stimulus to Fertility in Puerto Rico," *Demography*, II (1965), 233-239.

and anomie, in which the weak seek to advance or protect themselves by this special type of contract with the strong, than in situations of isolated traditional stability.[24] In once caste-like societies, such as Peru, *compadrazgo* functions to alleviate tensions and perceived abuses for those on the bottom and to enhance the status of those on top.

In our Lima mills the only recent acceptance of a worker–manager tie was on the part of the Peruvian-born son of a Jewish merchant who wanted to "see what it was like." Three late evenings of unexpected (and no longer traditional) serenading of his wife by the workers, in one of the recently developed modern upper-class suburbs, was sufficient to satisfy his interest in playing the part of a traditional Latin patron.

In La Inglesa, in the city of Arequipa, a young, part-English, part-Peruvian manager is determined to avoid the sick hangovers he has suffered as the patron or the *padrino* of worker fiestas. His understanding of what steps will successfully universalize his relationship to his workers is rather deficient, however; he plans to house workers on nearby company property while he himself lives ten feet from the main gate so that he can be available "in case anything happens." In Oropesa, the museum-like mill outside the city of Cuzco, the owner is the *padrino* of an unknown percentage of his labor force.

These isolated rural cases of *compadrazgo* are quite different in quality from cases in the urban setting. The paucity of actual manager–worker ties in Lima is misleading as to the vitality of at least the form of this institution. Requests to managers are a regular form of subtle harassment, since even if, as is usually the case, they are refused, the manager is expected to appreciate the honor of being asked. Some of

[24] See Alvin W. Gouldner, "The Norm of Reciprocity: A Preliminary Statement," *American Sociological Review*, xxv (April 1960), 165.

Sidney W. Mintz and Eric R. Wolf, "An Analysis of Ritual Co-Parenthood (Compadrazgo)," *South Western Journal of Anthropology*, vi (Winter 1950), 341-368.

George M. Foster, "Cofradía and Compadrazgo in Spain and Spanish America," *South Western Journal of Anthropology*, ix (Spring 1953), 1-28.

those managers who accepted such a relationship did so to obtain a *soplón* (spy) among the workers. It is for this reason that in the Lima factories the union leaders ostracize any worker seeking or accepting such a tie to a manager.

Where in force, this institution clearly could affect the extensity of the labor market by making prior ties a prerequisite of employment or promotion. The purity of the labor–management relationship would, of course, be compromised.

Provincial Variations

The preceding discussion has analyzed variations between *Limeños* and migrants to Lima for the nine mills in the Lima–Callao area. As the United Nations report on labor productivity notes, Peru not only has the most efficient cotton textile industry among the five countries studied (the others being Mexico, Brazil, Chile, and Ecuador) but it has, in comparison to the other four, the most concentrated location, 90 percent of the textile industry being located in Lima.[25]

In many respects the situation in Arequipa was similar to that in Lima. It is the second largest city (approximately 130,000 in 1959) in Peru, although less than one tenth the size of Lima. Like Lima, and unlike most other Peruvian cities, it has also been the goal of heavy migration, although the migration commenced more recently. For the past decade a severe drought in the south has finally dislodged[26] the Indian population in this part of Peru. Puno, the next most populous department after Lima, with 9 percent of Peru's population, accounted for only 1 percent of the textile workers in the Lima mills of our sample, none of whom were women.

With respect to the individual plants in the south, except for El Misti, one of the MacGregor mills, it seems that those

[25] United Nations, Department of Economic and Social Affairs, *Labor Productivity of the Cotton Textile Industry in Five Latin American Countries* (New York: 1951), p. 4.

[26] See Appendix A on Aguilar, Interview with Two Arequipenian Labor Leaders.

plants deliberately located in isolated areas have done very poorly.[27] Two of the four woolen mills near Cuzco have failed, the third limped along until recently with a restrained labor force (thanks to the "sweetheart" pact with the Communist union chief mentioned below), and the fourth, Oropesa, is outstanding for its extraordinarily stable structure, both technological and social.

Oropesa is Limenian in only one respect—its low percentage of women, the lowest in any Peruvian mill. The reason, in this case, has nothing to do with the labor welfare laws, which are not enforced there, but to a local tradition whose origin is unknown even to the owners of the mill.

At the time of its foundation, this mill was a symbol of adventurous entrepreneurship par excellence. The recently immigrant Spanish merchant who had the machinery packed in on llama-back in 1860 was 40 years ahead of the textile entrepreneurs in Lima. Subsequently, his heirs lost the founder's spirit of enterprise and allowed the surrounding environment to stereotype the mill in such a manner that it is of interest today largely as an operational museum. All of the equipment (except for a very recently acquired electric generator) antedates 1900, and many of the looms are well over 100 years old, limping along with wooden replacement parts under the full-time care of three men, a *maestro* and his two assistants. This contrasts with Lima, where in the most efficient woolen mill studied (La Plata), one weaver oversees eight looms (still a very low work load by United States expectations).

Almost all the males and all the females at Oropesa were recruited locally. The only outside labor comes from nearby towns and involves moving in at the top in a manner analogous to the general pattern of foreign migration to Peru. That is, unlike the low-status jobs provincial migrants to Lima usually obtain, the few migrants to Oropesa were experienced textile mill workers who were hired directly into

[27] See Appendix A on Oropesa.

master mechanic positions. It seems that what little migration occurs out of urban areas involves the exodus of experienced or trained workers who presumably enjoy a relative if not absolute (in monetary terms) rise in class status comparable to that already described in the case of European technicians coming to Peru.

There were several types of information available in Arequipa which were not obtainable in Lima. In the El Misti files the precise residence of all the workers was listed; this data could be fruitfully analyzed because it was possible to visit each of the nearby villages. The oldest workers, if among the better paid, lived in a development on the other side of the stream from the factory, which, in a manner typical of Andean towns, has a separate name and identity, although to North American eyes they are hardly separate communities.

Outside the factory town there are three villages in which factory workers live. The nearest, one and a half miles up the road toward Arequipa, provided a transitional life for those largely low-status factory males who maintain *chacras* (small farms) there. The only females resident outside the factory town itself are also found in this village, but as their seniority and young age on employment indicated, they are the survivors of an earlier era of recruitment.

The next community, Derrumbe, is an independent (of the factory) roadside town, three miles away, also on the railroad as well as on a highway. All but one of its eight worker-residents have low-status beginners' jobs. The pattern of movement of other Derrumbanos at El Misti indicates that this group will soon quit or move closer to the factory. The same is even more likely for the more recently hired worker from Baranquilla, which is five and a half miles away.

Another type of information was contained in El Misti's "black book," a dossier of "crimes" committed by workers which the former Spanish owner had kept until the firm was sold in 1932.[28] The pattern of labor recruitment and protest

[28] See Appendix A on El Misti.

suggested by this admittedly spotty data is that the earliest workers in this relatively isolated plant were mestizos from Arequipa (15 kilometers away along the railroad). Only later did workers migrating from the sierra come to El Misti. This latter group accounts for the "reactionary" types of protest noted in the "black book."

In Aguilar, the marginal rug-weaving mill located near La Inglesa in a slum suburb of the city of Arequipa, unusual co-operation on the part of the union leaders and management made a questionnaire possible. It was also necessary in view of the poor state of the company's personnel records. (The questionnaire dealt with the same facts obtained from personnel records in other factories.) It revealed that the survivors of the starting cadre were all nonagricultural workers from the nearby suburban village, in spite of a persistent managerial preference for *serranos*.[29] This original group, by virtue of the usual rigid adherence to seniority in promotions, was filling the top weaver positions. Unlike nearby La Inglesa, Aguilar has suffered a high rate of turnover, due primarily to its preference for female and *serrano* workers, as well as to its irregular production and piece-rate payment system. La Inglesa, on the other hand, has had an extremely stable labor force. The median seniority of both sexes at La Inglesa is the same as, and is equal to, the age of the firm (ten years in 1959). This perhaps can be explained by La Inglesa's unusual preference for a time-rate system as well as for experienced workers.

The mills around Arequipa do not hire from each other because there is a managerial agreement against "pirating." Since there are very few comparable employment opportunities in Arequipa, this agreement serves to increase the stability of the textile labor force within the city.

A special feature of Aguilar's social structure is the high proportion of working couples, who amount to a quarter of

[29] See Appendix A, on Aguilar, Interview with Two Arequipenian Labor Leaders.

all workers and half of those from the city of Arequipa. While there are Indian[30] men and women at Aguilar, none of the Indian women is married to a *serrano* male. The wives of the male Indian workers remain at home, while the husbands of the *serranas*, if they are married, are working on nearby haciendas or on construction projects. In short, factory work means something different to the women from the sierra from what it does to the men. It represents a much more radical break; hence, the migrant females are the least representative group of workers with respect to their home populations of either sex from either general origin.

An especially interesting fact was revealed about secondary occupations among the Aguilar work force. *Serranos* choose to, or must, live entirely on their factory incomes, while over half of the Arequipenian males have *cachuelos*, usually a small mercantile or repair shop which is run during the day by their wives or female relatives.

The same differentials in the age on employment by sex and origin were found in Aguilar as in Lima. An additional fact noted was that only the Arequipenian women exhibited a bimodal age on employment. The *serranas* at Aguilar all work in the rug-cutting room, where, because of the nature of their work, their children can play beside them. The women from Arequipa, on the other hand, all work at highly skilled jobs in the modern mechanized end of the plant.

The family status in transit of the migrants showed females being brought by their families, while men often came alone, especially the younger "pulled" migrants. The latter, as expected, also had the shortest time lapse between arrival in Arequipa and employment at Aguilar.

The Market Rationality of the Textile Wage Scale

The most important source of market irrationality in the average wage level of Peru's textile workers arises, as has been

[30] Defined here as speaking little Spanish, going barefoot, chewing coca, and dressing in a consistently traditional manner.

explained in Chapters 3 and 4, from government and union pressure. The Peruvian constitutions since 1920 have declared that the government's moral duty is to establish wages and working conditions. In Peru a market-determined wage and set of working conditions would generally be called "exploitation," since the Anglo-Saxon ethic of the justice of the market test finds little popular support.[31] Catholic doctrine even in the United States has made much of a "living" rather than a market wage.

Probably the more widespread ideological basis for rejecting the market mechanism is what North Americans would call cynicism as discussed in Chapter 3. Peruvians from all points of the political spectrum tend to feel that if they receive low wages or low profits it is not the result of any objective impersonal (and hence, in North American eyes, just) mechanism, but rather the result of a conscious plot by their enemies —or the powerful—to take advantage of them or to cheat them. This is to some extent a projection of their own behavior with others as a part of the vicious circle of *desconfianza* discussed in Chapter 2. The more sophisticated can, of course, easily marshal evidence to demonstrate that there are few markets in fully industralized, so-called capitalistic countries which are in fact free and pure. But the depth of this rejection of the market test goes far beyond the matter of empirical evidence.

As a result of legal action and political pressure, Peru's textile wage level has risen steadily irrespective of business cycles (except for World War II when this rise was rationally accelerated) and has risen in spite of the growing surplus of

[31] A useful definition of "exploitation" could be an inescapable relationship involving the exchange of unequal values as viewed by one of the parties. The inescapable part of the relationship could arise from a lack of alternatives, or an emotional commitment to the "exploiter." This definition could then apply in both directions. Management could "exploit" workers or workers "exploit" management. See the discussion of *compadrazgo* for some examples of the latter possibilities.

labor. The internal differentials in the wage scale are, nevertheless, another matter.

The wage system for any workers employed full-time in a formal organization is always under the influence of at least three major pressures: (1) supply and demand in the labor market; (2) the hierarchy of authority and skill within the organization; and (3) the stability or instability of the system of technology in use and, hence, the demands for skill. If the demands for skill are constant and skill is produced beyond a minimal level by on-the-job training, then seniority would vary directly with competence, thus justifying a regularly rising wage scale, assuming comparable jobs were constantly available in similar firms. These are actually rather special conditions which do not exist today in Peru's textile mills.

First of all, the type of machinery in use is being changed constantly, some machines, as in finishing and drying, requiring more skill than in the past and others, namely, automatic looms, requiring less. In the case of jobs requiring more skill, the younger recruits tend to be favored, either because they can be more easily trained after employment or because they arrive with more education. Similar conditions in the United States, whether in missile plants or in universities, have tended to compress the pay scale by raising the salaries of entrants while leaving "old timers" unchanged on the grounds of relative incompetence, an obsolete skill, or a self-imposed loss of mobility.

In Peru, on the other hand, changes in technology have not altered the rigid seniority-based pay scale. This conforms, nevertheless, to the low general mobility of textile workers and the young age on employment which precludes much industrially relevant experience.

A major complication in calculating wages arises from the popularity in Peruvian textile mills of piece rates, which presumably would favor the more efficient workers. In fact, the rates are constantly modified so that the resulting average wage approximates what would be a much simpler and more rigid system of hourly rates graduated on seniority. A detailed analysis of the rationale behind each of these modifications would reveal a frequent lack of justice or logic. The productivity of most jobs in a textile firm is dependent on the collaboration of other workers and successful production planning by management. It could be, and has long been, argued on these grounds that piece rates are unfair in any flow-process or assembly-line factory, but in Peru labor as well as management prefers piece rates to time rates.[32] As things are generally arranged, the workers with the most seniority are promoted to the weaver positions where piece rates make more sense. The two kinds of workers generally on a time rate basis are peons and mechanical maintenance workers.

Another source of market irrationality in the wage scale arises from the amazing level of ignorance generally observed throughout all the mills visited as to the prevailing wage level by occupation, even on the part of union leaders. Since, with the exception of a few mechanics and dyers, few skilled, experienced textile workers in recent years have changed firms and been taken into the same type of job, only the starting wage is relevant to most recruits. The great surplus of labor, however, makes it unnecessary for firms to compete for this latter group.

Another nonmarket factor is the legally required higher cost of female workers. As stated above in various contexts, it is not felt that these market "irrationalities" are necessarily irrational in terms of the overall goals of industrialization.

With respect to the market rationality of the level of Peru's textile wages, it would appear that it clearly bears little relation to the overall supply of workers. The most rationally selected and rewarded workers are those few at the highest levels of manual skill, the maintenance mechanics.

The rationality of the wage scale bears on questions of the

---

[32] See Appendix A on Aguilar, Interview with Two Arequipenian Labor Leaders.

purity and of the extensity of the market, although more directly on the former. Any system of wages which tends to decrease mobility, other things being equal, would provide more opportunities for particularism to invade the relationship between employers and workers. That is, a certain minimal level of turnover at all levels is required to universalize social relationships quite aside from its function in providing a continuous market test of the rationality of the level and differentials of the wage scale. This would be especially true in small firms, which would include most of those in our sample, the median size being approximately 200.

A contrary factor tending to favor purification is the law of *derecho adquirido* by which any benefit awarded two years in succession becomes an "acquired right" and no longer a *noblesse oblige* favor. Consequently, management is deprived of the leverage of a conditional bonus. Of course, if Peru's textile managers personified the norms of an efficient industrialist, any additional means such as the conditional bonus with which they could more effectively control their labor force would be "good" from their point of view. Few of the managers, however, could qualify for this role. This is not to say that their actions are not quite rational in terms of their personal interest or realistic in terms of conditions in Peru. All that is meant is that their official positions do not have built into them ideal industrial norms. Just being an industrial plant manager is not a universally "deterministic" situation.

The edges (extension) of the blue-collar and white-collar labor markets are, of course, somewhat different. Female white- and blue-collar workers can leave the labor market for a domestically dependent status, while only relatively few male blue-collar workers have, or feel they have, the option to return to independent farming. At what wage level or under what circumstances either would leave the labor market is hard to determine because an intervening category of occupations exists, i.e., marginal service and vending jobs, which fractionalize units of work to the point of irrationality. Women tend to be drawn out of the labor market when their husbands' or breadwinners' incomes rise, while men, as in the case of the United States during the Great Depression, are driven back to the land and "out of work" by a decline in wages.

At the level of technical and administrative skills, the situation should be different. Much has been written about the scarcity and strategic value of these abilities in underdeveloped economies. Hence, salaries at this level should be relatively high. In the case of foreign-born and foreign-trained technicians, and a few Peruvian mechanics, this is the case. But for native creole or mestizo Peruvians, even with adequate training, the salary level does not reflect this rationale. This is so because in many firms the job specifications and the corporate organization do not separate administrative, technical, and clerical functions as sharply as in the "West," speaking, of course, of firms of such a size as to make such a division of labor rational. This functional vagueness thus seems to make a vast army of clerks available for responsible administrative and technical posts. The very few who win such promotions suffice to keep the rest in individualistic motion rather than in collectivistic resistance.

The market for technicians is apparently quite international, with salaries varying not with respect to national boundaries but with the cost of living, distance from birthplace or last job, and the "cultural level" of employing areas. Latin engineers who insist on working in their home towns or national capitals generally earn less than foreigners even when the latter are nationals of neighboring countries. The act of crossing the frontier legally and emotionally puts them in a more rationalized labor market. The higher salaries paid foreign employees in the provinces still amounted on the average to apparently only $2,216 a year (see Table 17). However, in this category of labor we find an extreme case of payments being made on the side to avoid taxes, both national and in their home countries. Paying dividends from "ownerless" *acciones al portador* (bearer stock) is the most convenient method, but there are many other ways in which the salaries are supplemented.

The major factor which keeps textile technicians' wages so low is the superannuation and commercial crises in the textile industries of a number of European countries, especially England. In addition, the effects of the dislocation of Eastern and Central European refugee technicians are still being felt. Those with passport problems or those admitted under special refugee quotas generally end up in Peruvian firms or companies owned by other refugees, while English, German, and North American technicians are employed largely in British and North American firms, which have usually sought them out and brought them to Peru. A constant trickle of this latter group from the larger foreign to the smaller Peruvian firms has been observed. While this has the virtue of giving these locally based firms indirect access to the world labor market, it represents the type of immigration at the top which slows Peruvian upward occupational and social mobility. However, the recent political pressure on the foreign firms to hire nationals means that the Peruvian whose promotion was blocked in a Peruvian firm by the hiring of a foreigner (or a relative of the owner) can now look to the foreign firm for better opportunities.

THE PATTERN OF EMPLOYMENT

Of the 72 textile plants in Lima (not firms but separated buildings) covered by this 1954 survey (Table 17) only 41 have over 50 employees. In this latter category, the total employment is 12,652, giving a plant average of 308 workers (*empleados* and *obreros*). It is virtually impossible to determine exactly how many corporate entities this represents—in all probability there are 30 to 40. The various legal and architectural ruses used to escape the eye or at least the hand of the Ministries of Finance and of Labor have greatly lessened the significance of these figures for the purposes of organizational

TABLE 17

Textile Salaries and Wages in 1954, by Nationality, Occupational Status, Sex, and Location*

Location	Number of plants	Number of empleados	Empleados per plant	Ratio empleados per 100 obreros	Average annual per capita salary (S/25 = $1)	Total obreros	Obreros per plant	Average annual per capita wage (S/25 = $1)	Percentage empleados are of total labor force
All of Peru:									
Total	89	1,943	21.8	10	$1,006	18,932	213	$384	9.3%
Foreign		327	3.6		2,063	65		412	
% female		3.1%				17%			
Peruvian		1,616	18.1	9	792	18,867	212	384	7.8
% female		17.5%				21%			
Lima–Callao:									
Total	72	1,529	21.2	12	1,054	13,261	184	442	10.3
Foreign		297	4.1		2,047	65		412	
% female		3.4%				17%			
Peruvian		1,282	17.1	9	815	13,196	183	442	8.5
% female		19%				22%			

Provincial:

Total	17	414	24.3	7	825	5,671	333	250	6.8
Foreign		30	1.7		2,216	0			
% female		0%				0%			
Peruvian		384	22.5	7	716	5,671	333	250	6.3
% female		13%				18%			

In Lima Peruvian *obreros* receive 54 percent of Peruvian *empleados* wages.

In the provinces Peruvian *obreros* receive 35 percent of Peruvian *empleados* wages.

Peruvian provincial *empleados* receive 88 percent of Lima *empleados* wages.

Peruvian provincial *obreros* receive 57 percent of Lima *obreros* wages.

Peruvian *empleados* receive 38 percent of the wages of foreign *empleados*.

Perú Ministerio de Fomento y Obras Públicas, Estadística industrial año 1954 (Lima: 1956), pp. 52, 56, 60, 66.

analysis. Only for the larger foreign-owned firms are the legal and functional ties fairly clear. The two largest, Blessing Company and MacGregor, together own 11 of the 72 plants.

The provincial plants, which are more often separate firms except for several plants controlled by Lima firms, are fewer in number but are on the average larger. Only one of the five textile plants in Arequipa, for example, has less than 100 employees.[33] Consistent with our earlier finding on the employment pattern in larger plants, we find that while, in the provinces, there are fewer *empleados* per *obrero*, there are more *empleados* per plant. One could call this the fruits of economies of scale, but another factor is that *empleados*, like *obreros*, are cheaper than in Lima. This relatively larger percentage of *empleados* per plant in provincial areas, however, refers only to Peruvian *empleados*. There are relatively fewer foreign *empleados* per plant in provincial areas than in Lima. Perhaps as a result, foreign *empleados* earn more working in provincial mills than working in Lima, while Peruvian *empleados*, like *obreros*, earn less in the provinces. But again the size of plant (the provincial average being larger than Lima's) may be more significant than location. Larger plants presumably pay more.

The use of Peruvian female *empleadas* in the provinces is lower (13 percent) than in Lima (19 percent), which fits the misogynistic sex-stereotyping found in conservative Peruvian offices. This figure, however, considerably overestimates the proportion of males which actually would be found among the clerical *empleados*, since this category includes all the usually male technicians, many foremen, and even some highly skilled blue-collar employees.

The United Nations study of Peru's industrial growth problems found that Peru's textile industry (yarn and flat goods) [34]

[33] Peru, Ministerio de Fomento y Obras Públicas, *Padrón de industrias manufactureras* (Lima: 1956), p. 133.

[34] United Nations Department of Economic and Social Affairs, *Analysis*

had almost its "proper" quota of engineers and professionals, i.e., 2.8 percent (2.9 percent United Nations ideal) or one technician for each ten skilled workers. This report estimated (1959) that Peru would have a deficit of 3,000 engineers by 1965.

The percentage of properly skilled textile workers was currently too low according to the United Nations study. Only 28.8 percent were skilled workers whereas 40 percent should have been. This percentage was still above the 21.7 percent average for all branches of manufacturing. The expected rises in productivity plus the currently overextended capacity of the textile industry would call for no increase in employment by 1965, unlike the situation in almost every other branch of manufacturing. Consequently, the U.N. report predicted that the textile industry would continue losing its relative importance in Peru's industrial labor market.

---

and Projections of Economic Development. VI: The Industrial Development of Peru (Mexico D.F.: December 1959), p. 293.

CHAPTER 8

Conclusions and Speculation

The Development of an Industrial Labor Force

Since a central focus of this study has been the process of industrialization, it will be worth while to summarize those factors in the Peruvian textile labor situation which influence conformity to industrial norms.[1] The factors we have considered are: (1) the average size of the plants; (2) their location; (3) the social distance between labor and management; (4) the rate of labor turnover; (5) the existence of particularistic or universalistic institutions such as kinship, *compadrazgo*, unions, collective bargaining, etc.; (6) labor and welfare legislation; and (7) managerial employment policies. We will discuss each of these in turn.

Although the average *size* of all textile plants in Lima–Callao (97) or in Peru (111), or even in the sample of 13 of the largest plants (301), placed textiles second among major groups of manufacturing plants, they are, in worldwide terms, small factories. Since by itself the absolute size of any group probably has certain minimal organizational

[1] There is no general agreement as to what "*the* norms of an industrial society" are. This is because any concrete industrial society has a social structure which is a mixture of the general consequences of industrialization and its unique history and because industrialization is an apparently endless process of internally generated change. Therefore, it is not even possible hypothetically to abstract definitely the *essential* industrial norms from the currently most developed societies, asserting that these represent the structure of a completed industrial society. Nevertheless, the following norms have been tentatively employed in this evaluation as relevant to the data available: universalism in recruitment, specialization and division of labor, functional specificity or purity in labor–management relations, an increase in size of producing organizations, a widening participation of all types of adults in the labor force within a shrinking age range, and a rising level of labor-market mobility of the various types mentioned in Chapter 3.

consequences in any culture, it is thus assumed that the small size of these mills makes adjustment to them less difficult for Peruvian workers. Because these mills are not obliged to have elaborately impersonal bureaucratic systems of administration, traditional expectations of personalism can be partially maintained. Therefore, the size of these mills, per se, has not favored the development of a modern industrial labor force. On the other hand, their small size has eased the adjustment of workers to this industry. Perhaps too easy an initial adjustment means that a more painful change in behavior has only been postponed. I believe this is the case in this industry. Excessively high prices and a low level of labor efficiency (as well as other deficient business practices) probably mean that the sharpest labor–management conflicts are yet to come.

The urban *location* of the majority of Peru's textile mills, I believe, has been the major factor in the ease of labor recruitment. Moreover, painful as the postponed second stage of adjustment to industrial efficiency will be, it will be easier to carry out in a large city than in factory towns where, as Kerr and Siegel have pointed out, the "propensity to strike" is inevitably high.[2] Lima's employers are not obliged to provide housing, schools, churches, etc., for their workers as are isolated rural employers. In this and other respects the amount of traditional paternalism is far less in Lima–Callao.

Although the published data on the entire industry are suspect, both the data and personal observation indicate that the *social distance* between labor and management in textiles, while great from a North American point of view, is not as great as in many other fields. The *obreros* in Lima textile factories are the sixth best paid of the top nineteen branches of manufacturing while the *empleados* are ninth. Since the least pure relationships occur in those factories in which

[2] Clark Kerr and Abraham Siegel, "The Interindustry Propensity to Strike—An International Comparison," in Arthur Kornhauser, Robert Dubin, and Arthur M. Ross (eds.), *Industrial Conflict* (New York: McGraw-Hill Book Co., 1954), pp. 189-212.

social distance is the greatest, it would appear that a narrowing of labor–management social distance tends to create a more functionally specific or contractual relationship.

I mean by this not that normal industrial labor–management relationships are between social equals but that such distance as exists arises primarily from different occupational roles rather than an external status. When a large social chasm exists between labor and management compounded of caste-like ranks and differing cultures and even languages, modern industrial relationships cannot develop.

Consequently, the preoccupation with problems of recruiting and holding industrial workers appears to be relevant largely to the primary sector of the economy, especially to commercial haciendas and mines. This fact suggests that any effort to avoid the emotional problems of modernization by decentralizing industry or emphasizing labor-intensive domestic or cottage manufacturing is, at best, a desperation measure useful only to "buy time" while an urban manufacturing sector is established. The social costs of such a policy seem exorbitant, as well as inconsistent with the personal values of many of its proponents. In the first place, no more effective strategy could be devised to commercialize the family than to expose intrafamilial relationships to the market, especially in what tends to be a highly competitive field. Such "enterprises" would become rural sweatshops as in the notorious English "putting-out" system. In addition, the political strains attendant on the process of "persuading" the petit bourgeois class presumably created by such a cottage-industry policy to give up this fractionalized under-scale type of activity eventually would probably produce a fascistic or Poujadist type of reaction.

The low rate of labor *turnover* is, per se, an unfavorable influence on the process of modernization. It is, however, so rational a reaction on the part of the workers that it cannot be attributed to an uneconomic perspective on their part. Only an increase in employment opportunities would justify a higher rate of interfirm mobility. On the other hand, this low rate of turnover reveals that the process of labor recruitment was not a difficult one. Of course, it remains to be asked whether worker adjustment was deceptively easy. Have these factories overaccommodated themselves to uneconomic worker behavior and thus put off a showdown? It should be recalled that many employers took considerable advantage of the dictatorial Odría era to assert managerial initiative in structuring their labor relations. However, it cannot be said that all of them concentrated on increasing labor efficiency. Many merely fired disobedient workers and sought to replace them with more docile types.

The problem of turnover and absenteeism in general appears to be peculiar to isolated rural employers and marginal types of urban occupations. As Bonilla observed about urban workers throughout Latin America, "Problems of turnover and absenteeism seem to be clearly more a function of the existing structure of employment than of any cultural hangover or built-in incapacity to adjust. . . . Commitment and productivity prevail where working conditions support them."[3] Moreover, much of what labor instability exists in the city is more a response to managerial actions than to a worker inability to adjust to factory discipline.

The Lima mills were not burdened with numerous *compadrazgo* and kinship networks, which would be an obstacle to modern labor–management relations. On the other hand, neither did the workers feel capable of collectively confronting management through elected leaders. Instead they relied on the government, in a *patrón*–peon type of relationship, to fight their battles for them. This, of course, is due not simply to well-established tradition and the preference of many political leaders but also to the workers' objectively weak situation.

The legal and political environment in which workers and

---

[3] Frank Bonilla, "The Urban Worker," in J. J. Johnson (ed.), *Change and Continuity in Latin America* (Stanford, Calif.: Stanford University Press, 1964), p. 197.

unions operated would have to be described as carrying workers from traditional paternalism to welfare-state paternalism without, in theory, an intervening period of "rugged individualism." Of course it is only a minority of Peru's proletarian elite who are missing this "emancipating" experience. But for those favored few, I am not sure that Peru's lower-class culture provides them with any viable basis for such autonomy. In the case of English industrialization, Bendix reminds us of the role of the Chartist Movement in emancipating British workers from a desire to rely on obsequious individual ties to *noblesse oblige* aristocrats.[4] In Peru, Protestantism has not made much headway, especially in comparison to Brazil and Chile, nor does there appear to be a functional substitute. The few converts encountered were, to be sure, lower class, but they were found largely in the department of Puno, and they paid dearly in social ostracism for their rigid emphasis on alcohol and smoking as the primary vices. Only one Protestant convert was encountered in any of the textile mills visited, and he subsequently left for a white-collar job, thanks to his North American missionary contacts.

Perhaps more to the point in evaluating Peru's welfare state paternalism would be the avoidance of an obsolete capitalist bias. State-provided benefits constitute in principle the most universalistic manner of redistributing income, which at present is a major requirement for Peru's further economic development. The textile industry in particular has a large amount of unused productive capacity because its high prices do not permit it to reach more than two thirds of Peru's population. Progress would consist in both reducing prices and raising mass income.

In practice, however, welfare benefits in Peru are not enjoyed on anything like a universalistic basis. To begin with, the government could not afford to begin to fulfill its welfare promises. Those who do receive benefits, such as entry to

[4] Reinhard Bendix, *Work and Authority in Industry* (New York: John Wiley & Sons, 1956), p. 45.

a university or a bed in the appropriate class of hospital, need the intercession of a powerful patron, be he a government official or their employer. Therefore, the way in which Peru's welfare system actually operates does tend to perpetuate personalistic paternalism. But given the absolute scarcity of the various benefits, it is to be expected that the current sociopolitical structure, rather than the letter of the law, will determine how the programs actually operate.

Management employment policies varied from the highly modern tactic of hiring away valuable skilled workers from competitors to concentrating on docility at all costs. The latter policy has not usually been very successful. With a rigid seniority system enforced, the on-the-job system of apprenticeship was far more important than initial worker selection to the performance of the workers. Very little use was made of either the employment service or vocational school graduates. However, in view of the way these two institutions functioned, I feel that management does not deserve "industrial demerits" for not utilizing their services.

On balance, although no attempt has been made to assign numerical values to the pro and con factors in the development of a modern industry, it would seem that the favorable influences operated more saliently during the early phases of labor recruitment. In the future a more difficult period of industrial labor force development appears to be inevitable.[5]

[5] It is interesting to note the strategy employed by the MacGregor management in its efforts to raise productivity in the face of "the labor problem." Faced with the competition of the Blessing textile mills after World War II, this locally owned British firm (by long-resident British citizens) found itself saddled with several old mills: El Futuro and La Junta in Lima, and El Misti in Arequipa. From the point of view of the strategy of "industrial reformation" in a laboristically limited situation, it has faced the following possible settings in descending order of pliability.

1. First is a new plant in a worker suburb of Lima–Callao with new machinery and new workers, which would allow "efficient" work loads to be established at the beginning and, in general, the restoration, if only

The Commercialization of Labor:
Stages and Processes

In terms of the conceptual framework described in Chapter 2, the following summary statements can be made.

In the earliest stages of industrial labor recruitment, largely involving mines and decentralized agricultural processing plants, the widest extension of the lower-class labor market was found. This arose from the nearly total participation in work in the preindustrial setting by all the physically able. The number of types of workers, as well as the type of services demanded of them, has been reduced, especially since 1940. In the early period (1900 to 1920), the majority of textile workers were women and children working 10 to 15 hours daily, as well as frequently being on call for domestic service, construction, and other manual labor by the owners and managers of the mills. Today the age on employment is universally between 20 and 25, and in response to the higher cost of female workers, the percentage of women has been cut down to that deemed necessary to fill unavoidably stereotyped "female" jobs.

These restrictions on the type of workers employed and the services expected of them are not a feature of the entire labor market but relate predominantly to manual factory

temporary, of managerial initiative in structuring formal and, to some extent, informal plant organization.

2. If faced with an old mill, it is preferable that it be in an isolated rural location where traditional paternalism can be "exploited" to permit some freedom for restructuring work loads and plant organization. In this case, management must ride out the diffuse unorganized type of reaction of the "new against the old." This type of labor unrest, while "exasperating," can be overcome successfully, as the El Misti situation demonstrates, while the same efforts directed at a more organized and sophisticated urban labor force in an old factory could prove impossible.

3. The least desirable situation, then, from the point of view of raising industrial productivity or making any type of "progressive" change, would be an old downtown urban plant with a strongly organized, politically influential labor force, which is the situation management faces at El Futuro.

labor. The white-collar labor market, on the contrary, is experiencing an expansion in female employment, as well as in the type of services available for purchase from both sexes.

In terms of labor mobility, Peru is experiencing, as in the case of the United States during the 1920's, a high level of migration and interindustry movement (agriculture into manufacturing and urban services), but, unlike the United States, a low level of interfirm mobility. That is, in Peru too many workers, in terms of the development of a flexible labor force, are making one important move from rural areas and agricultural occupations to the largest urban areas, but then "staying put" occupationally and residentially. The least mobile are the highly skilled manual workers, while the most mobile are the lower-status white-collar workers, not only from firm to firm, but, in the case of women, in and out of the labor market. The double entry of women into the labor market also occurs in Peru, but far more for Limenian than for migrant women.

This latter observation suggests a general pattern with respect to migration and selectivity. It seems that the greater the cultural distance between the textile workers' role in Lima and the norms existing in their home areas, the more atypical these workers will be of their home population in terms of age, sex, marital status, and, no doubt, many other respects. Thus, the least representative type of worker is the migrant female.

A related inference from this analysis is that social discrimination against categories of workers, as, for instance, against women for legal reasons, or against Negroes and Orientals for cultural reasons, is not, per se, antithetical to the process of industrialization[6] if two conditions can be assumed: (1) the

[6] Hoselitz observes that in the case of the virtually unlimited supply of unskilled labor in Egypt and India, ". . . the factory manager *must* [my italics] use certain non-economic criteria to select among the applicants." Bert F. Hoselitz, "The Development of a Labor Market in the Process of Economic Growth," in *Transactions of the Fifth World Con-*

excluding trait is not directly related to industrial work, that is, the skilled workers are not specifically excluded; and (2) a large enough pool of recruits remains so that a sufficient number of qualified workers can be obtained. Moreover, it is my contention that, were all physically capable workers to be available for any specific type of work in a surplus labor situation, the wage level would be under pressure to drop so low as to jeopardize the whole process of industrialization.

On the other hand, it is highly likely that a society which practices employment discrimination would apply the same biases in other areas where positive economic irrationality would result. At the same time, as will be argued below, large segments of such societies are likely to be left behind during the early stages of economic development. The political issue then is: How will the losers be selected and how will their resentment be handled?

In terms of the purity of the labor market and the labor–management relationship, my general conclusion is that because urban factory labor is operating in the extreme climate of insecurity, injustice, inefficiency, and anomie which dominates Limenian society, many workers seek to advance or at least to protect themselves by individually establishing kinship-like ties to their employer, or to any other powerful person who will accept their proposal.

However, in the case of the textile workers, most overt invitations to employers to become the *padrino* of a worker's child come from migrant rather than locally born workers. Moreover, few Lima managers accept such offers. A major source of opposition to this traditional institution is the union. In the first place, the leaders oppose such action on the part of the rank and file as an obvious diversion of loyalty from the union. Secondly, and probably more important, the Textile Workers Federation has been able to provide its members

---

gress of Sociology, Vol. II (The Sociology of Development) (Louvain, Belgium: International Sociological Association, 1962), p. 67.

with a much greater degree of protection than that enjoyed by most of Peru's *obreros.*

In terms of other characteristics which are per se irrelevant to productive efficiency, kinship and nationality are greater sources of impurity and barriers to labor mobility at the white-collar level than *compadrazgo.* The family as an active influence in industrial production is much more persistent on the managerial level than at the so-called more backward manual-worker level. The capitalist institution of private property is, of course, the "loophole" here. In this respect, the structural inconsistency between private property norms and the requirements of large-scale industrial enterprises is revealed. In the United States this conflict has been handled, if not resolved, by so dispersing corporate ownership that the so-called owners have lost most of their rights of possession except that of the dividends allotted them.[7]

Corporate enterprise in Peru, however, is entirely different. The secrecy of company ownership, along with numerous other problems, has prevented the development of an internally rationalized money market. This is significant, since it is probably generally assumed that it should be easier to mobilize the market for something as impersonal as money than for any other good or service. (I am not referring to the international flow of capital out of Peru, which presumably is governed by much more rational considerations.)

Organizational Structure

Although the central focus of this study has been on the development of the industrial labor force at the manual factory level, some of my observations relate to white-collar workers.

1. The process of industrialization appears to involve an early phase of topheavy manufacturing establishments—with

[7] Wilbert E. Moore, *Industrial Relations and the Social Order* (New York: Macmillan, 1951), pp. 51-64.

a ratio of white- to blue-collar workers similar to that of much more highly developed societies. The majority of these employees are not, however, carrying out the type of technical and administrative functions so essential to a large, efficient, industrial enterprise. They are largely involved with carrying out routine and often dysfunctional clerical operations, some of which may have no relation to the enterprise's official business.

Subsequently, a tightening-up phase may occur as much of the "Parkinsonian" bureaucratic surplus overhead is eliminated before the firm reaches the point of automation at which most of its employees are doing nonmanual work. Such a tightening-up phase in Lima is being postponed by the surplus of lower-level clerical help and the small, family-owned and -managed firm structure. It may also be the case that the subsequent development of technical personnel in firms in underdeveloped countries will be retarded by (1) their ability to borrow technology from developed nations rather than having to develop it themselves and (2) their inability or unwillingness to pay salaries sufficient to attract highly skilled technicians from developed nations or to retain their own nationals with such training.

2. A multiple-occupation pattern among many white-collar and professional workers is apparently a labor market characteristic of this stage of industrialization. Along with the fractionalization of petty services demonstrated by street vendor–beggars selling a single orange at a time, this irrational extension of the market for services clearly impedes the specialization of labor so central to the development of an advanced industrial labor force.

The tendency of white-collar workers to take on several occupations is related to the blurred status system during the transitional stage of industrial labor recruitment discussed in Chapter 2, and it suggests another topic to which some of the data gathered are indirectly relevant. One of the most frequent observations made about Latin Americans at all levels, except in the case of some Indians, is that they are "leisure-oriented," a polite term for "lazy."[8] Another way of explaining this apparent fact would be to say that a large proportion of Latin American workers are alienated from "work"—a condition that can be explained as much by current social "pathologies" as by tradition. The two explanations happen to coincide: upward mobility to middle-class status in Latin America has meant mimicking traditional elite patterns of behavior, as imperfectly perceived by the emulators, rather than the creation of an independent bourgeois ethic in terms of which some elite behavior could be looked down on. However, it could also be suggested that middle-class "laziness" is deceptive in view of the common urban phenomenon of middle-class multiple-job-holding. Under these conditions, little as a man may be paid by any single employer, none of them may be getting his money's worth, since the employee is so fatigued and distracted by his fractionalized life. Any serious commitment to any one occupation will be diluted by the demands of his other jobs.

The practice of taking on *cachuelos* unrelated to the person's training or primary occupation (if there is one) is highly irrational behavior on the part of the new professional middle class. It denies the basic logic of occupational specialization, which is the basis of an industrial economy, and it is self-defeating. In the second instance it is analogous to the behavior of farmers in producing more goods when prices drop, in hopes of at least maintaining their standard of living. "Moonlighting" is rational in an industrialized society during periods of a labor shortage. But in Peru's case the multiple-job-holders are further overloading an already surplus labor market. (I am referring, of course, only to instances in which a skilled professional takes on other jobs which are unrelated to his profession and not of a labor-shortage nature.)

The fact of multiple-job-holding bears on the frequently

[8] Richard N. Adams, "Rural Labor," in J. J. Johnson, *op.cit.*, p. 76.

demonstrated observation that in apparently all industrializing societies the "reputational" prestige ranking of occupations is similar—hence sociology has achieved a kind of technologically determined "law." But if the question of status ranking is focused on actual people rather than on the reputation of abstracted activities, a different or much less clear prestige pyramid would emerge. Moreover, in Latin America, where social mobility based on economic achievement is so difficult, symbolic mobility is widely resorted to. Honorific and high-status titles are therefore rapidly depreciated by abuse. In provincial towns lower-middle-class people "rise" in their own eyes by taking on large numbers of lower-class *compadres*. Those with university degrees become Doctors in the eyes of non-university graduates. *Huachafo* behavior (a Peruvianism for *cursi* or pretentious vulgar ostentation) is said, by the old upper class, to characterize the entire middle class as well as the newly rich.

In the case of the factory worker the problem of occupational morale is more one of alienation than multiple-job-holding. His relatively well-paid position and full-time temporal commitment do not encourage or permit other "full-time type" jobs such as is common in the middle or upper classes. How many of them are "alienated" in general, assuming a cross-culturally useful definition could be agreed on and standardized, I would not presume to estimate from any secondary "behavioral manifestations" such as strikes, divorce, mental illness, etc. Alienation from work could be measured in terms of behavioral conformity to "ideal type" industrial norms, such as regular, on-time attendance and performance with a minimum of close supervision. This, however, would require that such workers be presented with employers already functioning as ideal models in this respect, and such is not the case. It is my observation that Peru's textile factory workers are, if anything, overcommitted to their specific employers. The deficiencies in their conversion to industrial labor arise from managerial behavior, or a quite rational reaction to job insecurity in an oversupplied market.

Contrasting Evidence

There are a number of other studies of textile factories in Latin America, but few present comparable data or are focused on the same problems. One, however, offers some evidence on several of the points discussed above. Rottenberg found that while reputedly "in some dominantly rural communities, recruitment for factories is difficult because workers refuse to accept jobs either because they involve a regime of discipline or for other reasons," no such problem exists in Tumbo (a one-plant town of 1,500 in Colombia) "where the people are wage oriented and job-hungry and seem to have a great desire for work in the factory."[9] Management, however, felt that there was a "high rate of absenteeism" (no figures were given). This arose in part from the concerted and apparently successful effort on the part of management to raise labor productivity. The work load of the largely female labor force was continuously increased.

This finding surprised Rottenberg, who assumed, on the basis of the famous Mayo industrial relations experiments, that workers always connived to prevent an increase in work loads or production standards. Therefore, Rottenberg was forced to conclude that in Colombia, unlike in the United States, where productivity and morale are supposed to be directly related, these phenomena are inversely related. The workers at Tumbo "are more productive when directed and 'driven' than when they have discretion and are permitted to set their own pace." (Actually, Rottenberg had no basis for the latter conclusion since he had not seen any experimental effort at the permissive approach. However, the comparable plant in Peru, namely, Oropesa, revealed the same style of

[9] Simon Rottenberg, "Problems in a Latin American Factory Society," *Monthly Labor Review*, LXXI (July 1954), 756-760.

labor discipline, except that its management did not "drive" very hard.)

In the United States between 1900 and 1955 somewhat comparable trends in labor-force participation were observed.[10] In general, proportionately fewer men and more women were working at the end of this period, especially married women. The average age of workers rose, partly because of the general increase in longevity but even more because of the delayed entry into the labor force due to prolonged education. As the structure of the economy shifted, the percentage of workers in tertiary services rose while that in manufacturing and especially primary activities fell. Women moved out of the first two sectors into clerical and professional work even faster than men.

In Peru, on the other hand, women are moving out of manufacturing before it has really developed, while their entry into white-collar work will undoubtedly be slowed by the surplus of male workers and the higher cost of child-bearing workers to management.

INDIAN PARALLELS

Because of the numerous and significant respects in which the Peruvian case parallels that of Bombay's cotton textile industry as described by Morris, they will be enumerated.

1. Early labor recruitment was not a significant problem[11] in Bombay or in Lima.

2. Labor turnover was low, and a major share of the responsibility for what instability did exist lay with management in both Lima and Bombay. In the Indian case, however, the latter problem arose from the jobber system of subcontract-

---

[10] Gertrude Bancroft, *The American Labor Force* (New York: John Wiley & Sons, 1958), pp. 28-48.

[11] Morris David Morris, *The Emergence of an Industrial Labor Force in India, A Study of the Bombay Cotton Mills, 1854-1947* (Berkeley and Los Angeles: University of California Press, 1965), pp. 39, 51.

ing the hiring function. This technique was not in evidence in Peruvian textile firms.

3. Even within the city of Bombay, as well as in Lima, wide differences in wages existed for the same type of work in similar firms.[12] However, Morris found that the overall level of wages did respond more readily to changes in supply and demand than has been the case in Peru since about 1945. Morris' evidence comes largely, however, from the pre-World War II period, when labor legislation was not as significant a factor as it has since become.

4. In both India and Peru, the sharpest era of labor conflict was not during early labor recruitment but much later as management was forced to attempt improvements in labor efficiency.[13] In both cases most of the strikes may be interpreted not as a Luddite type of anti-industrial reaction, but as a sign of a modern type of industrial labor commitment.

5. Willful absenteeism in Bombay was reputedly not over 10 percent.[14] In the case of the Peruvian mills "hard" evidence was not available on this point, but all reports from the Lima mills indicated that it was "low" or "not a big problem." The situation in Oropesa, the most rural mill, was one of a high rate of both absenteeism and turnover but the owner-manager did not feel this was anything he could or should try to change.

6. In both cases there was a low proportion of women and children. Adult males in Indian mills were always at least 70 percent. After 1931, when night work for women was prohibited, the proportion of females fell even lower. Female turnover in Bombay was, as usual, higher. However, their wages were not significantly lower than those of male workers.[15]

Unemployment

Throughout this study it has been asserted that manufacturing activities and services offer the only long-run employ-

[12] *Ibid.*, p. 159.
[13] *Ibid.*, pp. 202-205.
[14] *Ibid.*, p. 200.
[15] *Ibid.*, pp. 65, 70.

ment opportunities for Peruvians, given their desire to industrialize and their rapidly increasing population. However, as
Jaffe has observed, the effect of a rapidly growing population,
the greater efficiency of manufacturing compared to artisan
methods, and the redundant underemployment in white-collar
work means that for a period of time an increase in manufacturing will "create little if any additional employment in
supporting industries . . . [namely] retail trade, services, agriculture. . . . It is entirely possible that the total volume of
goods and services produced (gross national product in constant monetary units) may have to double or triple before the
economy may require additional workers."[16]

This observation appears to be borne out by a decrease in
the percentage of the economically active population, which,
as was pointed out, arose not because of an increase in the
proportion of dependents, but because of a decrease in market
participation by the working age groups. It appears that in
Peru lower-class women have borne the brunt of this closure,
or delayed replacement, of employment opportunities. The
combination of the mechanization of commercial agriculture
and the reduction of women in manufacturing means that

[16] A. J. Jaffe, *People, Jobs and Economic Development* (Glencoe, Ill.:
The Free Press, 1959), p. 18.

Land reform is relevant at this point in that among its various goals
is holding in tolerable rural employment a greater number of independent
farmers than would otherwise be the case. The Peruvian land reform
system does not offer much of a prospect for accomplishing this goal.
It is one of the most cautious and conservative of such efforts seen in
Latin America and promises to be too little too late. Moreover, even if
it were successful in this respect it can be argued that such programs
are really reactionary in terms of the pattern of required industrial labor
mobility assumed here. A temporary relative increase in peasant well-
being would probably result in even higher fertility, thus aggravating
the problem of surplus labor as well as reducing the per capita ratio of
available land. Moreover, the extremely conservative "kulak" petit
bourgeois mentality created by the Soviet and Napoleonic land reforms
suggests that the subsequent rationalization of agriculture will be agoniz-
ingly difficult. See Karl Marx, *The Eighteenth Brumaire of Louis Napoleon* (London: George Allen & Unwin, 1926), pp. 135-157.

female lower-class employment opportunities are shrinking. The humane way to handle such a displacement is to ensure that the affected group becomes securely dependent on some other source of reputable support, such as the state, the family, or even charity. But it is not at all clear that any of these institutions is doing or can do this job. Since the government is unable to provide unemployment compensation, or even more make-work activities than it already does, lower-class adult urban females, the majority of whom are not married, are largely dependent on themselves for their own and their children's support.

Perhaps it can be said that urban lower-class women are the most exploited group at this stage of industrialization, with rural workers in general a close second. The urban lower-class males are divided between a proletarian elite and a marginal mass. The former have been relatively well cared for all over Latin America, especially by dictators such as Perón, Batista, and Odría. For this reason this favored group has responded by behaving in a relatively conservative manner.[17]

Summary

In terms of "hard" data, the following summary picture can be drawn of the Peruvian textile labor force. Unlike the development in most other Latin American countries, Peru's textile labor force developed slowly and largely in the capital metropolitan area. It was also afforded considerable protection in the face of the general surplus of labor. On balance its early stage of labor recruitment and organization was not plagued by the recruitment and commitment problems reputedly inevitable in such countries. The relative facility of this stage, however, suggests that the most painful adjustments to the requirements of an industrial economy have yet to be made, namely, worker willingness to permit a higher level of change in employers and in the organization of work.

[17] See Victor Alba, *Historia del movimiento obrero en América latina* (México D.F.: Libreros Mexicanos Unidos, 1964), p. 80.

The primary responsibility for what early level of labor instability did exist seems to belong to management rather than labor. Moreover, the inability of these workers to commit themselves to industrial norms is primarily due to the failure of management to impose such demands upon them.

The other major influences in the structuring of this branch of the industrial labor force have been (1) the enormous and rising surplus of labor and (2) the political "interference" of the government in protecting these workers from the potentially depressing effects of this excessive supply.

In general no fixed universal sequence of stages of industrialization can yet be established. In Peru most of the usual stages occur greatly compressed in time and in a somewhat different order from that of "Western" experience. No doubt, the later a country begins industrializing, the faster will be the process and the more stages bypassed. Whether the resulting culture will be more industrial—or even less so—than "Western" cultures remains to be seen. Many of the latter differ from the ideal type of industrialized society because they stabilized their economic systems at an earlier stage of general industrial progress. This is especially so in the case of England and France. It remains to be seen whether the cultures of underdeveloped areas, by virtue of facing a more rapid and powerful pressure to industrialize, will capitulate more fully, or, on the other hand, preserve a distinctive way of life more effectively, or whether, eventually, all distinctive differences between cultures will be wiped out by the homogenizing consequences of industrialization.

Vignettes of the Thirteen Textile Mills: Brief Histories and Current Structure

ᘓᒒ

In the following plant and company vignettes the names of the plants, companies, and company personnel (but not public officials) have been fictionalized. Future United States social science investigations in Latin America have already been sufficiently damaged by the way in which espionage, politics, and scientific research have been confounded in this area. There has also been a case in which a prominent Peruvian was named in an academic article on politics in such a manner that he is no longer willing to confide in North Americans. Factory owners are especially guarded about their "valuable" trade secrets and confidential games with official regulations. It required several months of appropriate introductions for the various doors to be opened and to allow me to examine company files on my own.

SANTA MARÍA—AVENIDA GARIBALDI

History. The Avenida Garibaldi plant of the Santa María Company is today the second largest and second oldest woolen plant in Peru. It was founded in 1896 by Bartolomeo Bolognesi, who was born in Italy in 1853 and had recently immigrated to Peru. Like most of the textile entrepreneurs, he entered the Peruvian commercial world as an importer. Having undertaken a textile mill, he found himself also involved in financing an electric power plant as well as a wool hacienda to supply the mill.

By 1906 the firm was in need of more capital, so the Russo family, also Italians, entered the picture. Shortly thereafter some Peruvian financiers became involved, one being the father of a recent president of Peru. This body of stock, said to constitute 25 percent of the effective control, places Santa María in the dubious position of being part of the empire of the ex-president's cousin, generally known as the country's leading commercial and financial oligarch.[1]

The Bolognesi family, as the plant managers and technicians, lived in the factory enclosure that covers a block on what is now the slum edge of Lima's central business district. During World War II, when most Peruvian mills enjoyed unprecedented prosperity, the Garibaldi plant was still under the control of the founder, 79 at the time (1942), who was unable fully to adjust its operations to the higher demand. The various other owners of the company then decided that all future expansion would have to take place under physically, legally, and above all administratively separate auspices, viz., the Avenida La Plata plant, especially since the founder's middle-aged son was to inherit control of this little empire.

Current Situation. The Garibaldi plant's current equipment consists of 2,800 spindles and 115 looms. Were the latter not largely old mechanical looms this combination would be extremely unbalanced, i.e., the spindles could not keep up with the demands of the looms.

There is almost universal agreement on the mill's poor situation. The outstanding exception to this view is that of the current manager, Sr. Bolognesi. It would be incorrect and oversimplified, however, to blame him for all the plant's problems. The sales organization is extremely conservative, pre-

[1] One of the most widespread rumors about the family of President Prado (1939 to 1945 and 1956 to 1962), and one accepted as much by his friends as his enemies, is that his father started the family fortune by absconding with money raised in Lima during the war with Chile for the purchase of French warships from, among other things, melted-down family heirlooms donated by the first families of Lima. On arrival in Paris it seemed, say his defenders, too late to save Peru so he put the money in a bank in his own name. One of his warmest supporters explained Prado's desire to serve his country as an effort to clear his father's name.

ferring special orders for all but the most popular proven items.

On the labor front, the Garibaldi plant is endowed with a quarter of the top directorate of the Textile Workers Federation. It rates this distinction by virtue of its age and the continuity of its operations and a resulting high average seniority. One of its weavers is the grand old man of the textile union, a veteran of the organizing campaign of the 1920's and of the APRA's early years. He is still at work as a weaver except for his trips to Geneva as Peru's labor representative to the International Labor Office conventions.

The Santa María management has given up trying to reform the Garibaldi plant from above in view of the manager's entrenched position and his stock holdings. Sr. Bolognesi's policy is first of all to continue the "humane" practices inherited from his father, who died at work as manager at 89 in 1952. He keeps his desk drawer full of his own petty cash for loans to workers because "the Directors won't provide company funds and I am not a 'hard-hearted banker' (*banquero metálico*)." He feels his main problem is the evil commercial policy of the directors and views himself in his father's footsteps as fighting the good fight for quality work and humanity.

Another side of his character is shown by the role his family has played for the small wave of Italian immigrants to Peru after World War II. Several dozen were given makework employment in the plant to help them get their feet on the ground; afterward they either left or served to replenish the all-Italian technical and administrative staff at Santa María. He prefers Italians fresh from Italy even to second-generation Italian-Peruvians, in spite of the constant difficulties this creates with his workers. His Italians are mostly from Milan and have an attitude toward Peruvians not unlike that of the Germans or the English. He finds his Italian foremen cannot stand the local "mañana" philosophy and "do not treat the workers with the courtesy their delicate personalities demand."

233

The manager has never accepted the affront to his authority and humanity the union represents despite its 39 years of existence. The plant thus suffers from a maximal number of petty grievances, most of which are settled through the good offices of the Ministry of Labor, located ten blocks from the factory, rather than through direct negotiations.

One of the manager's good works on behalf of the workers was the establishment of a cooperative store in the plant. He picked its two managers, but, after several years of operation at a loss, he feels they are cheating him or the workers or both, but he cannot figure out a way to catch them nor will he allow the union to take over this responsibility.

He has no definite hiring policy at the moment; his main problem since 1955 has been who to try to let go. In the past, he says, he let workers hire their relatives, and he preferred to have jobs and even machines pass from father to son if possible. But "all this is changing." As was more the case at the new Avenida La Plata plant, he would occasionally obtain a batch of experienced workers on hiring away a foreman from another plant or mill when it closed, for instance, Fabrica Maragnani near Cuzco. Generally, the Garibaldi plant loses its good administrative and technical personnel to their overwhelmingly superior rival Lima woolen mill, El Mar, also run by Italians.

SANTA MARÍA—AVENIDA LA PLATA PLANT

The basis for the decision of Santa María's owners to establish a new factory separate from the old Avenida Garibaldi plant has already been explained. Along with their desire to be free of an incorrigible and irreplaceable management, their immediate goal was to take advantage of the unparalleled prosperity during World War II. Having decided on this course too late to obtain any new machinery from the United States or Europe, they were forced to begin with second-hand equipment. This was especially difficult to obtain, because, in addition to the excess demand, most mills will not sell their discarded equipment for fear of establishing low-cost marginal rivals. Each factory in Peru has its own pile of rusting junk which it will not sell even to a foundry until its usability has been completely destroyed.

The plant was located well outside the city of Lima between the parallel highways which connect the capital to its port city, Callao, eight miles away. The latter city, now over 100,000, has long been Peru's most industrialized and pro-letarianized community. It is somewhat insulated by Lima against the Indianization which recent migration has effected on the east side of the capital. Callao is very much a coastal community with no cultural Indians and a relatively heavy concentration of Negroes, Chinese, and non-Spanish whites and mestizos descended from generations of sailors beached and transient.

Countering the plant's nearness to Callao, however, was the fact that by 1943, when the plant opened, the wartime labor shortage had begun to pull into Lima many migrants on whom new firms were forced to rely for recruits.

Nevertheless, we find a higher percentage of *Chalacos* (citizens of Callao) in this plant than in any of the others studied. In spite of adequate transportation, the distance between Lima and Callao has prevented much commuting or migration between these cities by *obreros*. The cost in money and time and the opportunities available in Callao have kept the percentage of *Chalacos* working in Lima textile mills far below the level found even in the case of distant departments.

Managerial Policy. In a number of respects the management of this mill was the most "progressive" encountered in Peru. Their personnel policy included the following unusual features:

1. The summer employment of students in textile engineering from the National Engineering University.

2. A preference for workers with previous industrial experience especially in textile factories.

3. A corresponding dislike of *campesinos* (farmers or country "hicks"), who are "all right for the first six months" but are "worse than city boys once they become creolized."

4. A preference for formally trained technicians from whatever country.

5. Use of the recently established Employment Service of the Ministry of Labor, which is patterned exactly after United States federal and state employment services.

As far as *obreros* were concerned, this has meant relying on the following sources:

1. Two groups of experienced workers from textile mills in Callao which had closed (these sources, however, were not available until the early 1950's).

2. Workers selected from the construction crews which had built the factory and installed the machinery.

3. Recommendations from "good" workers, managers, and technicians hired away from other factories, and recently the government Employment Service.

4. When none of these sources is functioning, workers are hired *de la calle* (from the street), but often as *eventuales* (temporary workers) ostensibly, as the law requires, on construction work. In this manner the usual or legal trial period of 90 days is extended indefinitely. This is one of the many ruses practiced by various firms to circumvent the complex and extensive labor legislation described in Chapter 3. In general, however, the Textile Workers Federation has more than held its own in preventing such games from becoming the primary basis for labor–management relations.

MAC GREGOR & SONS—EL FUTURO

History. The El Futuro plant of MacGregor & Sons combine was founded in 1901 by two British engineers, James Bemis and Thomas Scanlon, who had come to Peru in 1870 to establish an iron foundry for an Italian coal importer,

Giovanni Battista, in order to produce cannon balls for the war with Chile. El Futuro was originally a small cotton knitting mill turning out lantern and candle wicks. When it later expanded into a fully integrated knitting and weaving mill, its Italian and English co-owners quarreled over nepotism in hiring. The two groups then split, the Italian one becoming the San Juan mill, and the other El Futuro.

The latter company relied on an independent British import and mercantile house for their machinery and cloth distribution. When El Futuro's owners were asked to expand and diversify production and refused, the mercantile house built a rival factory, La Junta, in 1918. By 1919 El Futuro was ready to sell out. The process of growth of the Blessing Company complex was similar to this in that a number of already functioning independent mills were bought out by their distributors in default of loans for operating capital, but here the similarity ends. The Blessing mills had a number of Peruvian owners who sold out only under conditions which still burden the company with a high overhead of Peruvian vice-presidents and stockholders with generous preferred stock, i.e., with a guaranteed dividend. The MacGregor & Sons combine, on the other hand, is owned largely by Englishmen who are all residents of Peru, which gives this firm a freedom and unanimity of action which all the Blessing operations in Peru lack. As a result, the MacGregor & Sons combine is rapidly overtaking the Blessing mills in sales; it has already developed the most efficient cotton spinning, weaving, and finishing operations in Peru.

The El Futuro mill, however, is this firm's downtown white elephant. It is located only four blocks from the Plaza San Martín on land which in a free real estate market would support one of the new "skyscraper" luxury apartment houses in which so much Peruvian capital is invested (rather than in industrial enterprises). The company has been trying to close the mill for years, but, as usual, the Ministry of Labor will not give them permission. As a second-best policy they are transferring their best younger workers to newer mills near Lima and letting operations decline as their older workers die off or retire.

Managerial Policy. Originally El Futuro's management adhered strictly to "the Lancashire system" of sex-stereotyped mill jobs. This consisted in giving all the "heavy" work to men and the "light" work to women. Their criteria of heaviness was by no means based solely on rational technological factors. In fact, it can be argued, in view of the wide variety of sex stereotypes found throughout the world in textile mills, that very few operations are actually so "heavy" as to require male workers. Some women are weavers, and some are operators of carding, combing, and finishing machines in most of the older Peruvian mills. The "Lancashire system" assigned women to spindles, to the older mechanical looms in small numbers, i.e., one or two looms per worker, and to all inspection work. It also favored the father-to-son inheritance of jobs and even machines and the hiring of whole families, but, as a Lancashire foreman observed, "in England you can fire easily." The recent disciplinary problems arising from a three-way conflict among managerial, union, and family prerogatives have left this recruitment criterion in disfavor. The current policy is now to avoid hiring anyone related to those already employed. This policy, however, is known to the workers and hence, of the few workers recently hired, those who had relatives in the firm were forewarned not to reveal this fact.

In general, El Futuro's managers prefer "green country workers." When asked, "Why not experienced urbanites?" their answer was that (1) urbanites with previous industrial experience, like all workers, would have to start at the bottom of the skill and status hierarchy in view of the strength of the seniority system, and hence would be unhappy; (2) their availability for employment suggests to El Futuro's managers that they were fired for "good reasons"; (3) their training would not suit "our way of doing things"; (4) if they had already worked in a textile mill they were certain to be members of the Textile Workers Federation. Furthermore, the managers' preferences for rural workers are quite specific. "I used to try to get them from Piura, but then the irrigation project up there spoiled them; now I prefer them from around Huaras in [the department of] Ancash."

Technical school training is viewed as being worse than useless. "All they want is a white-collar job, to say nothing of all the political ideas they pick up."

Along with other employers, El Futuro is reducing its female employment. Women now are limited to a 45-hour work week but must be paid as much as men on the same jobs, which in the case of El Futuro's 48-hour work week means that women are paid for three hours they do not work.

MAC GREGOR & SONS—LA JUNTA

The current La Junta mill was put in operation in 1918 by Juan Bemis, the son of one of the founders of El Futuro, James Bemis. By 1920 it had a work force of 260 *obreros* and a high average daily wage of 4 soles (1920 exchange 2 to 3 soles to $1.00). It has been run from the start by English foremen-technicians as was the case with the other MacGregor and the Blessing mills.

Managerial Policy. The peculiarities, relative to El Futuro and the Garibaldi plant, of the various characteristics of La Junta's labor force are the result of the MacGregor directorate's decision to restructure at least this one of their older Lima plants. El Futuro is regarded as a lost cause, but La Junta's location and equipment offered some hope of a "reformation" in line with the company's post-World War II modernization plan. Their major opportunity came in the last years of the anti-Aprista Odría regime when they were able to discharge and pension off enough workers to give them a relatively free hand in restructuring their productive organization. This meant not only getting rid of incompetent or unruly workers but in temporarily being able to disregard the generally sacred seniority institution which not only controlled promotions but was a major obstacle to lateral transfers within the plant from section to section.

The La Junta management followed up this breakthrough by favoring migrants from certain departments and even provinces, notably Ancash and Piura, over experienced *Limeños*.

In addition to a highly selective discharge and hiring policy, their labor force is further affected by the transfer of a cadre of their "best" workers to a new finishing and a new thread-spinning plant on the northeast side of Lima.

The final feature of La Junta's strong "reform" policy is a heavily foreign administrative and technical staff made up largely of ex-foremen from Lancashire cotton mills. This group works on the floor and "on the backs" of the workers in a manner unapproached in any other mill in Peru. It is doubtful whether their work force, once stabilized, will put up with this pressure if the experience of other mills is comparable. The manager of the newer (1943) Santa María plant on Avenida La Plata found serranos "a la primera, son humildes, pero después de seis meses, se ponen acriollados y peores que los vivos de Lima" [at first they are humble, but after six months they become "creolized" and worse than the wise guys from Lima].

BLESSING COMPANY—EL INDIO MILL

History. The Blessing Company was established in Peru in 1854 as a ship chandlery and later "under Blessing's energetic management, it went into foreign trading on a large and profitable basis." The company did not venture into textile manufacturing until 1905 and then in order to buy out rather than to initiate an enterprise. In 1905 the company purchased a mill known as La Providencia, owned by the brothers Quiroga, which is today El Indio cotton mill. Then in 1917 the Blessing Company purchased a major interest in a mill located eight miles east of Lima in a one-factory village on the central highway which links Lima to the sierra. This mill was the resuscitated survivor of an unsuccessful attempt to start a cotton textile mill in 1848 in the town house of one of the last Spanish viceroy's mistresses, "La Pericholi." It was second only to El Desastre, as of 1959, as a "white elephant" investment.

El Desastre had been founded in 1899 by José Pardo, a prominent Peruvian,[2] who managed it until 1903, when his brother Luís took over with a group of Italian and English technicians.[3] One of the latter, Flavio Germani, went on to become a director of this firm as well as one of the many wealthy Italian-Peruvian financier-merchants. It was also in this mill that the well-known Peruvian engineer, Ricardo Tizón y Bueno was the "radical" manager from 1919 until the middle 1920's, when he was exiled by the dictator, President Leguía. He was replaced by a foreign manager after purchase by Blessing in 1927. Only very recently have any Peruvians again attained positions of administrative responsibility and now only under political pressure from the government and a drive to lower white-collar labor costs.

El Desastre was finally closed in 1959 after years of negoti-

[2] Ricardo Tizón y Bueno, *El Perú industrial* (Lima: Sociedad Nacional de Industrias, 1924), p. 66.

[3] Since José Pardo y Barreda has been virtually the only creole Peruvian to found and personally manage a textile factory and since he was clearly one of Peru's national elite, some additional biographical material would be of interest. His father, Manuel Pardo, had been President of Peru from 1872 to 1874 and had sent his son to a local German school rather than to an English or French one in Lima. After finishing the usual law courses at the University of San Marcos, he was sent as Ambassador to Spain in 1889. He returned, after the relatively progressive Civilista party had at last brought peace and order to Peru in 1896, to run the family sugar plantation, Tuman, and arrange for a short rail line and a wharf at Eten on the northern coast of Peru to export his sugar. In 1903 he resigned his post of manager of the El Desastre mill to become Minister of Foreign Affairs and the next year, President, until 1908. He again gained the presidency in 1915, having in the meantime organized the first national steamship company and a dock-building program in Callao. His strongly pro-German sympathies during World War I deprived the Allies of Peru's active support and, in view of Britain's overwhelming influence in Peru at that time, led to his downfall and exile in 1919 by the very pro-British dictator President Leguía.

ations with the union and the government. From the company's point of view, it really "lost" because it had to transfer, rather than release, the whole El Desastre crew to El Indio cotton mill as a second shift. This was commercially unnecessary at the time in view of the poor market for textiles.

Up to 1940 all of Blessing's textile mills had been acquired in the same manner. The first step involved Blessing's handling the local sales and import needs of an independent firm. Then, as each of the independent firms got into financial trouble, Blessing bought a controlling but never complete stock interest in their former customer. The result is that today these old second-hand mills are each burdened, from the point of view of local American managerial initiative, by a complex of special concessions granted to Peruvian owners involving guaranteed dividends in the manner of preferred stock and an obligation to employ as many of the Peruvian owners as possible.

This duty has had its rewards in local political influence, since most of the recent presidents or cabinet ministers have been schoolboy chums if not relatives of Blessing's Peruvian stockholders. Other foreign firms starting afresh in Peru have to build up a local group of influential supporters because of the personalistic aspect of Peru's legal-commercial situation. On the one hand, the government today attempts to regulate closely a great many aspects of business activities in spite of its official private-enterprise economic policy. However, the government does not embody the degree of efficiency or honesty to make such a system of control function as it was intended. As a result, "political influence," never irrelevant to business even in economies most favorable to free enterprise, is often more valuable to owners than efficient internal management. In Blessing's case, it was crucial in their successful fight to close down their El Desastre plant. However, in spite of still being burdened with a comparable relic, El Futuro, Blessing's locally owned British rival, MacGregor & Sons, is fast overtaking Blessing as the leader in textiles.

BLESSING COMPANY—EL CHOLO

History. In 1940 the Blessing Company departed from its policy of expansion through the purchase of second-hand mills by constructing a large annex to its El Indio mill building. To gain the various legal advantages of corporate independence, this new plant was organized as a separate company. For this reason, and from a desire to prolong the period of managerial initiative in labor organization, no select cadre of experienced workers was hired or even borrowed from any of their older mills. In the opinion of Blessing's ex-textile officials and most of those still employed who were involved with the event, this strategy meant only delaying the full functioning of the mill to such an extent that much of the extraordinary wartime business was lost.

Current Situation. This plant's current labor problems, however, dwarf the problems it has had. When the Blessing Company received permission in 1958 to close its downtown Desastre mill, it had to promise to transfer the workers from this Communist-run local union to the Aprista-run El Cholo as a night shift. In addition, although the general level of efficiency at the Desastre mill was very low, the work loads on looms were actually higher than those at El Cholo. Furthermore, the latter's wage scale was higher. Needless to say, the Desastre workers were considerably mollified by this agreement, which in effect reduced the work load for weavers while paying all a higher wage, especially since the average level of seniority of the Desastre workers was almost twice that of the Cholo labor force.

The only managerial preference which survived this transfer was that disfavoring the employment of women. The "complete" stereotyping of women in an integrated mill means that they work only in the repetitive, meticulous, manual finishing operations such as cloth inspection and label sewing. This stereotyping raises the otherwise lower age on employment of women.

The 1952 decline in business worsened in the next few years and resulted in a series of abortive attempts by Blessing at technical and administrative reforms. The most outstanding was the employment in 1954 and 1955 of a new Swiss manager and a United States-trained (in educational philosophy and psychology) Peruvian managerial consultant, Juan Sánchez, who later became, rather briefly, the Minister of Labor. The Swiss manager rapidly upgraded the quality of Blessing's production only to find that the Peruvian market, or at least Blessing's distribution system, could not absorb it. Sr. Sánchez meanwhile presented a report on Blessing's textile labor problems and was then allowed to carry out his own recommendations. After two years of rising costs and friction between the "new regime" and the "establishment," Sánchez and a number of other officials were discharged and a new, "more business-like" British manager was hired to reorganize again the whole textile operation. More recently Blessing negotiated with a Swiss firm to sell off their entire textile holdings, but their whole situation has not proved very attractive to potential buyers.

Up to this point we have been dealing with mills having during any one period a fairly consistent labor recruitment policy, even if it is to let the workers recruit themselves. In the case of the Blessing textile mills, however, we are dealing with a confused situation owing to frequent drastic changes in all company policies initiated from the highly centralized headquarters in New York. Furthermore, as far as labor relations are concerned, new directives are not implemented in Lima by any single responsible official or office. The company's situation is not a happy one. As the largest as well as the oldest cotton textile company in Peru, it is the best known or most obvious. In addition to its age and size, its clearly American ownership makes it even more a target for political harassment.

As a result, although its workers are among the best-paid textile workers in Peru, it has the most militant and hostile union to deal with. This aggressiveness arises in part from the challenge to Aprista leadership constantly made by Communist dissenters. However, these Communists are not infiltrated "professional" provocateurs but workers who became Communists while working for Blessing. Some, like the group of old weavers in El Futuro, are "leftover" Trotskyites from the dissension which was part of the organizing era of the Textile Workers Federation.

LA PERFECTA

La Perfecta is a fully developed but not extreme example of the multiplication of corporate entities all operating within the same building. In 1936 some Eastern European Jewish textile-importing merchants opened a small rayon-weaving plant in Lima with 60 looms. In 1938, the owners, in debt for the plant's equipment, sold it to a German and Spanish-Jewish refugee family, who have operated it ever since. Until 1954 no new looms were added, but much vertical expansion took place, each new unit or process taking the form of an ostensibly separate company. By 1959 the company had the following physical and legal structure:

1. Inmobiliaria Greco—the holding company for its real estate.

2. Textiles Juntadas—its distribution branch.

3. La Junta Industrial del Perú—a spinning and dyeing plant owned jointly with another independent rayon weaving mill. (The last entity is an exceptional example of industrial collaboration between two firms, neither of which, while they are definitely competitors in the sale of rayon cloth, could operate their own spinning plants economically.)

4. Prisa—La Perfecta's finishing room which buys its plain cloth from the weaving section as a separate company. The 24 men in this "company" are the best paid in the plant and so far have kept an informal understanding that they will not unionize.

5. Nylontec—an added weaving room on one end of the main building. This "company" became unionized, but not before the highest loom work loads (20 per worker) in Lima had been established.

Without going into the intricacies of Peruvian business and labor laws, it can be stated that financially this is a highly rational arrangement. Moreover, all these units are run functionally by the same management as one organization.

The cautious growth of the company since 1936 arises from the same problems which face all Peruvian companies:

1. Commercial loans for manufacturing operations can only be obtained at an exorbitant interest rate and often at the price of giving company stock to the lenders.

2. Tax and labor laws make it convenient to understate drastically the capital value of the firm, in the case of La Perfecta as one sixteenth of its real assets. But this policy in turn makes it impossible to get any public loans for industrial development.

As a result, all of their development has come from reinvested profits. Until the devaluation of the sol to the S/26 = $1 level their 46 percent mark-up had enabled them to amortize all new equipment within three years.

Managerial Policy. At the staff level La Perfecta relies heavily on hiring away proven experts from competing firms, especially larger ones with European connections.

As far as the *obreros* are concerned, their policy consists of the following:

1. A "warm, personal, but strict" approach to discipline which accompanies the almost constant presence in the factory of one or another of the owner-brothers, all of whom attended textile schools in the United States. This constant managerial presence does not mean, however, that they carry out the fore-

man's function. On the contrary, they have been especially successful in recruiting effective foremen, who, it appears, are especially difficult to obtain in Peru. Their "formula" is to hire light-skinned mestizos from Lima or coastal urban centers who are "reformed radicals." The foreman of the weaving section is an ex-Aprista expelled from the military officers' school for his political beliefs. All of their foremen have an attitude toward their workers which can be paraphrased as follows: "Fundamentally these workers are lazy children, especially the *cholos*, but if you weed out the worst and stay on their backs you can get a good day's work out of them." The foremen's wages are more than twice those of the average worker, so their feeling of social distance is not simply a product of a racial-cultural bias.

2. A lenient or neutral policy as far as the backgrounds of male recruits are concerned, with reliance on their governmental contacts to enable them to discharge undesirable workers. The turnover of males, however, has been very low according to managerial memory, although no records of discharged workers were available.

3. The minimal use of women in view of their higher real cost.

4. A policy of promoting workers only within sections, except for the transfers of the best workers to newly formed "companies."

LUSTRADA

History. The history of this firm is typical of most of the small and middle-sized mills established since 1930. The founders are a family of Syrian merchants, who in 1937 left a partnership in a Syrian import firm in La Paz, Bolivia, to go into business for themselves in Lima. Their first step was the purchase of a third-hand Syrian-owned rayon-stocking–knitting mill. By 1950, with the help of a loan from the Banco Industrial, they had created a little textile knitting-mill complex of legally independent firms which included, besides the above, a cotton-underwear mill. The legal and political advantage to this deliberate miniaturization and fractionalizing of corporate organization has already been described. Knitting mills, for technological reasons, especially lend themselves to this process.

In view of this background it represented a daring and unusual step for the sons of this Syro-Bolivian merchant to establish the largest, most modern, independent, specialized, cotton-spinning mill in Peru. It was second only to MacGregor in the quality of its yarn and the efficiency of its production. This was due in part to the pirating away from MacGregor of an English foreman and various skilled workers, and in part to the guaranteed sale of a "break even" quantity of yarn to the family's various knitting mills.

By 1965 this company had gone into bankruptcy under circumstances which I was unable to investigate.

Managerial Policy. After an initial period of direct management by the owner's sons, it was decided that the size and complexity of their operations called for an experienced textile manager. For this purpose one of MacGregor's technicians, who only three years before had been brought from England by the company, was hired. His own limitations and, as he viewed the matter, the limitations of most English textile men in his position are those resulting from the Lancashire system, i.e., the extremely specialized "applied" background of English textile technicians because of the persistence of apprenticeship in highly specialized mills.

Thus the Lustrada mill enjoyed two advantages: (1) a manager with a variety of experience, part of which was in Peru; (2) an operation sufficiently specialized to be within the competence of this manager.

In 1959 the owners decided to retire the English manager and replace him by a second-generation Italian-Peruvian. The latter is an ex-instructor of economics from the Catholic University in Lima who was forced into a full-time reliance on his position as assistant manager by his failure to complete his degree work. As a Peruvian, he received considerably less than his predecessor. Furthermore, he was not related to the owners, nor had he any stock in the company. Whether his management was responsible for the firm's demise, I could not ascertain.

With respect to the labor force, the most striking difference between this mill and all those yet studied was its high percentage of women. An observer unfamiliar with the usual Peruvian practice would find this situation "normal" in terms of English and American sex-stereotyping, since this is only a spinning mill. However, as we have seen in the other "modern" Peruvian mills, very few women are used any longer in spinning, most of them being employed only in manual finishing operations. In a few more years Lustrada would have ceased to be an exception to this pattern, since it ceased hiring women in 1957, two years after the higher cost squeeze became generally effective.

Another difference in Lustrada from the usual pattern noted was the employment of experienced *obreros* as well as managers and technicians. Their mechanical maintenance workers were among the best paid in Lima, although neither the manager nor the workers in question realized this.

Their plant office also was "modern" in several respects; most of the clerks were women who received lower weekly wages than the average operative although, due to steadier work, they received an equal yearly income. The best paid male accountants received the same pay as the maintenance mechanics.

In general, skilled *obreros* had more opportunity for promotion to all but the highest responsible administrative and technical jobs in Lustrada than in any other plant. This was a major factor in the high degree of job satisfaction observed in this mill. Conversely, the blockage to *empleado* positions is the primary factor in turning ambitious skilled workers in many other mills into implacable unionists.

This was the last and the least of the Lima mills to be studied. It is a marginal spinning venture operated by some of the younger scions of several wealthy and related textile-mill–owning Italian families. Like Lustrada and La Perfecta, it is financially tied in to a variety of other small and large family-owned textile spinning, weaving, and knitting plants. The building, with a few hundred spindles, had been purchased from another Italian in 1938. At that time the Banco Industrial was functioning effectively and loaned them the capital to install 2,000 more spindles and other yarn-processing equipment just before World War II shut off supplies of textile machinery. The primary function of the mill had been to provide an extremely wide range of yarn for the various firms owned by the relatives of the owners, such as the large woolen mill, El Mar, and the cotton mill, San Juanito. Mario Scaloppini, the founder's son, like the sons of most of the other non-English immigrant owners, received his university education in the United States and has recently returned very desirous of "building the place up."

Managerial Policy. In comparison with the "respectable" Lustrada, El Fideo is a back-alley "speakeasy" sweatshop which reveals no outward sign of its function. An attractive facade and an active public relations program are, to be sure, a feature of very few firms in Peru, but below the level of the average "modest" but known plants in Peru there exist many firms whose functioning is not a part of public knowledge. El Fideo had been one of these until recently. It pays low wages and has operated almost continually on a three-shift schedule. Such an operating schedule is rational from a technological and financial point of view but is very rare in Peru because of lack of demand, labor resistance, and the level of administrative efficiency and mechanical maintenance required for continuous operation. A spinning process, however, lends itself to such a schedule much more readily than an integrated mill.

The sex-stereotyping of occupations at El Fideo is unique. Men operate the basic machines, the banks of spindles (usually a female specialty), while women are limited to winding, a prespinning operation, and to operating some of the finishing machines, usually a male job.

EL MISTI

History. El Misti was started in 1895 by a Spanish (Catalán) carpenter named Miguel Lorca, turned wool exporter in Peru. The plant is located in a desolate gully about 15 kilometers outside Arequipa, Peru's second largest city (135,358 in 1961). It was well located in the prehighway days to receive raw cotton from the coast and to sell finished cloth to what was in effect a captive market in the southern third of Peru, i.e., Arequipa, Puno, and Cuzco. La Industria, as it was called under Lorca's control, enjoyed this local monopoly in cotton goods until the early twenties. Then foreign and domestic competition, and mismanagement by Lorca's squabbling sons after his death, forced the firm into the hands of its British machinery suppliers in 1932. At that time the locally owned British firm of MacGregor took control.

One of the more exotic techniques Lorca used to handle his labor problem was the importation of 50 to 100 Japanese girls under the control of a Japanese ex-army officer. They were kept by themselves in a locked dormitory in a divide-and-conquer effort to break the series of strikes and organizing effort plaguing the factory during the 1920's. Eventually, however, they all escaped to disappear into Peru's already polyglot coastal population.

Current Situation. El Misti, now under the close and aggressive supervision of a resident (in the factory itself) British manager supported by a staff of British and German technicians, presents the paradox of a mill in an extremely unfavorable location with the highest labor productivity of any plant in Peru.[4] It is the only exception to my general finding that the decentralized, isolated mills have proved to be uneconomic and hostile to industrialism in most of its cultural manifestations. Therefore, this case demands further explanation. Briefly, what has happened is that the managerial advantage of labor docility has been exploited to the limits allowed by Peru's political situation. I do not mean exploitation in a crude Marxist sense. El Misti workers are relatively well paid in view of their location. There is no company police force, nor do the local police any longer support managerial authority—not even in cases of petty robbery.

From the El Misti managerial point of view, having made most of their desired organizational changes, they are now anxious to get out from under a load of paternalistic obligations. They are trying to sell the factory-owned homes to the 150 workers who live in them (about half the labor force) and get rid of the obligations to supply free water and electricity to the others. The law is a major obstacle here, since it requires that the company maintain other services such as a school (three years of public education) and a clinic.

Another problem the management feels it faces is an "excessive" proportion of women in view of their higher cost, especially since 1956.

Their personnel policy is avowedly to hire into sections and promote up within each section by seniority and capacity except to top positions, where "technical ability only is considered." Promotions end with *maestro operario* (master operative) positions. All foremen are English. "We don't encourage bright natives. They are fine on simple repetitive work but can't plan ahead, take responsibility or initiative."

Management in El Misti also faces the problem of obtaining good Peruvian clerical help. Since they do not provide enough schooling locally, and since no middle-class *Arequi-*

---

[4] According to unpublished studies by Roger Haour, the United Nations textile expert.

peño would be willing to live in this mill town, they must transport them daily from Arequipa.

Workers' Point of View. There is no longer any unified workers' attitude toward management, if such ever existed. The most obvious division of opinion is between the old-timers, those hired before World War II, who still doff their hats each time they see *el director* (no matter how often each day), and the younger generation. The old-timers will have no part in "politics," remembering the police repressions of their youth. They also can and do compare favorably the new administration (especially since 1945) with the old Lorca regime. "A lo menos, ahora hay justicia" (At least now there is justice). The workers of the older generation also form a major part of the 30 percent who live nearby in their *chacras* and thus do have an additional source of income to fall back on.

Those of the younger generation offer no more than a formal "Buenos días" once a day. They feel they face a group of *gringos vivos* (unscrupulous gringos) who, with the help of *tinterillos criollos* ("shyster lawyers"), have somehow or other pulled a "fast one" on them. The top group of weavers, however, know that they are as well paid as Lima weavers (because they handle twice to three times as many looms[5]), and so this crucial group is somewhat mollified. All the workers at El Misti still take for granted the obstacle to promotion presented by the exclusive employment of Englishmen as foremen.

The overall effect of the El Misti management's policy has been a technical success from their point of view. One inevitable result has been the highest rate of *reclamos* (grievances) passed on to the Ministry of Labor of any textile plant in Peru. However, this laborious grievance machinery functions

[5] From the "traditional" ratio of one worker to every 4 to 8 looms the El Misti plant finally stepped the load up to one worker to 24 looms when a new shipment of the latest automatic looms arrived in 1958. They then paid their workers 40 percent extra.

so slowly that, like the situation in the United States Federal Trade Commission, which attempts to police advertising, the situation has already changed if and when any action is ever taken.

Further changes are in prospect. Within the past five years a "bus service" (an open 2½-ton truck) has finally been independently formed and offers for the first time transportation to Arequipa. Now workers spend weekends with relatives in Arequipa, and a persistent number never return from such visits. All new employees, however, are still drawn from those available near the factory. Currently the company, as in Lima, is systematically attempting to hold down the average plant seniority by fostering a higher turnover, since the cost of discharge or retirement payments rises sharply with seniority.

Labor Protest. A tantalizingly skimpy but interesting bit of data was available from El Misti—a "black book" (the *Libro negro*) kept by the Lorca management from 1907 to 1930. Assuming that the quotations cited below are a fairly full, if not an unbiased, account of their major labor problems, with the probable exception of robbery, we may draw the following speculative conclusions.

1. The early labor force was headed, in skills and in protest, by mestizos or at least acculturated *cholos*, judging from the Spanish names. Name-changing, of course, is even more common and easier for Indians in Peru than for non-Anglo-Saxon immigrants to the United States. But at the factory-worker level, even today, workers born in Indian communities with Indian names usually adopt only a Spanish Christian name, leaving the dropping of their Quechua or Aymará last name for a subsequent generation. The *serranos humildes* (humble mountain Indians) currently working in Aguilar and hired 25 years after those mentioned here, have Indian last names.

2. The majority of the "insolent, forward, ill-bred" actions of the workers appear to be "modern" types of labor protest.

254

Those clearly "reactionary" actions, i.e., a worker who returns home during harvest time, and the one who "only obeys [his] father," seem few and far between. The "rationalizers" of the labor market, those recruiting for other employers, were certainly agents of modernization.

3. The three "reactionaries" and the objectionable *serrano* from Cuzco came to El Misti or at least got into trouble between 1927 and 1930, almost 30 years after the factory opened. Perhaps, as in the Lima factories, it is the later workers who come fresh from the farm, the early recruits being largely urbanites.

No examples of organized protest crop up before 1921, the year after the Lima textile workers had successfully formed a relatively strong union and had enjoyed some temporary success in winning a promise of an eight-hour day. The two previous types of trouble are typical of the first stage of factory-labor recruitment in such countries: (1) robbery, in this case against foreign workers imported to hold down wages and increase discipline, and (2) competition for labor in 1908, the year the last leg of the nearby railroad was being completed.

A full transcription from the *Libro negro* (my translations) of all the available information on labor problems of the period follows:

1907

"Robó a las Japonesas, fué despedido" (He robbed the Japanese women, [so] he was fired).

1908

"Se fueron sin motivo, enganchando gente, dejaron 30 telares parados" (They left without reason; pirating[a] people, they left 30 looms stopped).

1921

This was the year after the creation, in Lima, of the Textile Workers Federation.

[a] Literally, "hooking."

255

"Se retiraron sin motivo alguno de la fábrica para irse a Lima, cabecillas de huelgas" (The strike leaders left the factory without any reason to go away to Lima).

1927–1930

"Martínez, Alicia, pabilera, fué la instigadora en las pabileras, dejaron el trabajo y una de las más exaltadas en el reclamo, tambien un día se oponía a que su marido Chaguilla pusiese la correa" (Martinez, Alicia, spindle-operator, was the instigator in the spinning-room of the walkout and one of the most excited in the protest;[b] also one day she objected to her husband Chaguilla's working).

"Mendoza, Antonio, pasador lizos, era uno de los que se oponía a que la gente entrase al trabajo y los silvaba en el portón" (Mendoza, Antonio, spindle-operator, was one of those who opposed the entrance of the people to work and hissed at them in the main gate).

"Veliz, Enrique Pabilero (Cuzqueño). Muy atrevido en sus reclamos y en esta vez lo mismo que en el paro anterior es el que siempre habla de sus derechos" (Veliz, Enrique, spindle-operator, Cuzcan. Very forward in his complaints, and this time, the same as in the previous stoppage, he is the one who always talks about his rights).

"Torres, Juana, insolente, muy intrusa, trató de entrar a la oficina a ver el aviso, no sabía leer, incitaba a las otras a que ellas tambien hablasen" (Torres, Juana, insolent, very aggressive, tried to enter the office to see the notice, could not read it, incited the others to complain too).

Names unavailable for this group:

"Ladrón de tocuyo, huyó en las averiguaciones" (Sheeting thief, fled during the investigations).

"Cabecilla e instigador de huelgas, estropeó a una obrera que trató de volver a su trabajo" (Leader and instigator of strikes,

---

[b] *Reclamo* today is translated as "grievance."

molested a female worker who tried to return to her work).
"Se le sorprendió tambien moviendo los relojes" (He was also
surprised changing the meters[c]).

"Insolente y malcriado en huelgas" (Insolent and ill-bred in
strikes).

"Enganchando gente de la fábrica para el Sur" (Pirating people from the factory for the South).

"Abandona su trabajo frecuentemente y viene sólo cuando
no hay labor en la chacra" (Quits work frequently and comes
only when there is no work on his farm).

"Despedido por no reconocer otro jefe que su papá" (Fired for
not recognizing any other chief than his father).

"Cabecilla huelgas, en 1930 pronunció discursos subversivos
en ambas ocasiones en el patio de la fábrica, *muy mal elemento*,
fué apresado por la prefectura el 6 de noviembre 1930" (Strike
leader, in 1930 he gave subversive speeches on two occasions
in the factory yard, *very bad element*, he was jailed by the
prefect on November 6, 1930).[d]

AGUILAR

History. In 1940 a creole family, which had moved to Lima
from their hacienda in the southern highlands, decided to
establish a wholesale wool house in Arequipa to buy from
their own and other haciendas. Their desire to export wool
after the war required the sorting and cleaning of the raw material, especially necessary in Peru's case because the herds and
hence the shearings are of mixed quality. In addition, the

[c] For measuring the amount of cloth each worker produced under the
piece-rate system.

[d] The short-term caudillo Sanchez Cerro started his revolution against
Leguía in the nearby city of Arequipa on August 22, 1930. There followed
a series of brief regimes, culminating in Sanchez Cerro's inauguration
December 8, 1931. This jailing, therefore, occurred during a period of
chaotic oligarchic re-establishment during which the labor movement
engaged in open protest after a decade of suppression.

257

government-regulated price of raw wool by weight encourages the Indians to mix as much fine sand into the greasy raw material as possible.

By 1953 the owners of this small processing plant decided to push integration to the limit by weaving their own rugs and blankets as well as selling them. The only wholesale outlet today is in Lima, run by one of the owners. The factory in Arequipa is managed by a Peruvian employee director and a mixture of marginal and refugee English, German, and Polish technicians. Among the smaller mills, this owner–manager split correlates very highly with poor management and low productivity. As was observed in Lima, smaller plants can command competent and dedicated technical and managerial talent only through using kinship obligations of the owner's family. Nepotism does not guarantee efficiency, of course, as the Cuzco mills demonstrate. Given the low salaries they offer even their foreign technicians, only those unacceptable to the Lima mills for various reasons are left over for such provincial employment. Their morale is correspondingly low.

The first weaving operation was begun in 1944 using traditional hand techniques. By 1950, however, it was decided to mechanize the process and so all the workers were fired. This was possible then because the Odría coup in 1948 had effectively suppressed the Apristas for the time being, thus giving employers, especially in the textile industry, a breathing spell from union "interference."

Currently the mill is operating near its capacity, but even so its productivity and profitability are low. This is due to its excessive degree of integration in view of its small size. It sorts, washes, spins, weaves, and finishes a wide variety of rugs, blankets, and cheap woolen cloth, preferably all on specific order. The washing machine could service a plant with three times Aguilar's capacity. Their finishing operations, an area of commercially essential mechanization today, are primitive and form a major bottleneck. Thus, the already low wages of its workers are further lowered by frequent stoppages in production which, to the outside observer, make their piece-rate system especially irrational and unjust. Frequently whole sections are idle for a day or more during the week only to be asked to work overtime when things are finally straightened out by Saturday. Only the humble patience of the majority of Aguilar's *serrano* work force prevents labor protest. They willingly work overtime to make up lost wages, or, in relatively few cases, they leave.

Managerial Policy. Aguilar's manager said, and all other evidence concurred, that he preferred *serranos* to *Arequipeños*. It was this policy, he maintained, that had given him a record of no strikes against his administration (the workers had several times gone out on sympathy strikes on behalf of one of the other textile mills in Arequipa). He made no effort, however, to recruit actively but took workers *de la calle* demanding some evidence of minimal literacy but desiring no more formal education. The manager was a soft-spoken *caballero* (gentleman), a creole well-educated in local schools whom family misfortune had forced to work out as an *empleado*. He had rather limited formal authority in view of the relative isolation of the plant from Lima. On the other hand, the Lima office demanded primarily production and labor peace. The price of the finished goods in Lima was determined by what the limited and irrational market would bear, while the price of labor in Arequipa was determined by supply and governmental intervention. The labor cost of production, and, in fact, the overall costs of production were not and, in view of the accounting procedures used, could not be calculated. Unlike the managers of the other mills, the manager of Aguilar did not live at the factory. This was quite understandable in view of his local origin, the slum location of the mill, and the fact that no house was provided him by the owners. It was consistent also with his attitude toward fringe benefits. Aguilar provides no nursery or bus service as La Inglesa does. The work most of the women do, i.e., wool-sorting in a large shed and rug trimming in a separated room, provides a natural play area for their children. The factory is close enough to Arequipa to avoid the other obligations of isolated mills, i.e., schools, hospitals, etc.

Aside from rejecting any Limenian and disfavoring *Arequipeños*, the manager also held to an informal understanding not to "pirate" workers from the other Arequipa textile mills.

Like the managements of most textile plants, Aguilar hires workers into sections and promotes them up only within these areas. Transfers within the plant are made only if a worker cannot get along with his fellows. The manager felt that in general internal transfers upset too many people—the individual, the group left behind (more work for those left?), and the group added to (Where is he coming in—at the top?). If more workers were needed, adding on at the bottom of a section from the outside made everyone happy, for it usually raised the status of those already employed.

The strongest barrier of all, as usual, was between the *obrero* and *empleado* categories. No worker had ever been promoted at Aguilar from the plant floor to the front office, although a few had been given symbolic promotions by changing to clerical work in the plant.

The Data. Unlike most textile plants, even the others I studied in Arequipa, Aguilar's personnel records were very sparse, including only birth date and place, sex, year of entrance, and salary. The labor force was so small that the management knew personally all the other relevant facts about each worker. An effective introduction from the Lima owners and, by good luck, a trusting and helpful union leader (see the following interviews), made possible the only complete use of the questionnaires. Production was stopped for an hour at a time in each section of the plant so that the union leader could explain what I wanted. Each worker then filled out the form on the spot with my help where questions were not clear to them. Some requested that they be allowed to take them home to return them filled out (presumably by someone who was more literate) the next day. Fortunately, either the union chief or I was able to elicit the necessary answers on the spot to prevent uncontrolled pressures for lying, confusion, or joking to creep in. A further advantage to this on-the-spot answering was that the workers all knew that their union *jefe* knew the answers to many of these questions, so they were intimidated into answering correctly and fully.

After this collection process had been completed, which took a day and a half, the union leader and later the personnel clerk and I checked over each form.

In addition to the data discussed in Chapter 7, I also obtained taped autobiographies of the two top union leaders in Aguilar. Their deep apoliticism, due to their having entered the labor force in the late 1940's under the anti-APRA Odría dictatorship, later won them an all-expense State Department tour to the United States. They were disturbed by the intensive cross-examination they had to undergo to ferret out any radical aspects of their careers, but they returned to Peru even more strongly pro-United States. As a result of their two-month absence and gringo views they were subsequently voted out of office.

TAPE-RECORDED INTERVIEW WITH
TWO AREQUIPENIAN LABOR LEADERS FROM AGUILAR

CHAPLIN: Does management prefer *Cuzqueños* and *Puneños* or *Arequipeños*? (The two former being *serranos* in this context and the latter from the city of Arequipa.)

MORENO: Management prefers *Cuzqueños* for the top posts. They are more humble and adapt themselves better to the foreman.

PARDO: And they don't insist, for example, on an increase in salary. On the other hand, the *Arequipeño*, he insists.

MORENO: We don't like overtime work . . . while the *serranos*, when the foreman says, "You are going to work overtime this Saturday," say, "Very well, sir. We shall work overtime." There are a lot of squealers in that group who run to the foreman or the director and say, "Sr. Alemán, this worker is a bad egg, he is disobedient, we ought to fire him."

CHAPLIN: Do you find that many workers are unhappy having to work in a factory, especially those who were independent artisans before? Do many want to leave the factory to return to their homes?

MORENO: No, on the contrary, instead of feeling worse the *serrano* he feels better; all he knows, he has learned in the factory. Those who talk of leaving want to do the same work on their own account . . . for example . . . one fellow learned how to weave rugs here, then he worked out a wire tool to do it at home. . . . Another washed rugs, and when he leaves the factory he can do it cheaper at home in competition with the factory. . . . Of course, many exaggerate about what they could do with the property they left behind. They say, "I have an hacienda in my village, and near the lake 100 llamas and 100 sheep and 50 head of cattle." We say, "You are losing time here. Go home. There no one will punish you or give you a hard time." They *do* have land, but lost land . . . arid . . . the *sequia* [drought] had caused thousands to flee to the city in search of work.

CHAPLIN: Could you give me a short history of your life?

MORENO: Well, without exaggerating much, after I had finished school, very young, my childhood was a bit sad because I lost my parents early. Then I had no one to help me. I believe that I could have made something of myself otherwise. . . . I began working as a store clerk's helper.

My father and grandfather were blacksmiths. My father used to be gone on long trips to repair mine machinery . . . but he earned very little in this way.

By the time I was eighteen, my older brother returned from the jungle. . . . He arrived with money, luxury, lots of clothes . . . as a worker in gold-workings . . . his own site. . . . It's easy to open a claim since all this unknown land belongs to the government. According to all the foreigners I met there, Canadians, North Americans, Italians, Germans . . . there's gold there. . . . It's the purest kind . . . no quartz. We call it *charpa* . . . pieces of pure gold.

When my brother said to me, "Do you want to come with me?" . . . "Delighted. I want to become rich." Thus, at eighteen I went to the jungle. We hired five peons to help us—Indians from Cuzco. (*We* are *cholos*). . . . We had to travel 150 kilometers by road and another 150 kilometers by foot. I began to work with my brother, and it turned out he was something of a tyrant. He exploited me for a year; he did not help me start my own independent operation. He thought that because I was his younger brother and a boy, I was only there to serve him. A cousin of mine was also working there as a merchant. He had a rice shop. One day he told me, "You are losing time here. Come to work for me. I shall pay you a salary and you can make yourself independent of your brother . . . make yourself a man." . . . By the time I was twenty I had saved up 1,500 soles. In those days that was real money.

I had a younger brother and two older sisters without husbands . . . so with good intentions I opened a store, a good store with a radio in it since at that time the radio had first appeared in Arequipa. . . . I wanted to be independent of the jungle but it turned out that my sisters lacked experience, and I too. . . . The first thing we knew, I did not have a shop. I returned anew to the jungle to work on my own. I had luck. I returned with 8,000 soles, got married, had a son, and opened a rice shop in Cuzco. Again, it failed. Finally I had to return to the jungle again, in 1946. I lost everything, had to work for others. I fought it out 'til 1950 in the jungle without success. Finally I got malaria . . . I had to borrow again from my brother to return to Arequipa. I returned and finally came to the factory. I was making very little until Aguilar. In this company, I began to work methodically to raise myself. Now I have two boys; my wife helps me by working to give them an education, which is my obsession.

CHAPLIN: And your story, Sr. Pardo?

PARDO: I started to work at fifteen as a telegraph messenger boy in the railroad. . . . My father was a superintendent in the railroad. I studied half a day in the industrial school and I worked half a day. Then I went to work in the carpenter shop at the Salesians School in Arequipa. . . . The next year my uncle died and my mother took in all my cousins and paid no attention to me. She did not make me matriculate into the school. Later when she tried to get me in, it was too late. I went that year without studying . . . and finally I decided to go to work. . . . Finally I came to Aguilar in 1952. Since then I have been trying to get hold of myself (poco a poco fuí controlandome para evitar el mal camino, digamos, porque todo lo que ganaba a veces derrochaba). I used to waste all that I earned . . . I was a bachelor. . . . It's the truth that one must enjoy and make the most of youth but not to extremes, because you have to save to acquire some things. . . .

The union was formed in 1952 and my first post was in 1956 as secretary of social service. In 1957 I got the job of secretary of economics. In that opportunity I did nothing, the *jefe* then did not tell me what to do, and as I did not know what unionism was about, I didn't bother. Then I met Sr. Moreno and he put me on the right path.

CHAPLIN: Would you prefer to be paid on a time or piece-rate basis?

MORENO: Well, from the point of view of experience, I believe piece rates are convenient as much for the worker as for the *patrón* himself. . . . For example, if a worker works harder he can earn more. If he works hard the boss can leave him alone. Also, there is no use working up to a strike—they only lower our already bad pay. . . . The time-rate worker (*jornalero*) is too often a worker without a conscience who just tries to pass away the time. . . . Often they are shameless. . . . We have to recognize that there is a bad element in our midst.

CHAPLIN: Have you gone on strike often?

MORENO: Happily there have never been strikes against *el patrón*. . . . There have been various strikes but always supporting other unions, since we are all affiliated to the Central Zone. . . . Another interesting thing is that the *patrón* wanted to close the factory . . . due to the intransigence of the workers . . . but we had the luck to pressure the government to refuse to leave a thousand families without work.

LA INGLESA

History. This plant, the most modern of the three Arequipa mills studied, was gradually put into operation between 1944 and 1950. Its long delay in becoming fully operational was due to the slow arrival of new machinery after the war, poor administration, foreign competition, and the simultaneous demoralization of the woolen market, which caused two of the Cuzco woolen mills to close. The owners constitute a rather large and mixed group of European-oriented, English- and German-descended Peruvians. They have the necessary political influence to back up so risky an enterprise as a factory, as well as a desire to make money primarily through efficient production and broad distribution rather than high mark-up and controlled markets. The original interests were two large commercial importing wholesale and retail houses, one German and the other English.

The plant is located one and one half miles west of Arequipa in a slum suburb, which in turn is less than a mile from the Aguilar mill. It is one of the two postwar woolen mills to be established, the other being a small Italian spinning plant in Lima; so although its wages are about the highest of any woolen factory, it should eventually be able to undersell most of the much older and less efficient mills.

Like most of the other textile firms in Peru, La Inglesa's operation involves a completely integrated spinning, weaving, and finishing process for the production of blankets and cloth in the usual wide variety of designs, qualities, and even types of wool, i.e., sheep wool as well as llama, alpaca, and vicuña.

Managerial Policy. A major change had been made in the person of the manager, which should greatly improve the firm's situation. The previous and first manager of La Inglesa was one of the ex-playboy sons of the founder of La Industria, the predecessor firm to El Misti. A worse choice could hardly have been made. The only reason for having hired him was that he had been "available" in Arequipa for such a job since La Industria failed in 1932. He had, of course, had a wing of that factory under his control for some years but with disastrous results. It is still not easy to persuade the few available competent native plant managers Peru has to leave Lima. In the case of La Inglesa the half-British, half-Peruvian and British-educated nephew of the president was talked into "going up there [8,000 feet] to straighten out the mess."

The first objective of his administration he has declared to be the elimination of paternalism. One step will be to rent, hoping to sell later, the large amount of adjacent land the factory owns to the workers who are now squatting there free of charge. In order to persuade them to collaborate, and to avoid the politically very undesirable necessity of eviction, the factory will first build the homes, thus hoping to lure the workers out of their squatter status. It would seem that he is more likely to solidify a dependent mill town situation which would burden the firm until Arequipa expansion swallows up their locale.

A further illustration of his determination to avoid paternalism was his order to all subordinate officials to avoid involvement in *compadrazgo* ties with workers. The new manager was speaking from painful recent personal experience as he went on to describe how such ties involve one in mandatory invitations to all the *compadre's* major family parties at which the *padrino* must answer all toasts, ending up "drunk on cheap wine. . . . From then on they address you familiarly and expect you to hire all their relatives . . . and they become cocky and untouchable."

When asked why he lives on the factory grounds in the former manager's home rather than in the fashionably appropriate Miraflores section of Arequipa, he replied, "Well, I'm the only one who has the authority to make decisions—even petty ones—that can arise at any time of the day or night, especially in the country. For instance, a worker is hurt on the night shift. Of course, there are some younger men we have trained who could do this too, but now that it's established, we can't easily change."

The only concrete result of a new personnel policy was evident in the office and technical staff, which had been greatly increased. The clerical positions had been de-sex-stereotyped, with the result that La Inglesa had a transitional type of office staff, i.e., the clerks with the most seniority were dark-skinned mestizo males, while the more recent employees in comparable positions were creole or very light-skinned mestizo women.

OROPESA

Background. In order to place in perspective the special situation found at Oropesa, some background on all the Cuzco mills is called for. All of the textile mills in the department of Cuzco were in such a difficult situation by 1950 that above and beyond the various studies made of the entire textile industry, a special series was undertaken of this group.[6] Up to 1950 there were only seven woolen plants in Peru; four in Cuzco, and one each in Lima, Arequipa, and Huancayo. All were over 30 years old. By 1956 four new spinning and weaving mills had been established in Lima and Arequipa which could produce a higher quality and a cheaper cloth. Three of the Cuzco factories, excluding Oropesa, had unions which refused to allow any of the estimated 30 percent of excess workers to be discharged.

Their problems, however, were technical and commercial rather than due to their labor force:

1. Wool buying was done in a costly and inefficient manner (in some cases, however, this was an administrative ruse

6 James F. Pardue and Robert S. Ray, "Report on the Textile Industry in the Department of Cuzco," Report to the Ministry of Labor and Indigenous Affairs, September 10, 1956.

to bleed capital out of manufacturing enterprises into wool haciendas belonging to the same owners).

2. The initial processing required lengthy hand-sorting for quality and slow hand-drying outdoors during the dry season of the year.

3. Distribution was solely through the four to five retail shops which each factory owner maintained, one in Cuzco, one in Lima, and the others in various sierra towns. This attempt at complete integration, so that all profits to be made fall directly into the hands of the factory owner, has apparently sharply limited their potential market. Oropesa only recently has been willing to sell at a slight wholesale discount directly from its factory door, and, notwithstanding its isolation, sales have risen.

4. Their machinery is antiquated and, lacking the combing process, can only produce a coarse, heavy grade of cloth. This type of material, however, has long suited the Indians and *cholos,* who have been the Cuzco factories' primary customers. The process of acculturation may be their real problem. Western-style clothing, one of the primary symbols of acculturation, cannot be made of such heavy, coarse material.

5. The wide variety of colors and patterns they turn out to suit the tastes which vary traditionally by region, as well as by degree of acculturation, require uneconomically short runs of production. Again each factory attempts to control its whole world by vertical integration from the sheep to the consumer. A gentleman's "cartel" agreement on specialization was implicitly recommended.

History. In September of 1861, Francisco Cortuña, a Spaniard from Catalonia like Lorca in Arequipa, finally put into operation a horse-powered, integrated woolen mill at his hacienda in Oropesa near Cuzco. It had been packed in from the coast at Islay hundreds of miles away over the Andes on mule- and llamaback. This was 50 years before the railroad which now passes five miles away from his hacienda (37 kilometers south of Cuzco) was constructed. The original French and Belgian machinery, very little of which has been replaced, still functions to turn out the same 15 colors in three different fabrics for skirts, blankets, and ponchos. The plant consisted originally of two carding machines, eight looms, and 200 spindles, to which some second-hand looms and spindles were added around the turn of the century after years of a seller's market had convinced the founder's more timid successors that such an investment would be worth the risk. Their current functioning equipment consists of 1,000 spindles and 29 mechanical (nonautomatic) looms, the latter operating with numerous wooden replacement parts.

The original technician-manager was the French installer of equipment, who was persuaded to remain. He later married the owner's daughter. The current owner and his son are the descendants of this family and by now are firmly established as a family of the creole elite in the city of Cuzco, in part owing to the flight to Lima of the longer-established Cuzco elite.

Their original market consisted of Indians and *cholos* throughout the southern part of Peru and much of Bolivia. The director's son wistfully boasted, "We outfitted the Bolivian army until 1920." Shortly before World War I, other woolen mills were established nearby, largely by Italian merchants, to cater somewhat more to the growing mestizo demand for a finer grade of woolen cloth as well as cotton cloth. Anglo-Saxon entrepreneurial efforts in textiles have never reached into the sierra beyond Arequipa.

Current Situation. The two major technological advances which have been made were the change from horsepower to water power around 1900, and the change from water power to electricity in 1950. Unfortunately, since the same small river is being used for the hydroelectric plant, the mill is still forced to cease functioning five to six months of each year as the river flow slackens. This suits the labor force, however, as it facilitates the maintenance of the fields which nearly all of the workers own or rent on the same plantation.

To those objective textile experts who had an interest, Oropesa's persistent functioning was an economic mystery. Two of the other three nearby woolen mills had closed within the previous five years, presumably facing the same market and cost conditions. Oropesa's machinery made the factory a living museum. The looms were among the earliest mechanical looms exported to Latin America. The spindles ("mules") were one of the earliest models, which, in addition to their non-human-powered rotary action, required several men to push a frame of spools on a track toward and away from the main, bolted-down part of the machine every 30 seconds. The picking machine which tears at blanketing to give it a fluffy surface was coated not with the usual wire brushes but with the tacked-on spiny husks of an imported Spanish nut which now grows outside the factory doors. There were thus seven extra men having jobs that did not exist at any other mill, whose duty it was constantly to replace the husks, the spines of which often stayed with the blanket instead of on the machine. This, of course, created yet another job for the *revisadoras*, the women who inspected finished products. They had to watch out for the spines. Notwithstanding their efforts, one of their customers' persistent complaints deals with *espinas dentro la frazada* (spines in the blanket). Unfortunately, the company which once made the proper wire brushes has long since gone out of existence (as is true of the makers of much of their other equipment).

The work loads on the looms were the most striking feature of Oropesa's organization. In Santa María in Lima, the lowest load was four semi-automatic looms to a worker. In Oropesa each loom enjoyed the complete attention of three workers, the weaver and his two assistants. As a further example of Oropesa's inefficiency, we have the following from the Ray-Pardue report. The raw-wool-sorting process is made even less efficient because "selection in Oropesa is made on a platform outside the warehouse [which] is very narrow thus impeding the deposition of large quantities which could be worked at the same time. . . . [Moreover] the selection area is some distance from the washing tank, which requires additional personnel to transport the [seven different types of] wool."

The workers at Oropesa, however, take all this for granted. Oropesa is very much at "the end of the line." Only 8 of the 130 males and none of the female workers came from outside the plantation village. Two hundred of these work regularly on the hacienda itself, either in the fields or as one of the 18 virtually unpaid domestic servants (*pongos*) employed in and around *la casa grande* (the main house). The hacienda bakery, a charcoal-heated brick oven tended by an artisan baker and eight of his family and relatives, turns out over 1,000 small loaves a day for sale to the village as well as for the owner's consumption.

Unlike the practice at all the other textile plants in Peru, the owner-manager lives at the plant. In some other cases, i.e., El Misti and La Inglesa in Arequipa and El Indio and Santa María in Lima, hired managers live very near the factories— but the owners never do. This "personal touch" is perhaps the secret of Oropesa's "success" in avoiding bankruptcy. Of course, a major problem is the question of the firm's actual solvency. The owner-manager mixes together the operations of the factory, the hacienda, and several of his other businesses in such a way that it is impossible for him to tell which enterprise is subsidizing which. Generally such mixed "empires" function deliberately to drain profits out of politically observable enterprises such as a factory into real estate or trading firms. In this case the flow may be reversed, since the machinery, of course, was amortized over half a century ago, with the exception of the miniature hydroelectric plant.

Oropesa's success specifically rests in large part on the administration's strategy in maintaining its cultural as well as physical isolation. Until a few years ago, no school existed in the factory town, which by law is the owner's responsibility. The school now there functions very irregularly, offering education, in practice, only in Quechua. The owner as a matter of policy speaks to workers only in Quechua, even in those cases where the worker does speak Spanish. This policy paid off most dramatically during the wave of strikes in 1956 which the Aprista-backed textile unions staged at some of the nearby mills shortly after the end of the Odría dictatorship. Since that time, officials from the Ministry of Labor, rather than organizing agents of the union, have repeatedly tried to enforce unionization from the outside. Each time they have been met by the workers with a "signed" declaration to the government asking to be left out of wage increases and the *pachamanca* (mess) of unionization. Their weekly wages remain the equivalent of a day's income of workers in Arequipa, which in turn is lower than in Lima.

Another related facet of Oropesa's administrative policy is that today there are no foreign or even Peruvian "outside" technicians or managers with a technical training or education. The owner and his son run the factory with the help of locally born foremen.

The most highly paid workers at Oropesa are not the loom mechanics or any of the machine operators but the general overseers, whose duties range from guarding the doors against the unauthorized exit of workers, usually with stolen goods, or the entrance of any outsiders, to keeping track of the individual production of those paid on a piece-rate basis. In the absence of the owner or his son, they exercise managerial authority over their sections, but when either of *los señores* is present they take over from rather than working through these overseers. At various times in Oropesa's history, outside technicians were employed, but never to the satisfaction of the owner's family or apparently of those employees who were accustomed to working for absentee creole employers. In effect each stayed long enough to teach a few workers new skills or to temporarily upgrade the level of existing ability. Currently, in view of the salary offered and the reputation of the mill, it is no wonder that the owners have not been able to secure a new *técnico*. They are not, however, trying very hard to find one. "When one leaves, he always takes my best weavers with him," reported the owner's son.

Another crucial factor in Oropesa's isolation is the factory's shortened work year which allows—or requires—all of the workers to have *chacras* to fall back on. The price the factory pays for this policy is the high rate of absenteeism and turn-over that has so often been written of as a universal early-recruitment-stage problem. Here, however, we have an arrested state of commitment which has the sanction of one hundred years of operation. Of course, even this limited factory experience and these low wages encourage some workers to seek better textile-factory jobs. "Somos la escuela textil del Perú" (we are the textile school of Peru), boasted the owner. Each year they have lost about ten of their best younger apprentice weavers and machine operators, primarily to the other nearby mills, especially the woolen mill in the city of Cuzco. Spontaneously they have evolved an "up or out" system of promotions. Most of the weavers entered younger than the average worker and have as usual a seniority surpassed only by the manual artisans (carpenters, masons, plumbers, etc.) on the plant payroll and master mechanics.

Instead of a formal retirement system, those male workers too old for anything else are maintained as *secadores* (dryers). They spread and stir the washed raw wool and later the dyed yarn on a concrete patio to dry in the sun, since the factory has never installed drying machinery. This can be done during the five- to six-month dry season when the factory is idle due to the drying up of the stream on which they have always depended for power.

In addition to this exodus of skilled workers and the annual prolonged "vacations" which provide natural opportunities for changing personnel, the Oropesa management is also able to lay off and hire at will, unlike almost any other plant in Peru today. Here the manager's authority is paternal in every sense. His most reliable source of clerical help in this isolated location is the "pool" of locally born mestizo children. He also enjoys *padrino* relationships with most of his older factory workers and domestics. All hats are doffed and all conversation ceases when he enters the factory, and those spoken to bow slightly. All in all it would appear that a genuinely happy and stable situation has been established. The annual exodus takes care of those who cannot take this type of life, leaving behind those who resignedly or positively accept it.

Discipline against modern types of labor protest, therefore, is not a problem. The manager's greatest headaches are alcohol and coca-leaf chewing. The latter he personally feels more strongly about because it is a constant habit, although this drug does not create addicts. In this respect he differs from most Andean *hacendados*, who pay their peons in part in coca leaves.[7] Therefore, he forbids its use, with only moderate success. Apparently some "guilty" Indians have made themselves sick by having to swallow large wads of leaves for fear of being caught during unexpected visits. Alcohol, on the other hand, is only a periodic abuse too well integrated into the "fiesta complex" to be successfully combatted. Moreover, it is associated with a very low rate of alcoholism.[8]

[7] W. W. Stein, *Hualcan: Life in the Highlands of Peru* (Ithaca, N.Y.: Cornell University Press, 1961), p. 59.

[8] William Mangin, "Drinking among Andean Indians," *Quarterly Journal of Studies on Alcohol*, XVIII (1958), 55-66.

Methodological Procedures and Problems

THE SAMPLE

A total of 3,918 "biographies" of currently employed workers was obtained in 13 mills, nine in Lima, three in Arequipa, and one near Cuzco. In every case but that of La Inglesa in Arequipa, this represented all of the workers currently employed. (In this latter case a representative sample was studied.) This information was obtained in a majority of cases from the personal documents kept in each worker's file, a Peruvian custom of great utility to any labor researcher. These documents usually include (1) birth certificate, (2) school certificate, and (3) job recommendations, especially from the previous employer. Birth certificates are especially rich sources for research, since the occupations, ages, and residence of the parents are called for, as well as the occupation of "witnesses," in addition to information on siblings.

Access to these files required far more than a self-presentation. Once the rather considerable barriers of suspicion and the Peruvian restraint when dealing with strangers was overcome, all desired information (and more) was made available. A usual question, in effect a trap, was, "Can you tell me how I stand relative to 'X' Company?" Whether intended consciously or not as a test of my professional ability to keep confidential anything I learned, I viewed it as such. There is very little communication between textile mills at any level in Peru.

Estimation of Coverage. Just as it is difficult to determine what proportion of the manufacturing sector could legitimately be called factory workers, it is also a matter of conjecture as to what portion my sample was of the total 1959 Peruvian textile factory labor force. The census bureau employs two definitions which refer to textiles—one to economic activities and the other to occupations. The latter probably comes closest to the relevant universe.

The 1961 census lists 12,481 workers in textile spinning, weaving, and finishing operations for the department of Lima (21 percent of whom were women). Under the parallel occupational category there appear 13,746 workers (23 percent female) for the department of Lima. Very roughly this suggests that the sample of 3,043 Lima–Callao textile factory workers included at least 25 percent of this universe. It should be recalled, however, that this was a purposive sample in that it covered all but one of the large mills. It was not intended to represent the entire industry, defined as spinning, weaving, and finishing (not knitting mills, garment shops, etc.) but rather to cover the largest plants as presumably the "most industrial."

In Arequipa three of the four mills were covered. In Cuzco one of the five mills was visited in 1959. Two of the others had recently ceased operations, and the two other functioning mills were not available for personnel analysis owing to an understanding between the owner and his Communist union chief. The latter objected to any "spying on his men."

The only other functioning textile mills in Peru in 1959 were a woolen mill in Huancayo and a cotton mill in Sullana. Neither was visited, but they are known to be small and inefficient.

THE "SNAPSHOT" PROBLEM

One phase of this study appears to involve a cardinal sin in social analysis, namely, an attempt to describe the history of real cohorts from the residual survivors available for enumeration in the factories in 1959. This problem is most salient with reference to our observation that there is a secular rise in the age on employment of all Limenian workers and a decline in the case of provincials. Of course, the survivors in 1959 of those hired before 1920 will be only those hired younger than the average age on employment in that period. The only survivors of the American Civil War to live past 1950 were the drummer boys who were too young to have fought.

To counter the irrefutable charge that in principle this is a prime statistical error, I would like to state the following:

A. For two mills, Garibaldi and La Plata, data are available on all workers ever employed.

B. Most of our analysis concentrates on differentials between various groups with the same seniority, thus partially controlling for the temporal factor.

C. No firm generalizations are made which would be affected by this problem unless they seem justified in a wide variety of firms (thus making it unlikely that so constant a pattern arose by chance) and on the basis of other information.

For instance, we should go more deeply into the matter of the rising age on employment. This generalization, of course, requires some modification with reference to the extent of the rise due to the effect of age attrition. However, it is the fact of the rise, not its extent, which is of primary interest. The supporting and, in such a case, the crucial evidence for this idea is the following:

1. Descriptive material on the history of these firms referring to the employment of many children under 15, especially before 1920.

2. The existence today of some 40 workers out of our sample of some 1,500 from the older mills who were hired under age 15, whereas no workers hired after 1945 were so young.

3. A great deal of material on labor laws and social policy which indicates that a number of age-raising factors are now at work, such as education and the strict prohibition of child labor in all the mills studied except Oropesa in Cuzco.

4. The existence of a contrary trend in spite of the effect of age attrition. Provincial migrants entered at a higher age in the past than today—even though many arrived in Lima young enough to have been employed at the same age as *Limeños*. In some cases a clear decline is evident; in others we can see only an irregular variation around a level usually higher than the age on arrival of Lima males. In this case what we have is a slight decline counterbalanced by the effect of age attrition.

Consequently, our longitudinal generalizations are essentially based on data supplementary to our surviving cohorts, while the statistical material is used primarily to observe variations between the sexes by origin and occupation, holding age or seniority constant.

THE USE OF THE MEDIAN

All of the averages employed in this analysis are medians unless otherwise stated. The rules followed in deciding on the value of a median were as follows:

A. If the distribution was approximately "normal" and consisted of an odd number of workers, a whole number appears. In the case of an even number of workers, the difference between their ages was halved, sometimes resulting in a decimal of 0.5.

B. If the distribution was markedly bimodal, a slash was used, such as 18/38, in which each age was the median for its part of the distribution.

THE CODING OF OCCUPATIONS

The textile factory occupations were coded as follows:

WEAVERS: All regular loom operators excluding their assistants, if any, who were placed in the operatives' helper category.

OPERATIVE: The most conglomerate category but consistently restricted to workers directly responsible for and tied to a machine which was part of the main flow of materials. The majority are spinning-frame operators.

MECHANICAL MAINTENANCE: All of these workers repaired machinery and set up looms for new runs of cloth. This category was restricted to highly skilled workers who were not machine tenders but who, nevertheless, were not traditional artisans, such as masons or carpenters.

OPERATIVE'S HELPER: This is a category which unavoidably mixed together those already slated to become weavers with those who would be limited to operative positions. In most mills recruits move directly into the department where they will ordinarily spend their entire careers.

LIGHT MANUAL WORKER: This group consists of seamstresses, finished-cloth inspectors, and stockroom clerks.

PEON: This category consists of janitors and yard men for cleaning and pushing hand carts of materials from one stage of processing to the next.

A NOTE ON THE USE OF THE 1940 AND 1961 CENSUSES

A census is a politically sensitive document in any country but especially so in an underdeveloped nation. In the Peruvian case there are two outstanding biases which are relevant to present interests. The definitions lead to highly inflated urban and manufacturing populations. In the former case any capital of any district, no matter how small, is automatically urban. In the case of the 1940 census the imposition of a 2,500 cut-off point reduced the percent urban from the official 36 percent to a more realistic 18 percent.

In the case of manufacturing it is clear that the bulk of the workers in this category are not factory workers but rather manual artisans. But both censuses make it very difficult to separate these two groups. The 1961 census does explicitly define some textile workers as factory workers and others as artisans but leaves a third group undefined. Apparently only about 22,000 of the 71,000 employed textile workers are factory workers. In other occupations it is difficult to come to as close an estimate. It seems evident that there is a desire to inflate those indices which would make Peru appear more developed than it is.

Another problem of great importance to a study of urbanization and industrialization in Peru is the legal separation of the Lima–Callao metropolitan area. Callao was allowed "home rule" to satisfy its community pride, with the result that all national compilations of data require the reuniting of the province or city of Lima with Callao if a valid view of Peru's major city is to be obtained. This is especially necessary in any study of internal migration. (See footnotes to Table 2.) A discussion of some of the other problems involved in using Peruvian migration data is contained in Juan C. Elizaga, "Assessment of Migration Data in Latin America," *Milbank Memorial Fund Quarterly*, XLIII, No. 1 (January 1965), 90-91.

THE ANNUAL REGISTER OF MANUFACTURING ESTABLISHMENTS

As explained in Chapter 7, the Annual Registers of Manufacturing Establishments vary in coverage from year to year and in any year among the various government agencies which publish data on this sector. Ideally the censuses of 1940 and 1961 provide an enumeration of the entire universe from which these rather capricious samples are drawn. However, the working definitions of an establishment also vary, owing partly to an unfortunate lack of collaboration among statistics-publishing agencies in Peru and partly to the peculiarities of corporate structure. The primary problems are the following: (1) The data are obtained from voluntary reports from employers. (2) Because of the use of *acciones al portador* (bearer stock) it would be a matter of commercial espionage to determine the ownership of a firm. Therefore, it is extremely difficult to link together correctly for meaningful analysis all the parts of one manufacturing enterprise. In the case of some textile firms, for instance, the spinning, weaving, and finishing plants may all be officially autonomous firms although they occupy the same or adjacent buildings. Moreover, the clerical staff for this complex may or may not be housed in the same location. In addition, a varying number of *empleados* may, in fact, be spending some or all of their time doing work for a completely unrelated enterprise belonging to the same owner. The factory then may be either missing *empleados* or burdened with some who should really be attributed to a different organization. In the latter case, the owners are deliberately subsidizing the outside activity from the textile payroll.

The *Primer censo nacional económico 1963* is explicitly a survey of *buildings* in which manufacturing operations are taking place and not enterprises. Yet the data presented— number of white- and blue-collar workers, salaries and wages, horsepower, gross value of production, costs and value added— make sense only as part of a corporate enterprise. Like the annual registers, it was not an enumeration by government employes but still a mail survey requiring employer collaboration. The results were described, in the introduction to the census, as burdened by "the reluctance of the major part of the enterprisers to provide the statistical information requested, the deficiency of accounting procedures, and the lack of statistical consciousness. . . ." Unlike the censuses of 1940 and 1961, no estimates of underenumeration were offered.

THE TURNOVER INDEX

Although social change is a major theoretical and empirical concern in sociology, a standardized index of organization turnover has yet to be developed. Most of the work on turnover has been done by labor economists and has been oriented largely around the Bureau of Labor Statistics monthly survey.

The history of turnover indices is reviewed by E. Y. Hartshorne in a pace-setting article in 1940.[1] Early efforts in this

[1] E. Y. Hartshorne, "Metabolism Indices and the Annexation of Austria: A Note on Method," *American Journal of Sociology*, XLV, No. 6 (May 1940), 899-917.

direction confused absenteeism with turnover and focused only on the "managerial problem" of those leaving rather than studying the arrivals as well. Subsequently, distinctions were made between different types of separations, with the basic distinction being the degree of voluntariness. To date no comparable distinction is yet made in accessions except for that of new hires/rehires in the Bureau of Labor Statistics series, even though equally significant differences exist here. However, in the case of both flows it has proved difficult on a mass survey basis to agree on definitions and obtain detailed information.

The most basic problem, of course, is that no single manner of constructing an index is likely to be relevant to everyone interested in the general problem of organizational change. Those studying organizational structure might focus more on voluntary separations as a problem for the organization, whereas anyone interested primarily in career patterns or unemployment is more concerned with involuntary turnover. In this respect the BLS series is helpful in that it offers two types of accessions and two types of layoffs.

In addition, as Parnes notes, "The proportion of *workers* who separate from jobs during a year is always smaller than the proportion of jobs from which separations have been

---

A separate and more recent discussion of turnover methodology, unfortunately limited entirely to British sources, can be found in H. Silcock, "The Phenomenon of Labour Turnover," *Journal of the Royal Statistical Society*, Series A, Vol. 117, Part 4 (1954), pp. 429-440. The author requests that British industry go beyond the formula:

$$\frac{100 \times \text{number of leavers in a year}}{\text{average number of persons employed during the year}}$$

His suggestions are interesting. He proposes an analogy with a life table, but this would require data not readily available. Also, some of the statistical assumptions underlying his formula reflect social beliefs about "drifters . . . misfits . . . industrial nomads" which assume that labor "wastage" is much more the responsibility of labor than management. Perhaps so in England, but certainly not in the case of Lima's textile workers.

made, for a minority of mobile workers account for a substantial majority of all job changes."[2] Since I am concerned
with job changes in firms, I am therefore concerned with the
larger number. Parnes concludes that in the period 1937 to
1950 between a fourth and a third of all workers changed
jobs voluntarily or otherwise.[3]

The problems which especially concerned Hartshorne were
(1) to develop an index which in one number reflected all
changes and (2) to obtain numerical results which "made
sense"—in particular to have a 100 percent turnover result
only when none of the original members of the organization
survived the period in question. All of the earlier indices
then in use would yield an apparent complete replacement,
i.e., 100 percent turnover with far less than a complete change
of personnel. His resolution of this problem is as follows:

$$\text{Turnover} = \frac{L + A}{G_0 + G_1} \times 100$$

where L equals leavers, A equals arrivals, G_0 equals the size
of the group at the start of the period, and G_1 equals its size
at the end. This index combines accession rates and separation
rates to give a total picture of change such that 100 represents
a complete replacement of personnel. There is thus a "complete correspondence between common sense expectation and
algebraic description." Such, however, is not the case. Suppose
an organization experienced the following "100% turnover":

$$\frac{100 + 100}{100 + 100} = 1.00 \times 100 = 100\%$$

This could have arisen from having all the leavers come from
that year's arrivals, thus by no means signifying a complete
replacement of personnel. Hartshorne's final index, a stability

[2] Herbert S. Parnes, "The Labor Force and the Labor Market," in H. G.
Heneman, Jr. (ed.), *Employment Relations Research* (New York: Harper
& Bros., 1960), p. 17.
[3] *Loc. cit.*

index, could be viewed as a solution to this problem. It is defined as follows:

$$\text{S.I.} \ = \ \frac{2\,R}{G_0 + G_1} \ \times \ 100$$

in which R is the stable remainder. However, the author's discussion of this "stable remainder" does not make it clear whether he defines it as those who remain of all who arrived that year, or those who remain of all who were already members at the start of the period—or both. Since he defines stability as complete (100%) if $R = G_0 = G_1$, it is still not clear how the leavers were recruited—from that year's arrivals or previous members.

In view of this ambiguity and the fact that comparability with Bureau of Labor Statistics data rules out a valid assessment of the "stable remainder," the turnover index was used instead, although a valid stability index would be preferred for purposes of evaluating organizational continuity.

There remain, however, limitations in this turnover index which it seems can only be handled by simultaneously presenting its component parts. For instance, there are three very different situations, each of which yields a turnover ratio of 0.5. If an organization doubles or halves in size or experiences accessions and replacements amounting to half of the combined starting and finishing populations, the same 0.5 figure results, viz:

A. Doubling

$$\frac{100 + 20}{80 + 160} = (+)\,0.5$$

B. Halving

$$\frac{20 + 100}{160 + 80} = (-)\,0.5$$

C. Balanced heavy turnover with no change in size (and possible complete stability among those already employed)

$$\frac{50 + 50}{100 + 100} = 0.5$$

One could of course impose, in a mathematically improper manner, a plus sign in Case A, a minus sign in B, and no sign or a novel one in C indicating its constancy in the face of change.

Bibliography

I. Peru

ADAMS, RICHARD N. *A Community in the Andes: Problems and Progress in Muquiyauyo.* Seattle: University of Washington Press, 1959.

———. "Change from Caste to Class in a Peruvian Sierra Town," *Social Forces,* XXXI (1953), 238-244.

———. "A Study of Labor Preference in Peru," *Human Organization,* X (Fall 1951), 37-38.

ALAYZA PAZ SOLDÁN, FRANCISCO. *La industria moderna.* Lima: Imprenta Torres Aguirre, 1927.

ALMENARA, GUILLERMO. "Causas y efectos del éxodo rural," *Informaciones sociales* (La Caja Nacional de Seguro Social del Perú), Año IX, No. 2 (April, May, June 1954).

ANDREA, JULIO DE. "La industria textil algodonera en el Perú," *Industria peruana,* September 1953, pp. 536-539.

ARCA PARRO, ALBERTO. *El medio geográfico y la población del Perú.* Lima: 1945.

———. "La ciudad capital de la república y el censo nacional de 1940," *Estadística peruana,* Año I, No. 1 (January 1945), 26-35.

ARCE MÁS, YOLANDA. "La composición familiar de los obreros textiles de Vitarte." Tesis de bachillerato de la Escuela de Servicio Social, Lima, 1945.

BARRIENTOS CASOS, LUÍS FELIPE. *Los tres sindicalismos.* Lima: Ediciones Continente, 1958.

BASADRE, FEDERICO. *Comparación entre ferrocarriles y caminos en el Perú.* Lima: Sociedad de Ingenieros, 1927.

BASADRE, JORGE. "El Perú actual," *Tierra firme* (Madrid), No. 3 (1935), 51-53.

———. *Meditaciones sobre el destino histórico del Perú.* Lima: Ediciones Huascaran, 1947.

————. *La multitud, la ciudad, y el campo.* Lima: Editorial Huascaran, 1947.

————. *La promesa de la vida peruana.* Lima: Librería Editorial Juan Mejía Baca, 1958.

BEALS, CARLETON. *Fire on the Andes.* New York: Lippincott, 1934.

BELAUNDE, VICTOR ANDRES. *Peruanidad.* Lima: Ediciones Studium, 1957.

————. *La realidad nacional.* Paris: Le Livre Libre, 1931.

BOURRICAUD, FRANÇOIS. "Algunas características originales de la cultura mestiza en el Perú contemporáneo," *Revista del Museo Nacional* (Lima), XXIII (1954), 162-173.

————. "Castas y clases en Puno," *Revista del Museo Nacional* (Lima), XXXII (1963), 308-321.

————. "Changements à Puno," *Étude de sociologie andine.* Institut des Hautes Études de l'Amérique Latine, 1962.

————. "Syndicalisme et politique: le cas Peruvien," *Sociologie du travail,* III, No. 4 (October–December, 1961), 33-49.

BOWMAN, ISAIAH. *The Andes of Southern Peru.* New York: Henry Holt, 1916.

BRADFIELD, STILLMAN. "Some Occupational Aspects of Migration," *Economic Development and Cultural Change,* XIV (October 1965), 69.

BRIONES, GUILLERMO, AND MEJÍA VALERA, JOSÉ. *El obrero industrial: aspectos sociales del desarrollo económico en el Perú.* Lima: Universidad Nacional Mayor de San Marcos, 1964.

BURGESS, EUGENE W., AND HARBISON, FREDERICK H. *Casa Grace in Peru.* Washington: National Planning Association Series on United States Business Performance Abroad, 1954.

BUSTAMANTE Y RIVERO, JOSÉ LUÍS. *Tres años de lucha por la democracia en el Perú.* Buenos Aires: 1949.

CANNON, MARY M. *Women Workers in Peru.* Women's Bureau Bulletin No. 213. Washington, D.C.: United States Department of Labor, 1943.

CAPASSO PERILLA, ROMANO. "Mercados reales y mercados potenciales del Perú." Unpublished Ph.D. dissertation, Department of Economic and Commercial Science, Catholic University, Lima, 1959.

CAPUÑAY, MANUEL A. *Leguía*. Lima: 1952.

CAREY, JAMES. *Peru and the United States, 1900–1962*. Notre Dame, Ind.: University of Notre Dame Press, 1964.

CASTRO POZO, HILDEBRANDO. *El yanaconaje en las haciendas Piuranas*. Lima: 1947.

————. "Social and Economic-Political Evolution of the Communities of Central Peru," in *Handbook of South American Indians*, ed. Julian Steward (Bureau of American Ethnology Bulletins, No. 143). Washington, D.C.: 1946, II, 483-499.

CAVANAUGH, JOSEPH A. *Socio-Demographic Characteristics of Lima, Peru*. United States Interoffice Publications, published in Peru by technical assistance operations, Foreign Operations Administration, June 8, 1955.

CHANG-RODRÍGUEZ, EUGENIO. *La literatura política de González Prada, Mariátegui y Haya de la Torre*. Mexico: Ediciones de Andres, 1957.

CHAPLIN, DAVID. "Industrialization and the Distribution of Wealth in Peru." Research Paper No. 18, Land Tenure Center, University of Wisconsin, August 1966.

————. "Industrial Labor Recruitment in Peru," *América Latina*, año 9, IV (October-December 1966).

CHIRINOS SOTO, ENRIQUE. *Contradicción entre los hechos y los textos en la historia del Perú*. Lima: Primer Panorama de Ensayistas Peruanos, 1958.

CHOCANO, EDUARDO A. *El desenvolvimiento comercial e industrial del Perú*. Lima: Sociedad Nacional de Industria y Asociación de Comerciantes, 1925.

CLAGUE, CHRISTOPHER. "Economic Efficiency in Peru and the United States." Unpublished Ph.D. dissertation, Department of Economics, Harvard University, 1966.

COLE, J. P. "Crecimiento de la Gran Lima," *La Prensa*, 5 January 1958, p. 8.

————. *Estudio geográfico de la Gran Lima*. Lima: Oficina Nacional de Planeamiento y Urbanismo, 1957.

————. "Geografía urbana del Perú," *Revista del Museo Nacional* (Lima), XXIV (1955), 50-80.

CORDOVA U., ADOLFO. *La vivienda en el Perú*. Lima: Comisión para la Reforma Agraria y la Vivienda, 1958.

CORONADO S., PEDRO P. "Génesis, evolución y estado actual de la legislación social peruana," *Revista de la Facultad de Ciencias Económicas y Comerciales* (Universidad Nacional Mayor de San Marcos, Lima), No. 9 (August 1937).

COSÍO, FÉLIX. "Realidad y ficción de las comunidades indígenas," *Peru Indígena*, II (June 1952), 212-215.

COSTA L., FEDERICO. "Perú: país sin gerencia," *La Prensa*, 19 September 1958, p. 7.

CUADROS, CARLOS FERDINAND. *Las relaciones individuales de trabajo en la legislación social peruana*. Cuzco: Ediciones del Centro de Estudios Jurídicos, 1959.

DAVENPORT, JOHN. "Why Peru Pulls Dollars," *Fortune*, LIV (November 1956), 130-134.

DE ANGELI, GIORGIO. "Ensayo sobre la industrialización del Perú." Unpublished Ph.D. dissertation, Department of Economic and Commercial Science, Universidad Nacional Mayor de San Marcos, Lima, 1947.

DE LA BARRA, GENERAL FELIPE. *La abolición del tributo por Castilla y su repercusión en el problema del indio peruano*. Lima: Ministerio de Guerra, 1956.

DELMAS, GLADYS. "The Paradox of Peru," *Reporter*, XIX (September 18, 1958), 30.

DE LUCA, RICHARD J. "Glossary of Terms used in Land Tenure and Related Labor Situations in Peru." Land Tenure Center, University of Wisconsin. Mimeographed.

ESCOBAR M., GABRIEL. "El mestizaje en la región Andina: el caso del Perú," *Revista de Indias* (Madrid), Nos. 95-96 (January–June 1964), 197-220.

FEDERACIÓN DE TRABAJADORES EN TEJIDOS DEL PERÚ. Issues of *Obrero Textil*, 1958–1959.

————. *Planificación sindical del gremio textil.* Lima: 1958.

FERRERO, RAÚL R., AND SCUDELLARI, CARLOS. *El derecho del trabajo en el Perú.* Lima: Centro de Estudios Económicos y Sociales, 1955.

————. *Legislación social del Perú y otros países de América Latina.* Lima: 1954.

FERRERO, ROMULO A. *Tierra y población en el Perú.* Lima: Banco Agrícola del Perú, 1938.

FERRERO, ROMULO A., AND ALTMAYER, ARTHUR J. *Estudio económico de la legislación social peruana y sugerencias para su mejoramiento.* Lima: 1957.

FORD, THOMAS R. *Man and Land in Peru.* Gainesville, Fla.: University of Florida Press, 1955.

FOX, K. V. "Pedro Muñiz, Dean of Lima, and the Indian Labor Question," *Hispanic American Historical Review,* XLII (1962), 63-88.

FRIED, JACOB. "Acculturation and Mental Health Among Indian Migrants in Peru," in *Culture and Mental Health,* ed. K. Opler. New York: Macmillan, 1959.

GARAYAR, GREGORIO. "Necesidad de una política de desarrollo," *El Comercio,* 1 February 1959.

GARCÍA FRÍAS, ROQUE. "Crecimiento de la población de Lima, ciudad, capital," *Estadística peruana,* Año I, No. 1 (January 1945), 55-59.

————. "Intensidad absoluta y relativa de la emigración provinciana al departamento de Lima," *Estadística peruana,* Año III, No. 5 (July 1947), 54-66.

GARLAND, ALEJANDRO. *Reseña industrial del Perú.* Lima: 1905.

HAMMEL, EUGENE A. "Wealth, Authority and Prestige in the Ica Valley, Peru." Unpublished Ph.D. dissertation, Department of Anthropology, University of California, Berkeley, 1959.

HAOUR, ROGER. *Estudio sobre la modernización de la industria textil en el Perú.* Lima: United Nations, Oficina de Operaciones de Asistencia Técnica, 1959.

————. *Informe preliminar sobre la industria textil peruana.* Lima: 1958.

HAYA DE LA TORRE, RAÚL. *Treinta años de Aprismo.* Mexico D.F.: Fondo de Cultura Económica, 1956.

HERMAN S., MAURICIO M. "Tipo de ingreso medio y distribución del presupuesto familiar del empleado en Lima." Unpublished Ph.D. dissertation, Department of Economic Science, Catholic University, Lima, 1954.

HERNÁNDEZ URBINO, ALFREDO. *Los partidos y la crisis del Apra.* Lima: Ediciones Raíz, 1956.

INSTITUTE OF INTER-AMERICAN AFFAIRS. *Industrial Hygiene Problems in Peru.* Washington, D.C.: 1947.

INTERNATIONAL BANK OF RECONSTRUCTION AND DEVELOPMENT. *The Current Economic Position and Prospects of Peru.* Report No. WH-70, February 26, 1958.

KANTOR, HARRY. *The Ideology and Program of the Peruvian Aprista Movement.* Berkeley: University of California Press, 1953.

KIRCHHOFF, PAUL. "The Social and Political Organization of the Andean Peoples," in *Handbook of South American Indians,* ed. Julian Steward (Bureau of American Ethnology Bulletins, No. 143), Washington, D.C.: 1946, II, 293-311.

KLEIN-SAX ECONOMIC MISSION TO PERU. Series of mimeographed reports to the Peruvian government, 1949–1951.

KUBLER, GEORGE. *The Indian Caste of Peru, 1795–1940.* Washington, D.C.: Smithsonian Institution, Institute of Social Anthropology, 1952, No. 14.

————. "The Quechua in the Colonial World," in *Handbook of South American Indians,* ed. Julian Steward (Bureau of American Ethnology Bulletins, No. 143). Washington, D.C.: 1946, II, 331-410.

KUCZYNSKI-GODARD, MAXIME. *Disección del indigenismo peruano.* Lima: Ministerio de Salud Pública y Asistencia Social, 1948.

————. *Estudio familiar, demográfico ecológico, en estancias indias de altiplanicie del Titicaca (Ichupampa)*. Lima: Ministerio de Salud Pública y Asistencia Social, 1945.

————. *Estudios médico-sociales en minas de Puno con anotaciones sobre las migraciones indígenas*. Lima: Ministerio de Salud Pública y Asistencia Social, 1945.

————. *La vida bifronte de los campesinos Ayacuchanos*. Lima: Ministerio de Salud Pública y Asistencia Social, 1949.

LAGUNA BENAVIDES, GERARDO. *Prontuario textil*. Lima: Federación de Trabajadores en Tejido, 1958.

LEGUÍA, AUGUSTO B. *Yo tirano, yo ladrón*. Lima: Editorial Ahora, S.A., n.d. (about 1930).

LONGMORE, WILLIAM, AND LOOMIS, CHARLES P. "Health Needs and Potential Colonization Areas of Peru," *Interamerican Economic Affairs*, III (1949), 71-93.

LÓPEZ, RENÉ HOOPER. *Leguía*. Lima: Ediciones Peruanas, 1964.

MACLEAN Y ESTENÓS, ROBERTO. *Democracia*. Lima: 1926.

————. *Sociología peruana*. Lima: 1942.

MANGIN, WILLIAM P. "Estratificación social en el Callejón de Huaylas," *Revista del Museo Nacional* (Lima), XXV (1956), 174-189.

————. "Haciendas, Comunidades and Strategic Acculturation in the Peruvian Sierra." Unpublished Ph.D. dissertation, Department of Anthropology, Yale University, 1950.

————. "The Role of Regional Associations in the Adaptation of Rural Population in Peru," *Sociologus*, I (1959), 23-35.

MARIÁTEGUI, JOSÉ CARLOS. *Siete ensayos de interpretación de la realidad peruana*. Lima: Biblioteca Amauta, 1957.

MARTÍNEZ, HECTOR. "El indígena y el mestizo de Taraco," *Revista del Museo Nacional* (Lima), XXXI (1962), 172-244.

MARTÍNEZ DE LA TORRE, RICARDO. *Apuntes para una interpretación Marxista de historia social del Perú*. 4 vols. Lima: Empresa Editora Peruana, S.A., 1947.

MATOS MAR, J. "Three Indian Communities in Peru," *International Social Science Bulletin*, VI (1954), 466-476.

MAVILA, CONSUELO. "Aspecto económico de las familias de los obreros textiles de Vitarte," *Servicio Social*, Año III, No. 3 (December 1943), 64-86.

MEANS, P. A. "Social Conditions in the Piura-Tumbes Region of Northern Peru," *Scientific Monthly*, VII (1918), 385-399.

MEJÍA BACA, JOSÉ. *Aspectos criollos*. Lima: 1937.

MENDIZABAL, PEDRO. "Las clases sociales en la historia de la economía peruana." Unpublished Bachelor's thesis, Universidad Nacional Mayor de San Marcos, Lima, 1955.

MIRÓ QUESADA C., FRANCISCO. *Las estructuras sociales* (2nd ed.). Lima: Tipografía Santa Rosa, 1965.

MOORE, SALLY FALK. *Power and Property in Inca Peru*. New York: Columbia University Press, 1958.

NUÑEZ ANAVITARTE, CARLOS. *El problema de la realización del producto en la economía capitalista*. Cuzco: 1952.

———. *El problema de la acumulación en la industria y el proceso de la economía nacional*. Cuzco: 1957.

PAN-AMERICAN UNION. *The Peruvian Economy*. Washington, D.C.: 1950.

PARTIDO DEMOCRÁTICO REFORMISTA. *Lo que el oncenio hizo por el Perú bajo el mando del Presidente Leguía*. Opúscula No. 2. Lima: Imprenta Gil, n.d. (after 1930).

PATCH, RICHARD. *Some Aspects of Peru's Economy* (American Universities Field Staff Reports). New York: April 1958.

———. *The Indian Emergence in Cuzco* (American Universities Field Staff Reports). New York: November 1958.

———. *An Hacienda Becomes a Community* (American Universities Field Staff Reports). New York: October 4, 1957.

———. *Modern Indians and the Inca Empire* (American Universities Field Staff Reports). New York: October 1958.

———. *An Oil Company Builds a Town* (American Universities Field Staff Reports). New York: March 12, 1958.

PAYNE, JAMES L. *Labor and Politics in Peru: the System of Political Bargaining*. New Haven: Yale University Press, 1965.

PAZ-SOLDÁN, C. E. *Lima y sus suburbios.* Lima: Universidad Nacional Mayor de San Marcos, 1957.

PERÚ, BANCO CENTRAL DE RESERVA DEL PERÚ. *Renta nacional del Perú, 1942–1946.* Lima: 1958.

———. *Renta nacional del Perú, 1942–1956.* Lima: Imprenta Casa Nacional de Moneda, 1958.

———. *Renta nacional del Perú, 1952–1960.* Lima: Imprenta Casa Nacional de Moneda, 1962.

———. *Actividades productivas del Perú: análisis y perspectivas.* Lima: 1961.

PERÚ, BANCO DE CRÉDITO DEL PERÚ. *Vademécum del inversionista.* Lima: Imprenta Torres Aguirre, 1956.

PERÚ, BANCO INDUSTRIAL DEL PERÚ. *Legislación.* Undated mimeographed collection of all laws pertaining to the bank.

———. *Veinte años de vida del Banco Industrial del Perú, 1936–1956.* Lima: 1956.

PERÚ, DIRECCIÓN NACIONAL DE ESTADÍSTICA Y CENSOS. *Censo nacional de población y ocupación, 1940,* Vol. I. Lima: 1944.

———. *Censo nacional de población, 1961: resultados de primera prioridad.* Lima: 1964.

———. *Resultados preliminares del censo de manufactura— primer censo nacional económico, 1963.* Lima: 1965.

———. *Censo nacional de población: Algunas características generales de la población, cuadros comparativos, distribución geográfica, edad y sexo, lugar de nacimiento.* Vol. I, Tomo I. Lima: March 1965.

———. *Censo nacional de población: Migración, nacionalidad legal, estado conyugal, religión, fecundidad.* Vol. I, Tomo II. Lima: June 1965.

———. *Censo nacional de población, 1961: características económicas.* Vol. I, Tomo IV. Lima: March 1966.

PERÚ, MINISTERIO DE FOMENTO Y OBRAS PÚBLICAS. *Estadística industrial año 1954 y padrón de industrias manufactureras* (Lima: 1956), pp. 52 and 66.

———. *Estadística industrial.* Lima: 1958.

Perú, Ministerio de Hacienda y Comercio. *Anuario estadístico del Perú, 1954.* Lima: 1957, p. 487.

―――. *Boletín de estadística peruana* (various years).

―――. *Censo nacional de población y ocupación, 1940,* Vol. I. Lima: 1944.

Perú, Ministerio de Salud Pública y Asistencia Social. *Censo experimental de población y vivienda : Trujillo, 1956.* Lima: June 1958.

―――. *Encuesta demográfico-sanitaria: Huacho, Perú.* Lima: 1954.

―――. *La demografía de las principales ciudades peruanas.* Lima: 1957.

Perú, Ministerio de Trabajo y Asuntos Indígenas. *Informe preliminar sobre las fábricas textiles del Cuzco.* Lima: 10 September 1956.

―――. *La industria textil en el Perú.* Lima: 1957.

―――. *Los problemas sociales del Perú y la organización internacional de trabajo.* Lima: 1958.

Perú, Oficina Nacional de Planeamiento y Urbanismo. *Distribución de la tierra agrícola.* Working paper, analysis of data from *Padrón de regantes del ministerio de fomento* and *Padrón de predios rústicos de ministerio de hacienda.* Lima: 1958.

Perú, Universidad Nacional Mayor de San Marcos, *Censo del alumnado.* Lima: 1957.

Pesce, Luis. *Indígenas e inmigrantes en el Perú.* Lima: Ministerio de Fomento y Obras Públicas, 1906.

Pike, Frederick B. "The Old and the New Apra in Peru: Myths and Reality." *Interamerican Economic Affairs,* XVIII, No. 2 (Autumn 1964), 3-45.

Plank, J. N. "Peru, A Study in the Problem of Nation Forming." Unpublished Ph.D. dissertation, Department of Political Science, Harvard University, 1958.

Ponce de León, Francisco. *Bosquejo del problema de la propiedad de la tierra en el Perú.* Lima: 1946.

QUIJANO, ANÍBAL. "La emergencia del grupo 'cholo' y sus consecuencias en la sociedad peruana," in *Sociología y sociedad en Latinoamérica*. Bogotá: Asociación Colombiana de Sociología, 1965.

RAMÍREZ GASTON, JOSÉ M. *Legislación industrial*. Lima: 1913.

RAMÍREZ OTAROLA, JORGE. *Codificación de la legislación del trabajo y de previsión social del Perú* (2nd ed.). Lima: Editorial Antonio Lulli, 1963.

————. *Codificación de la legislación de trabajo y de previsión social del Perú*. Lima: 1955.

RAY, ROBERT S. *Notas sobre la industria textil en el Perú*. Lima: International Cooperation Administration, 1956.

REAÑO GARCÍA, JOSÉ. *Historia del Legüismo—sus hombres y sus obras*. Lima: Ernesto E. Balarezo P., 1928.

REINAGA, CESAR AUGUSTO. "La fisonomía económica del Perú," *Revista Universitaria* (Cuzco), Año XLV, No. 3 (1956), 112-279.

RIPPY, J. F. "The Dawn of Peruvian Manufacturing," *Pacific Historical Review*, XV (1946), 147-157.

ROEL, VIRGILIO. *Problemas de la economía peruana*. Lima: 1959.

ROMERO, EMILIO. *Geografía económica del Perú*. Lima: 1939.

————. *Historia económica del Perú*. Buenos Aires: Editorial Sudamérica, 1949.

ROMERO, FERNANDO. *Evolución industrial y educación técnica*. Lima: 1951.

————. *La industria peruana y sus obreros*. Lima: 1958.

ROWE, JOHN HOWLAND. "The distribution of Indians and Indian Languages in Peru." *Geographical Review*, XXXVII (April 1947), 202-215.

————. "Inca Culture at the Time of the Spanish Conquest," in *Handbook of South American Indians*, ed. Julian Steward (Bureau of American Ethnology Bulletins, No. 143). Washington, D.C.: 1946, II, 183-330.

————. "The Incas Under Spanish Colonial Institutions." *Hispanic American Historical Review*, xxxvii (May 1957), 155-200.

Rowe, L. A. *Early Effects of the War upon the Finance, Commerce and Industry of Peru.* New York: Carnegie Endowment for International Peace, Oxford University Press, 1920.

Sabroso Montoya, Arturo. *Defensa del derecho sindical.* Lima: Ediciones C.T.P., 1959.

Saenz, Moises. *Sobre el indio peruano y su incorporación al medio nacional.* Mexico: Secretario de Educación Pública de México, 1933.

Samamé, Benjamín. "Manpower Problems and Policies in Peru," *International Labour Review*, xciii (February 1966), 127-142.

Sánchez, Luís Alberto. *El Perú retrato de un país adolescente.* Buenos Aires: Ediciones Continente, 1958.

Sánchez Palacios, Manuel. "Desaparición legal del yanaconaje en el Perú," *Perfil Económico*, Año ii, No. 15 (March 1958), 27-31.

Schwab, Federico. "Lo huachafo como fenómeno social." *Peruanidad*, ii (March 1942), 400-402.

Servicio Cooperativo Interamericano Plan del Sur. "Capacidades humanas." Cuzco: 1958. (Mimeographed.)

Simmons, Ozzie. "The Criollo Outlook in the Mestizo Culture of Coastal Peru." *American Anthropologist*, lvii (February 1955), 107-117.

Sinclair, Joseph T. "Lima, Peru: A Study in Urban Geography." Unpublished Ph.D. dissertation, Department of Geography, University of Michigan, 1959.

Sivirichi, Atilio, *Derecho indígena peruano.* Lima: Ediciones Kuntur, 1946.

Sociedad de Ingenieros del Perú. *Forum sobre desarrollo económico.* Lima: 1957.

Sociedad Nacional de Industrias. Issues of *Industria peruana,* 1958–1959.

————. *Directorio Fabril,* 1958.

Socio-Economic Development of Andean Communities. Reports 1–7, Cornell–Peru Project, Department of Anthropology, Cornell University, Ithaca, N.Y., 1963–1965.

Solis, Abelardo. *Once Años.* Lima: 1934.

Stein, William W. *Hualcán: Life in the Highlands of Peru.* Ithaca, N.Y.: Cornell University Press, 1961.

Stewart, Watt. *Chinese Bondage in Peru.* Durham, N.C.: Duke University Press, 1951.

————. *Henry Meiggs, the Yankee Pizarro.* Durham, N.C.: Duke University Press, 1947.

Tarnawiecki, A. "Peruvian Economic Outlook." Industrial Development Department, Grace Company, September 29, 1958. (Mimeographed.)

Thompson Company, J. Walter. *The Peruvian Market.* March 1957.

Titiev, Mischa. "The Japanese Colony in Peru," *The Far Eastern Quarterly,* x (May 1951), 227-247.

Tizón y Bueno, Ricardo. *El Perú industrial.* Lima: Sociedad Nacional de Industrias, 1924.

Tschopik, Harry, Jr. "On the Concept of Creole Culture in Peru," *Transactions of the New York Academy of Sciences,* Ser. ii, no. 10 (1948), 252-261.

Tudela, Felipe. *Las comunidades indígenas, la constitución del estado y el mundo histórico occidental.* Lima: 1949.

Ugarte, Cesar Antonio. *Bosquejo de la historia económica del Perú.* Lima: 1926.

Ulloa Cisneros, A. *Leguía apuntes de cartera, 1919–1924.* Lima: 1933.

United Nations, Department of Economic and Social Affairs. *Analysis and Projections of Economic Development VI: The Industrial Development of Peru.* E/CN.12/493. Mexico D.F.: December 1959.

Uriarte, Carlos A. "Un ensayo de la distribución de los habitantes de Lima, ciudad capital, por grupos socio-económicos." *Estadística peruana,* Año iv, No. 6 (March 1948).

UNITED STATES, CONGRESS, H.R. Doc. *The Putumayo Affair—Slavery in Peru*, 62nd Congress, 3rd Session, 1913, p. 14.

UNITED STATES, DEPARTMENT OF COMMERCE. *Basic Data on the Economy of Peru.* (World Trade Information Service, Economic Reports, Part I, No. 58). Washington, D.C.: May 1958.

————. *Investment in Peru.* Washington, D.C.: 1957.

UNITED STATES, INTERNATIONAL COOPERATION ADMINISTRATION. *Summary of the Labor Situation in Peru.* Washington, D.C.: October 1958.

UNITED STATES, INTEROFFICE PUBLICATIONS. *Informe del subproyecto "capacidades humanas" en el departamento de Puno.* Lima: Servicio Cooperativo Interamericano Plan del Sur, 1958.

VALCARCEL, LUÍS. *Ruta cultural del Perú.* Mexico D.F.: Fondo de Cultura Económica, 1945.

VÁZQUEZ, MARIO C. "A Study of Technological Change in Vicos, Peru: Cornell–Peru Project." Unpublished Master's thesis, Department of Anthropology, Cornell University, 1955.

————. "Cambios en la estratificación social en una hacienda andina del Perú." *Revista del Museo Nacional* (Lima), XXIV (1955), 190-209.

————. "Campesinos andinos en un valle costeño del Perú." *Extensión en las Américas,* IX, Nos. 1, 2 (1964), 12-16.

VELARDE MORAN, ERNESTO. *Indice geográfico e industrial de los pueblos del Perú.* Lima: 1950.

VELIZ LIZÁRRAGA, JESÚS. *El Perú y la cultura occidental.* Lima: Biblioteca de Ensayos Sociológicos, 1957.

VIRGIL, MANUEL A. "El fuero privativo de trabajo," *Perfil económico,* Año III, No. 25 (January 1959), 11-15.

WHITAKER, ARTHUR PRESTON. *The Huancavelica Mercury Mine.* Cambridge, Mass.: Harvard University Press, 1941.

WHYTE, WILLIAM F. (in collaboration with Graciela Flores). *La mano de obra de alto nivel en el Perú.* Lima: Servicio

Nacional de Aprendizaje y Trabajo Industrial (SENATI), 1964.

ZUZUÑAGA, CARLOS. "Sobre la tipología cultural del Perú," *Acta americana,* V (1947), 151-158.

II. General

ALBA, VICTOR. *Historia del movimiento obrero en América Latina.* Mexico City: Libreros Mexicanos Unidos, 1964.

ALEXANDER, ROBERT J. *Communism in Latin America.* New Brunswick, N.J.: Rutgers University Press, 1957.

————. *Labor Movements in Latin America.* London: Gollancz, for the Fabian Society, 1947.

AUBREY, HENRY G. "Deliberate Industrialization," *Social Research,* XVI (June 1949), 158-182.

BACKMAN, JULES. *Economics of the Cotton Textile Industry.* New York: National Industrial Conference Board, 1946.

BAKKE, E. W., *et al. Labor Mobility and Economic Opportunity.* New York: John Wiley & Sons, 1954.

BANCROFT, GERTRUDE. *The American Labor Force.* New York: John Wiley & Sons, 1958.

BANFIELD, EDWARD C. *The Moral Basis of a Backward Society.* Glencoe, Ill.: The Free Press, 1958.

BARLOW, FRANK D. *Cotton in South America.* Washington, D.C.: National Cotton Council, 1952.

BAUER, P. T., AND YAMEY, B. S. "Economic Progress and Occupational Distribution," *The Economic Journal,* LXI, No. 244 (December 1951), 741-755.

BEALS, RALPH L. "Social Stratification in Latin America," *American Journal of Sociology,* LVIII (1953), 327-339.

————. "Urbanism, Urbanization and Acculturation," *American Anthropologist,* LIII (1951), 1-10.

BENDIX, REINHARD. *Work and Authority in Industry.* New York: John Wiley & Sons, 1956.

BENEWITZ, MAURICE. "Migrant and Non-migrant Occupational Patterns," *Industrial and Labor Relations Review,* IX (January 1956), 235-240.

BLANKSTEN, GEORGE I. "Technical Assistance and the Political Instability of Latin America," *Economic Development and Cultural Change*, II (June 1954), 350-356.

BLOOMFIELD, J. J. *Latin American Labor Legislation*. Washington, D.C.: United States Department of Labor, August 1956.

BROWNING, HARLEY L. "Present Trends in Latin American Urbanization," *Annals of the American Academy of Political and Social Science*, CCCXVI (March 1958), 111-120.

BURNIGHT, ROBERT G. "Estimates of Net Migration, Mexico 1930–1950," International Population Union Conference (New York: 1961), Paper No. 42.

CAPLOW, THEODORE. "The Modern Latin American City," in *Acculturation in the Americas*, ed. Sol Tax. Chicago: International Congress of Americanists, 1952, XXIX, 255-260.

CARBIA, ROMAN D. *Historia de la leyenda negra Hispano-Americana*. Buenos Aires: n.d.

CARLETON, ROBERT O. "Labor Force Participation: a stimulus to Fertility in Puerto Rico," *Demography*, II (1965), 233-239.

CHAMBERS, J. D. "Enclosure and Labor Supply in the Industrial Revolution," *Economic History Review*, Second Series, V, No. 3 (1952-1953), 319-343.

CHAPMAN, SYDNEY J. *The Lancashire Cotton Industry*. Manchester: Manchester University Press, 1904.

CLARK, COLIN. *The Conditions of Economic Progress*. New York: St. Martins, 1957.

CLARK, M. GARDNER. "Government Restrictions to Labor Mobility in Italy." *Industrial and Labor Relations Review*, VIII (October 1954), 3-18.

COLLVER, ANDREW, AND LANGLOIS, ELEANOR. "The Female Labor Force in Metropolitan Areas: An International Comparison," *Economic Development and Cultural Change*, X (July 1962), 367-385.

COOPER, CLAYTON S. *Latin America, Man and Markets*. Boston: Ginn & Co., 1927.

DAVIS, KINGSLEY, AND CASIS, ANA. "Urbanization in Latin America," *Milbank Memorial Fund Quarterly*, XXIV (1946), 186-207, 292-314.

ELIZAGA, JUAN C. "Assessment of Migration Data in Latin America," *Milbank Memorial Fund Quarterly*, XLIII (January 1965), 76-106.

FORM, W. H., AND BLUM, A. D. *Industrial Relations and Social Change in Latin America*. Gainesville: University of Florida Press, 1965.

FOSTER, GEORGE M. "Cofradía and Compadrazgo in Spain and South America," *Southwestern Journal of Anthropology*, IX (1953), 1-28.

FRANCO, JORGE. "Productivity and Economic Development in Latin America," *International Labour Review*, LXXII (November 1955), 367-384.

FRIED, JACOB. "Jews in Latin America," *Jewish Affairs*, III, No. 1 (1949), 3-11.

GALENSON, WALTER (ed.). *Labor and Economic Development*. New York: John Wiley & Sons, 1959.

———. *The Problem of Industrial Productivity in Backward Areas*. Labor-Management and Economic Development Conference, Cornell University, Ithaca, N.Y., March 1954.

GERTH, HANS H., AND MILLS, C. WRIGHT. *From Max Weber: Essays in Sociology*. New York: Oxford University Press, 1946.

GILLIN, JOHN. "Ethos Components in Modern Latin American Culture," *American Anthropologist*, LVII, No. 3, Part 1 (June 1955), 488-500.

GOULDNER, ALVIN W. "The Norm of Reciprocity: A Preliminary Statement," *American Sociological Review*, XXV (April 1960), 161-177.

HARTSHORNE, E. Y. "Metabolism Indices and the Annexation of Austria: A Note on Method," *American Journal of Sociology*, XLV (May 1940), 899-917.

HAUSER, PHILIP M. *Urbanization in Latin America* (A UNESCO Survey). New York: International Documents Service, Columbia University Press, 1961.

HAWTHORN, H. B., AND HAWTHORN, A. E. "Stratification in a Latin American City," *Social Forces*, XXVII (October 1948), 19-29.

HEATH, DWIGHT B., AND ADAMS, RICHARD A. (eds.). *Contemporary Cultures and Societies of Latin America*. New York: Random House, 1965.

HENEMAN, H. G., JR. (ed.). *Employment Relations Research*. New York: Harper & Bros., 1960.

HOLMBERG, ALLAN R. "Some Fundamental Assumptions of Latin American Culture," International Management Association Pamphlet, 1949.

HOOKS, JANET M. *Women's Occupations Through Seven Decades*. (Women's Bureau Bulletin, No. 218). Washington, D.C.: United States Department of Labor, 1947.

HOSELITZ, BERT F. "The Development of a Labor Market in the Process of Economic Growth." In *Transactions of the Fifth World Congress of Sociology*, Vol. II, *The Sociology of Development* (Louvain, Belgium: International Sociological Association, 1962), p. 67.

———. "The Recruitment of White Collar Workers in Underdeveloped Countries," *International Social Science Bulletin*, VI, No. 3 (1954), 433-442.

———. *Theories of Economic Growth* (Working Paper). Glencoe, Ill.: Social Science Research Council, May 1956.

HUGHLETT, LLOYD S. *Industrialization of Latin America*. New York: McGraw-Hill Book Co., 1946.

INSTITUTO DE ECONOMÍA. *Movilidad de la mano de obra*. Santiago, Chile: 1960.

INTERNATIONAL LABOR OFFICE. *Indigenous People*. Geneva: 1953.

———. *Social Legislation of Latin America*. Vol. II. Geneva: 1929.

———. *Textile Wages*. Geneva: 1952.

JAFFE, A. J. *People, Jobs, and Economic Development.* Glencoe, Ill.: The Free Press, 1959.

JAMES, RALPH C. "Discrimination Against Women in Bombay Textiles," *Industrial and Labor Relations Review,* xv (January 1962), 209-220.

JEWKES, JOHN, AND GRAY, E. M. *Wages and Labor in the Lancashire Cotton Spinning Industry.* Manchester: Manchester University Press, 1935.

JOHNSON, J. J. (ed.). *Continuity and Change in Latin America.* Stanford, Calif.: Stanford University Press, 1964.

KANNAPPAN, SUBBIAH. *The Impact of the International Labor Office on Labor Legislation in India.* U.S. Department of Labor. Ithaca, N.Y.: Cornell University Press, March 1954.

KERR, CLARK, *et al. Industrialism and Industrial Man.* Cambridge: Harvard University Press, 1960.

KORNHAUSER, ARTHUR, DUBIN, ROBERT, AND ROSS, ARTHUR M. (eds.). *Industrial Conflict.* New York: McGraw-Hill Book Co., 1954.

KIMBER, ALBERT W. *Latin American Industrialization.* New York: White, Weld, 1946.

LAMBERT, RICHARD. *Workers, Factories, and Social Change in India.* Princeton: Princeton University Press, 1963.

LATIN AMERICAN DEMOGRAPHIC CENTER. "Differential Migration in Some Regions and Cities of Latin America in the Period 1940–1950, Methodological Aspects and Results." International Population Union Conference, New York, 1961, Paper No. 127.

LATIN AMERICAN ECONOMIC INSTITUTE. *The Cotton Textile Industry in Latin America.* Pamphlet Series No. 6. New York: 1942.

LEIBENSTEIN, HARVEY. "The Theory of Underemployment in Backward Economies." *Journal of Political Economy,* LXV (April 1957), 91-103.

LEWIS, OSCAR. "Urbanization Without Breakdown," *The Scientific Monthly,* LXXV (July 1952), 31-41.

————. "Further Observations on the Folk-Urban Continuum and Urbanization with Reference to Mexico City," in National Institute of Mental Health, *Proceedings of the Rural Urban Migration Conference, Bethesda, Maryland, May 11-16, 1964.* (Mimeographed.)

LIPSET, S. M. "Social Mobility and Urbanization," *Rural Sociology,* XX (September 1955), 220-228.

LIPSET, S. M., AND MALM, F. THEODORE. "First Jobs and Career Patterns," *American Journal of Economics and Sociology,* XIV (April 1955), 247-261.

LITWAK, EUGENE. "Occupational Mobility and Family Cohesion," *American Sociological Review,* XXV (February 1960), 9-20.

MAHONEY, THOMAS A. "Factors Determining the Labor Force Participation of Married Women." *Industrial and Labor Relations Review,* XIV (July 1961), 563-577.

MALM, F. THEODORE. "Recruiting Patterns and the Functioning of Labor Markets," *Industrial and Labor Relations Review,* VII (July 1954), 507-525.

MARKOWER, HELEN, *et al.* "Studies in the Mobility of Labor," *Oxford Economic Papers,* I (October 1938), 83-123.

MARX, KARL. *The Eighteenth Brumaire of Louis Napoleon.* London: Allen & Unwin, 1926.

MCNULTY, PAUL JAMES. "Labor Market Analysis and the Development of Labor Economics," *Industrial and Labor Relations Review,* XIX (July 1966), 538-548.

MECHAM, J. LLOYD. *Church and State in Latin America.* Chapel Hill: University of North Carolina Press, 1934.

MEYERS, CHARLES, AND MACLAURIN, W. RUPERT. *The Movement of Factory Workers.* U.S. Department of Labor. Ithaca, N.Y.: Cornell University Press, 1954.

MINTZ, SIDNEY W., AND WOLF, ERIC R. "An Analysis of Ritual Co-Parenthood (Compadrazgo)," *Southwestern Journal of Anthropology,* VI (Winter 1950), 341-368.

MOORE, WILBERT E. *Industrialization and Labor.* Ithaca, N.Y.: Cornell University Press, 1951.

———. *Industrial Relations and the Social Order.* New York: Macmillan, 1951.

———. "Migration and Social Opportunity." *Rural Sociology,* VII (March 1942), 86-89.

———. "The Migration of Native Laborers in South Africa," *Milbank Memorial Fund Quarterly,* XXIV (October 1946), 401-419.

———. "The Exportability of the 'Labor Force' Concept," *American Sociological Review,* XVIII (February 1953), 68-72.

———. "A Reconsideration of Theories of Social Change," *American Sociological Review,* XXV (December 1960), 810-818.

———. *Social Change* (Foundations of Modern Sociology Series). New Jersey: Prentice-Hall, 1964.

MOORE, WILBERT E., AND FELDMAN, ARNOLD S. *Labor Commitment and Social Change in Developing Areas.* New York: Social Science Research Council, 1960.

MORRIS, MORRIS DAVID. *The Emergence of an Industrial Labor Force in India, A Study of the Bombay Cotton Mills, 1854–1957.* Berkeley and Los Angeles: University of California Press, 1965.

MOSK, SANFORD A. *The Industrial Revolution in Mexico.* Berkeley: University of California Press, 1950.

NASH, MANNING. *Machine Age Maya.* Glencoe, Ill.: The Free Press, 1958.

ORNATI, OSCAR. *Organized Labor's Impact on Indian Industrialization.* U.S. Department of Labor. Ithaca, N.Y.: Cornell University Press, 1954.

OSBORN, HAROLD. *Indians of the Andes.* Cambridge, Mass.: Harvard University Press, 1952.

PAGE, CHARLES A. "Labor's Political Role in Latin America," *Virginia Quarterly Review,* XXVIII (Autumn 1952), 481-499.

PALMER, GLADYS L. *Labor Mobility in Six Cities,* New York: Social Science Research Council, 1954.

PARNES, HERBERT S. *Research on Labor Mobility.* Bulletin No. 65. New York: Social Science Research Council, 1954.

PARSONS, TALCOTT. *Structure and Process in Modern Societies.* Glencoe, Ill.: The Free Press, 1960.

PARSONS, TALCOTT, AND SMELSER, NEIL J. *Economy and Society.* Glencoe, Ill.: The Free Press, 1947.

PETERSON, WILLIAM. "The Demographic Transition in the Netherlands," *American Sociological Review,* XXV (June 1960), 334-346.

PIHLBLAD, C. T., AND AAS, DAGFINN. "Mobility and Industrialization," *American Sociological Review,* XXV (June 1960), 369-374.

POBLETE TRONCOSO, M. *Condición de vida y trabajo de la población indígena del Perú.* Series B, No. 28. Geneva: International Labor Office, 1938.

POBLETE TRONCOSO, M., AND BURNETT, BEN A. "Latin American Labor Law: A Synthesis," *Interamerican Economic Affairs,* XII, No. 2 (Autumn 1958), 3-18.

ROMERO, EMILIO. *El pensamiento económico Latino-Americano.* Mexico D.F.: Fondo de Cultura Económica, 1945.

ROSTOW, W. W. *The Stages of Economic Growth.* New York: Cambridge University Press, 1960.

———. "The Take-off into Self-Sustained Growth," *The Economic Journal,* LVI (March 1956), 25-48.

ROTTENBERG, SAMUEL. *Technical Cooperation in Latin America.* Washington: National Planning Association, 1956.

ROTTENBERG, SIMON. "Note on Economic Progress and Occupational Distribution," *Review of Economics and Statistics,* XXXV (May 1953), 168-170.

———. "Problems in a Latin American Factory Society," *Monthly Labor Review,* LXXI (July 1954), 756-760.

RYCROFT, W. STANLEY. *Indians of the High Andes.* New York: Committee on Cooperation in Latin America, 1946.

SALZ, BEALE R. "The Human Element in Industrialization," *American Anthropologist,* LVII, No. 6, Pt. 2, Memoir 85 (December 1955), 1-268.

Sánchez Luís Alberto. "Latin America and the War," in American Academy of Political and Social Science, Pamphlet Series ii (Philadelphia: 1942), pp. 5-9.

Service, Elman R. "Indian-European Relations in Colonial Latin America," *American Anthropologist*, lvii, No. 3, Pt. 1 (June 1955), 411-425.

Siegel, Jeanette G. "The Measurement of Labor Turnover," *Monthly Labor Review*, lxxvi (May 1953), 519-522.

Silcock, H. S. "The Phenomenon of Labour Turnover," *Journal of the Royal Statistical Society*, Pt. IV, Vol. xvii (1954), 429-440.

Smelser, Neil J. *Social Change in the Industrial Revolution.* Chicago: University of Chicago Press, 1959.

Solomon, Morton R. "The Structure of the Market in Underdeveloped Economies," *Quarterly Journal of Economics*, lxii (August 1948), 519-541.

Stein, Stanley S. *The Brazilian Cotton Manufacture.* Cambridge: Harvard University Press, 1957.

Thorp, Willard L., and Quandt, Richard E. *The New Inflation.* New York: McGraw-Hill Book Co., 1959.

Tumin, Melvin M. *Caste in a Peasant Society: A Case Study of the Dynamics of Caste.* Princeton: Princeton University Press, 1952.

———. "Reciprocity and Stability of Caste in Guatemala," *American Sociological Review*, xiv (February 1949), 17-25.

United Nations, Department of Economic and Social Affairs. *Labor Productivity of the Cotton Textile Industry in Five Latin American Countries.* E/CN. 12/219, New York, 1951.

———. *Processes and Problems of Industrialization in Underdeveloped Countries.* New York: 1955.

Vernengo, Roberto. "Freedom of Association and Industrial Relations in Latin America," *International Labour Review*, lxxiii, Pt. 1, No. 5 (May 1956), and Pt. 2, No. 6 (June 1956), 451-482.

WAGLEY, C., AND HARRIS, M. "A Typology of Latin American Subcultures," *American Anthropologist*, LVII, No. 3, Pt. 1 (June 1955), 428-451.

WEBER, MAX. *The Theory of Social and Economic Organization*. Glencoe, Ill.: The Free Press, 1947.

WHYTE, W. F., AND HOLMBERG, ALLAN R. "Human Problems of United States Enterprise in Latin America," *Human Organization*, XV, No. 3 (Fall 1956), 1-40.

WILKINSON, THOMAS O. "Urban Structure and Industrialization," *American Sociological Review*, XXV (June 1960), 356-362.

WIRTH, LOUIS. "Urbanism as a Way of Life," *American Journal of Sociology*, XLIV (July 1938), 1-24.

WITFOGEL, KARL. *Oriental Despotism*. New Haven: Yale University Press, 1957.

WOLF, ERIC R. "Types of Latin American Peasantry," *American Anthropologist*, LVII, No. 3, Pt. 1 (June 1955), pp. 452-471.

WOYTINSKY, M. S. "Auge y miseria en Latino-América," *Cuadernos*, XXXIV (January–February 1959), 31-42.

WYTHE, GEORGE. *Industrialization in Latin America*. New York: Columbia University Press, 1949.

Index

Subject Index

entrepreneurs, 100, 257. *See also criollo*

criollismo, 14-16; diffusion of, 14; as obstacle to development, 14

criollo, 58; exodus from provincial areas, 61; managers, 76, 259; and *serrano*, 120

Crown, as labor contractor, 58; as protector of Indians, 5, 60. *See also* colonial era; Spain

C.T.P. (Confederación de Trabajadores del Perú), 82

Cuban *guajiro*, compared to Peruvian sugar workers, 69

cultural inferiority, sense of, 28

cultural situs, 53

culture, as obstacle to industrialization, 15, 35

Cuzco, 25, 36, 118, 120, 126, 134, 136, 145, 193, 196, 234, 251, 261, 263, 267, 277; Communist strategy in, 77; sample coverage in, 276

cynicism and the market mechanism, 202

day laborers, payment in kind, 68

debt peonage, 64

decentralization, of industry, issue of, 24, 214, 252; of 19th-century government, 7

decommercialization of fiestas, 70

demographic growth, 32. *See also* population

demonstration effect, 37

dependency burden, in Lima, 24; time and space differentials of, 171

Depression, effects of, 9, 76

derecho adquirido, 85, 205

desconfianza, 15, 16, 95, 111

diffusion, of *criollismo* to local elites, 14; of female labor-force participation, 193

discharged workers, 85, 166

discretionary income and particularistic pressures, 44

discrimination, 219, 220; by sex and race, 185. *See also* sex, stereotyped jobs; Indian

distribution, of land, 36, 38; of wealth and income, 37; of welfare benefits, 216

docile workers, managerial preference for, 215, 217

domestic industry, *see* cottage industry

domestic servants, 17, 22, 122, 134; and female employment, 193-94; as *pongos*, 66, 271; some early factory workers required to be, 218

dues check off, absence of, 81

economic development, effect of U.S. Civil war on, 6; structure of in Peru, 34, 37; overhead projects in, 9

economically active, decline of, 170

education, effect on age first employed, 226; foreign, of the elite, 8; and labor mobility, 184; and social status, 54

efficiency, of labor, 215; less important than political influence, 242; low level of, 213; need for measure of by sociologists, x; and organizational change, 49

eight-hour day, fight for, 75

elite strangers, as entrepreneurs, 99. *See also* British; English; entrepreneurs; European immigrants; foreign; French; Germans; immigrants; Italian; Jews; Spain; Syrians; *Turcos*; United States

elites, 223; "exploited" by lower class, 21; orientation toward foreign cultures, 8, 14, 36; in provincial areas, 14

emancipation of Negro slaves, 61

empleado-obrero comparisons, 176-81; barriers between, 260; benefits, 83-87, 180; income, 184; mobility between, 44; payment differential, 178-79; ratio between in Lima and in provinces, 210; sex ratio, 190. *See also* obrero

empleados, labor market, 184-85; salary level and seniority, 185

employee compensation, 207

employment, of children, 140; of experienced *obreros*, 249; and fertility, 195; instability of females, 154; service, use of, 51, 217,

urban areas, life in and acculturation to, 21, 164; population of exaggerated in census, 33, 279
urbanization, 32; concentrated, 23-24, 260; and female employment, 188; and fertility, 125
utilities, public, 23, 174

vertical integration, 258
violence in labor-management relations, 81. *See also* labor, protest
Virú, 68
vocational school graduates, 217. *See also* technical school training

wages, and authority and skill, 203; equalization by sex, 105; and the market, 203; and market impurities, 220; poor communication about, 204, 249; and seniority, 203; and technology, 203
wealth, redistribution of, 70. *See also* income
weavers, 131, 137, 200, 233; and kinship, 142; and seniority, 204; sex ratio among, 192; work loads of, 114, 198, 243, 253, 270
welfare laws, 139; and the oligarchy, 78; and paternalism, 216
Western civilization, 230; influence on Indian property norms, 67;

19th century isolation from, 7; Peru's membership in, 29
white-collar work, 184, 221-22; and blue-collar skilled pay, 249; entry of middle-class women into, 186; proletarianization of, 184; salary level and pirating, 207. *See also empleados*
women, *see* female workers
wool, costly and poor quality, 109
woolen mills, problem of, 267
work loads, 132; of weavers, 114, 198, 243, 253, 270
workers, apoliticism of, 261; attached to land, 69; discharged, 85, 166; generational differences, 261; housing of, 199; overcommitted, 224. *See also* artisans; day laborers; docile workers; domestic servants; *empleados*; female workers; foremen; handweavers; light manual workers; maintenance workers; *obreros*; operatives; skilled workers; temporary workers; weavers; white-collar work
Worker Congress, First, 75
World War I, effect on textiles, 9, 65
World War II, effect on textiles, 11, 157, 232, 235

yanaconaje, 68. *See also coloniaje*